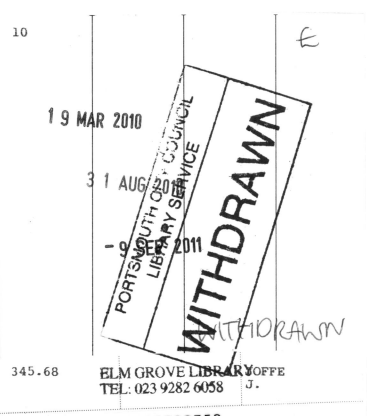

This book is due for return by the last date shown above.
To avoid paying fines please renew or return promptly.

Portsmouth
CITY COUNCIL
LEISURE SERVICE

CL-1

The State vs. Nelson Mandela

The State vs. Nelson Mandela

The Trial that Changed South Africa

Joel Joffe

ONEWORLD

OXFORD

THE STATE VS. NELSON MANDELA

A Oneworld Book
Published by Oneworld Publications 2007
Copyright © Joel Joffe 2007

ISBN-13: 978–1–85168–500–4

Typeset by Jayvee, Trivandrum
Cover design by D. R. Ink
Printed and bound by T. J. International Ltd.,
Padstow, Cornwall

Oneworld Publications
185 Banbury Road
Oxford OX2 7AR
England
www.oneworld-publications.com

Learn more about Oneworld. Join our mailing list to
find out about our latest titles and special offers at:

www.oneworld-publications.com

Pretoria Prison
Republic of South Africa
11th May 1964

TO WHOM IT MAY CONCERN

When our trial started in October 1963, none of us had ever met Joel Joffe before. All we knew of him at the time was that he had cancelled plans to leave South Africa in order to take up our defence. This alone, at a time when frenzied hysteria was being whipped up against us amongst the White population of this country, assured us that he was a man of rare courage and real devotion to the cause of justice.

Since getting to know him, we realise how fully our first impressions have been justified. Today we know him both as a lawyer and a friend, and have the highest regard for him in both capacities.

As the general behind the scenes of our defence, he has managed and marshalled this most complex case with understanding and skill. His judgement of the strength of our case, and of its weaknesses, has been keen and stated without hesitation. He has understood and accepted that, above all else, we would not compromise our beliefs or consciences for legal advantage; and in that understanding he has advised us along a course which we fully believe to have been politically correct, and legally so as well.

As a friend, Joel has taken on himself services far beyond the call of a lawyer's duty. He has assisted in all the personal and family problems that have beset us, as though our friendship had been long and close. Nothing has been too much trouble for him or fallen outside his concept of a lawyer's responsibility to his client.

We have come to admire and respect this quiet, courageous man, whose devotion to the cause of justice has been shown to be in the very highest tradition of his calling. We will be sorry indeed to end our close relationship with him. But we know that, wherever he is, wherever he may go, Joel's legal brain and services will be at the call of those in need of justice and defence as it has been so fully and well at ours.

THE RIVONIA ACCUSED: PRETORIA

NR MANDELA	GOVANMBEKI	RAYMOND MHLABA
WM SISULU	AM KATHRADA	A MOTSOALEDI
D GOLDBERG	L BERNSTEIN	A MLANGENI

Contents

Foreword

Joel Joffe had the most extra-ordinary vantage point on the Rivonia Trial. His record of the trial, therefore, can take us inside the courtroom as well as into the corridors of the courtroom and prison cells. *The State vs. Nelson Mandela* is based on an intimate and deep grasp of what happened in court, the strategy and tactics that the accused and their defence team employed, the machinations of the prosecution and the security branch. It is a story told in a way that shall immerse the reader in the atmosphere of the time.

The State vs. Nelson Mandela is a remarkable piece of contemporary historical writing that will serve as one of the most reliable sources for understanding what happened at that trial and how we came to live to see democracy triumph in South Africa.

The importance of this book is greater because there is no complete record of the Rivonia Trial, which was concluded on 12 June 1964. Fragments of the records are scattered in various public and private libraries and it is still uncertain that when all of these are put together they will make a complete record. Even if such a record were to be put together, Joel Joffe's book will be an indispensable guide to anyone seeking to wade through those records.

The stand we took during the Rivonia Trial was shaped by the knowledge that our struggle was morally just. We were aware that the cause we stood for would eventually triumph. We went into that courtroom determined to put Apartheid in the dock, even if this were to put our own lives in jeopardy. And we were assisted by a legal team led by the indomitable advocate Bram Fischer and managed by the tireless attorney Joel Joffe.

The arrests that led to the Rivonia Trial were an enormous setback to the struggle for freedom. The task of snatching victory from the jaws of death needed steadfastness from the accused, commitment and resourcefulness from our defence team, and a steady and growing stream of financial, moral and political support from people within South Africa and the world at large, up to and including the United Nations.

We write this Foreword with great gratitude and appreciation for all of these persons and institutions.

Nelson Mandela.
11 June 2006

Acknowledgements

Shortly after the Rivonia Trial, I left South Africa to settle in London. While looking for a job I had some free time and decided to write a book about the trial as a tribute to Nelson Mandela and his fellow accused, all of whom I expected to die while in prison on Robben Island and Pretoria Central jail. My objective was to ensure that their incredible courage and integrity in their trial should be remembered by future generations. As it turned out, I was quite wrong and happily they all survived Robben Island and did not need me to ensure that they were remembered.

Being a lawyer, what I wrote was accurate but needed livening up. Remembering that Lionel (Rusty) Bernstein, Accused Number 6, had been the propagandist for the National African Congress prior to his arrest, I sent the draft to him for comment. From then on both our memories fail us. Rusty remembered working on the draft but not exactly what he did to it. I, on re-reading the book, do not recognise much of the writing as my own and think Rusty must have substantially rewritten it, but he remained unconvinced. On further reflection, I am satisfied that Rusty, who has since died, was the co-author of this book.

Having written the book in 1965, I took no steps to publish it as the Accused were all still alive. However, after Nelson Mandela was released in 1990, friends who had seen the manuscript encouraged Mayibuye Books to publish it.

I then lost track of sales of the book as I had waived any royalties due to me. Out of the blue in September 2002, I received a letter from a lively New York attorney, Ann M. Schneider, who had just returned from Robben Island where she had picked up a copy of the book at the Robben Island Bookshop. She thought the book was important and offered to help get it published. She wasted no time and, fortunately for me, found the Literary Agent, Frances Goldin, who liked the book and worked incredibly hard to find a publisher, eventually tying up a contract with Oneworld Publications, to whom I am indebted for their support and advice.

I am also indebted to the late Edelgard Nkobi-Goldberg for producing the German version of the book and providing the photographs in the plate section.

That the book has now been republished is entirely due to Ann and Frances to whom I am most grateful. I also thank my wife Vanetta and my PA Elizabeth Smith for their support.

Swindon, England
April 2007

Introduction

Mac Maharaj
Minister of Transport 1994 to 1999, and a member of the National
Executive Committee of the African National Congress 1995–2000

From prisoner to president: Nelson Mandela has become part
of the warp and weft of the chronicle of South Africa's negotiated
transition from apartheid to democracy. His role has been so
crucial that the idea of such a transition without Mandela is
almost unthinkable.

Yet the prospect that Mandela and at least some of his colleagues would be sentenced to death in 1964 in the Rivonia Trial
was very real. And it is a certainty that Verwoerd, the prime minister and architect of apartheid, would have ensured that his government carried out that sentence. Verwoerd was never one to
heed world opinion: he marched apartheid South Africa out of the
Commonwealth Prime Ministers' Conference held in London in
1961 rather than listen to the counsel of his Commonwealth
colleagues.

The State vs. Nelson Mandela by Joel Joffe takes the reader into
the courtroom intrigues and drama. It is a story told with simplicity and eloquence, stripped of the legal jargon that often mystifies
the reader. It is all the more powerful as a contemporary document
for the insight it offers into the implications of the trial. It is this
kind of contemporary writing that becomes crucial for subsequent
analyses and on-going reconstructions of the past into the present.

Once the prosecution had outlined its case, the issue for the
defence team was "a battle to prevent the death sentence being

carried out".[1] The accused, of course, had a wider strategy which made the task of the defence far more difficult. Mandela and his co- accused were not prepared to restrict themselves to a straight legal defence; they wanted to go on the political offensive – to use the courtroom to explain precisely what they were aiming to do and why. They wanted to put the record straight and to answer in public the falsifications and distortions of the State.

The first pillar of this wider strategy was not to challenge evidence by prosecution witnesses in instances where they were telling the truth; rather to focus on exposing the lies and the slandering of organizations. This closed a whole field of cross-examination to the defence team. Also such restricted cross-examination involved implicit admissions of the main charges against the accused. This meant that there could not thereafter be any possible denials of guilt or attempts to evade conviction because the full proof of the offence had not been given in court. In the case of Mandela and some of the other accused this was tantamount to their signing their own death warrants.

The second aspect was that the accused had decided that in court, even where they were giving evidence under oath, "they would state the facts as fully as possible, but they would not under any circumstances reveal any information whatsoever about their organizations, or about people involved in the movement, where such information could in any way endanger their liberty".[2] The lawyers explained that this approach might antagonize the judge. The accused were unmoved.

This strategy formed the fabric of the statement from the dock by Nelson Mandela in which he explained the aims of the ANC and MK and defended the resort to sabotage. He ended with what was perceived by some to amount to inviting the death penalty when he said; "I have cherished the ideal of a democratic and free society in which all persons live together in harmony and with equal opportunities. It is an ideal which I hope to live for and to achieve. But if needs be it is an ideal for which I am prepared to die."[3]

[1] This book (Joffe). p. 76.
[2] Joffe. p. 147.   [3] Joffe. p. 160.

The prosecution certainly started with all the advantages. Its strategy not to charge the accused with High Treason but under the Sabotage Act removed a great deal of the onus of proof from the prosecution and placed it on the defence. Under a charge of treason two witnesses were required for every overt act; under the Sabotage Act an offence could be legally proved by a single witness. Despite these advantages, however, the prosecution botched its case. It could not resist the temptation to play to the media and instead of restricting itself to the legal terrain chose to enter the political fray. In this it tried to take on the accused on their own turf and it was hopelessly outmanoeuvred.

Furthermore, aside from throwing out the first indictment, the judge gave almost free rein to the prosecution. While Joffe is satisfied that the leader of the prosecution, Dr Percy Yutar, "took instructions quite definitely and without question from the political authorities of the State – and in this case, from the senior officials of the police", he believes that Mr Justice De Wet was "an obstinate and self-willed man, who would not, I think, have taken kindly to either direct government or even indirect political intervention in his domain." However, the judge "showed throughout the trial that he was a typical white South African, with all the prejudices that that implies . . . He was unquestionably sensitive to the needs of the white society which he believed in and upheld, and also of the government. He acted out their role, I think, unconsciously, in the firm conviction of his own judicial impartiality, and without the need for a direct word or intervention from any source whatsoever."[4]

White society was taking the lead from government. During the trial, the right-wing media were calling for the death penalty. Afterwards, the trial the prosecutor and the police commissioner were feted at functions and in media interviews. *The Sunday Times* splashed an account by Maj-Gen. Van den Bergh. *The Star* welcomed the life sentences as a lesson to anyone wanting to overthrow the established order. No media bothered to interview anyone from the defence team. Government was determined to

[4] Joffe. p. 66.

crush all black opposition and resistance and South Africa was in the grip of a reign of terror. If they could have their way white society wanted the men to hang.

Were there any countervailing forces?

There were protests and calls to 'stand by our leaders' within South Africa but the apartheid regime simply brushed these aside. If the internal dynamic of South Africa and the needs of white society favoured the death penalty, external forces, including allies among western governments, supported the call for the release of the Rivonia trialists and were concerned about the possibility of the death sentence being imposed.

By 106 votes to one, the United Nations adopted a resolution condemning apartheid repression and called on South Africa "to abandon forthwith the arbitrary trial now in progress, and grant an unconditional release of all political prisoners and all persons imprisoned, interned or subject to other restrictions for having opposed the policy of apartheid". The one vote against was that of South Africa.

As the trial progressed the UN representatives of thirty-two African states appealed to all countries that shared diplomatic relations with South Africa to "take all necessary measures to prevent the execution of African nationalist leaders now on trial in Pretoria." By the time of sentencing the group had grown to fifty-six and several countries used a meeting of the Security Council to condemn the court's decision.[5] Two days before the court's verdict the United Nations Security Council (with four abstentions including Great Britain and the United States) urged the South African government to end the trial and grant amnesty to the defendants.

The international trade unions staged protests and the dockworkers' unions around the world threatened not to handle South African goods. Members of the United States Congress protested and fifty members of the British parliament staged a march in London. Night-long vigils were held at St Paul's Cathedral in London. The students of the University of London elected Nelson Mandela president of their Students' Union.[6]

[5] *Memoirs* by Ahmed Kathrada. 2004. Zebra Press. p. 167.
[6] *Long Walk to Freedom* by Nelson Mandela. 1994. Macdonald Purnell. p. 358.

The prime minister of the Soviet Union wrote to Dr Verwoerd asking for leniency. Adlai Stevenson, the US representative at the UN wrote a letter saying that his government would do everything to prevent a death sentence.

We do not know what steps the US government took in this regard. But it seems that the British government did make some interventions, however circumspect these may have been, to prevent the death sentence from being imposed.

George Bizos, who was an advocate in the defence team, tells of his meeting the night before sentencing with the British Consul General, Leslie Minford, who assured him that none of the accused would be sentenced to death and that one of them, Bernstein, would be acquitted – which is what happened.[7]

Anthony Sampson in his biography of Mandela accessed records of the British Foreign Office. Although he did not find any direct intervention by the British government there is much suggestive detail. In particular there is a report in May 1964 from the Cape Town office of the British foreign service to London stating that Major General Van den Bergh, head of the Security Police, did not expect the death sentence and that the prosecutor, Dr. Yutar, would not ask for the death sentence.[8] Indeed, in his closing address Yutar did not ask for the death sentence to be imposed.

Another interesting titbit of what was or may have been happening behind the scenes is recorded in Stephen Clingman's biography of Bram Fischer, who was leader of the defence team in the Rivonia trial. Clingman says that Harold Hanson, an eloquent and impressive member of the defence team, went to see Mr Justice De Wet before Hanson presented the case for mitigation of sentence. "When he returned he said to Arthur Chaskalson (who was also in the defence team), 'He is not going to impose the death sentence.' Chaskalson asked, 'How do you know?' Hanson swore him to secrecy, and then said, 'I asked him.' Hanson had enquired

[7] *Mandela: The Authorised Biography* by Anthony Sampson. 1999. Jonathan Ball. P. 195; and *Bram Fischer* by Stephen Clingman.1998. David Phillips Publishers, Cape Town. P. 320.
[8] Sampson. P. 195.

whether De Wet was considering the death penalty, because if he was it might affect the nature of his argument. And De Wet had simply said, 'No.'[9]

The British government may have been sensitive to how it should be raising the matter. In May 1964 Sir Hugh Stephenson, the British ambassador advised the Prime Minister Sir Alec Douglas-Home that no more pressure should be applied on Pretoria. Are we allowed to assume that Sir Hugh Stephenson knew more than is found in the Foreign Office records? Douglas-Home seems to have adhered to his advice.

Sampson maintains that Stephenson was "not a man for bold initiatives . . . (He) never really grasped the realities of Africa . . . He dreaded offending Afrikaners." This, despite being warned by the Foreign Secretary "never to appear to condone apartheid."[10] However much Stephenson sought to be on good terms with the Verwoerd government, he would have absorbed the experience of British colonialism that in some of its colonies leaders such as Nehru, Nkrumah and Kenyatta emerged from prison to play a useful, if not a leading, role in the transition from colonial rule to independence. In short, his outlook would allow him both to sympathise with white South Africa and caution against the death penalty.

There can be no doubt that the prosecutor, Dr Yutar, conducted the case with venom and viciousness. Why did he then not ask for the court to impose the death penalty? He fawned on the police and we can assume that he was guided by them, quite likely by Van den Bergh. Secondly, there are enough pointers that sometime during the three week adjournment between the court's verdict and the resumption of the trial to hear arguments in mitigation of sentence the judge had already arrived at his decision that he would not impose the death sentence. Thirdly the decision not to impose the death penalty on Mandela, Sisulu and Mbeki had more to do with politics and external pressures than with issues of law. Joffe may be right that Mr Justice De Wet was not the kind of person who would countenance "direct . . . or even indirect political

[9] Clingman. P. 320.

[10] Sampson. P. 187.

intervention in his domain." But that does not exclude the likelihood that he may have licked his finger and held it up to determine whether there was a breeze and its direction.

That is how close we were not to having Mandela around to place negotiations on the agenda at a time when most of the evidence pointed to a bloody denouement to the crisis in South Africa.

It may well be that the British, and it would seem the US, stance of limiting public pressure and confining themselves to gentle allusions against the death penalty tipped the balance in favour of the court's decision. This may have happened more by accident than design. The British government appears to have been preoccupied by fears that pressures on Pretoria would be counter-productive.

None of these issues should detract from the pressures that were mounted by the defence team and the accused themselves, as well as the protests within South Africa and the condemnations and representations made by the outside world including governments and the United Nations. Without these pressures it is quite likely that Mandela and some of his colleagues would have been sentenced to death.

At the heart of "the battle to prevent the death sentence" was the strategy of the accused, the dignity and forthright way in which they gave their evidence, withstood cross-examination and championed the cause of freedom and democracy from within the courtroom and the magnificent performance of the defence team led by Bram Fischer. This is *The Rivonia Story* that Joel Joffe recorded in December 1965, the closest we shall get to know what happened as it happened.

Mac Maharaj
Johannesburg
2006

1 Arrests at Rivonia

On 11 July 1963 seven men were arrested in the Johannesburg suburb of Rivonia. The following afternoon the news of their arrest was blazoned across the front pages of South African newspapers. Looking back I suppose the news should have meant something to me, but it didn't. Perhaps the reason is that one had become too accustomed to raids and arrests in the South Africa of 1963. Amongst those arrested only one was known to me by name, Walter Sisulu. I had never met him, but had read of him. I was aware, vaguely, that he was a figure of considerable importance amongst non-white people. But apart from this I knew nothing either of the people involved or of their cause.

I was not to know as I read the papers on that July day that the arrest of these people was to become perhaps the most celebrated arrest in South African history. At the United Nations an unprecedented 106 nations gathered to call for the immediate release of these seven men even before any evidence against them had been heard; against this united world opinion would be found only the lone voice of the South African Government.

The South African press did its best to convince everybody that this case was unique amongst the many political cases which South Africa had witnessed over the years. The headlines were bigger, the excitement greater, the adjectives stronger, the claims by Government officials and spokesmen of the police more sweeping than ever before. Two days after the arrests the *Rand Daily Mail*, headline 'Subversion—End Near', reported the Commissioner of Police as saying 'We are following up clues which will undoubtedly lead to the end of all subversive elements' and describing the arrests as 'a major breakthrough in the elimination of subversive organisations'.

Just weeks before the arrests I had decided to leave the country where I had grown up and lived my whole life, and emigrate forever to Australia. Life in South Africa with its injustice, its cruelty, its arbitrary resort to force, its gradually developing worship of police, of authority and of strength had become so intolerable to me that I could no longer face the prospect of living in it or of rearing a family in it. I was going to spend the few weeks I had left winding up my legal practice.

I read about the Rivonia arrests and did my best to forget about them. Not for long. A few days later, Harold Wolpe, one of the partners of the legal office in which I had previously been a partner, was arrested near the borders of Bechuanaland. He, I knew, had been active in left-wing politics in South Africa for some time. He had acted not only as a politician, but also as a lawyer, for the banned African National Congress and the organisations of whites and Indians which worked together with it for a multiracial South Africa.

Wolpe was the brother-in-law of James Kantor, the principal partner of that firm. Kantor had taken him into the business some two or three years before. Until that time the business had been strictly legal, specialising particularly in criminal cases and in the handling of some of the most publicised divorces and criminal actions. After joining James Kantor, Wolpe, on his own behalf, had acted as attorney in a number of political trials, generally without charging fees. Kantor and everybody else in the office were aware of it. Nobody had objected.

Suddenly, a few days after the Rivonia arrests, Wolpe had disappeared from the office. Two days later he was arrested on the borders of Bechuanaland, apparently in disguise and attempting to leave the country illegally. The police statements indicated that Wolpe would join those arrested at Rivonia when the time for a trial came. For the time being he was lodged incommunicado in Marshall Square prison not far from our office, an old red brick building which stands surrounded by skyscrapers of the great Witwatersrand gold mining corporations. Marshall Square had been police headquarters ever since the days when the town was a mining camp. No charge was brought against Wolpe at this time. In the office, Kantor knew as little as I did of the whole affair.

Some months before, the law had been amended to allow a suspect to be detained on the say-so of any police officer for a period of 90 days, during which time he could be held completely incommunicado and interrogated, unable to speak to any other prisoner, relative or legal adviser, and not allowed to communicate in any way with any person outside the prison walls. Wolpe was held under the 90-day Detention Law. So were the seven who had been arrested at Rivonia, together with several others who had been brought in during the following days.

With Wolpe at Marshall Square was the occupant of the Rivonia house, Arthur Goldreich. I did not know Goldreich but learnt subsequently that he was a man of considerable talent in many different spheres. He had studied at the University of Witwatersrand as an architect for several years, but before qualifying had switched and become an industrial designer. He was highly regarded as an artist, managing to combine fine arts and painting with commercial art. He held down a major store-designing job for one of the largest chain stores in the country. Everyone spoke of his pleasing personality, of his humour, drive and enthusiasm.

Goldreich had not been at Rivonia when the police arrived on the afternoon of July 11th, but he was arrested when he returned home from work later in the evening. His wife was arrested at the same time and the two of them had been lodged at Marshall Square. All the other Rivonia detainees had been transferred immediately from Johannesburg to Pretoria Local jail. But at Marshall Square, for reasons still not clear, Goldreich and Wolpe were lodged together. They were old friends.

The arrest of Wolpe had come as a considerable shock to James Kantor. Naturally he had been aware of Wolpe's earlier political activities and of the part Wolpe had taken in many political trials, where his appearance to defend was entered in the name of James Kantor and Partners. Kantor was, perhaps even more than myself, a non-political man. Young and of pleasing personality, he had the reputation of being one of the social set who frequented the night clubs and whose doings were reported regularly in the social columns of the newspapers. He had a house in the suburbs and a weekend cottage at Hartebeespoort Dam about 40 miles from Johannesburg, where he and his friends enjoyed the boating and the fishing. He had a reputation as a successful criminal lawyer with a flair for the dramatic in court.

Kantor had never, so far as I was aware, been personally involved in any political law case and had certainly never taken part in any political activities. Some considerable part of Kantor's success as a criminal lawyer lay in his ability to make friends with members of the South African police force. He was on first name terms with many of them, and thus able to glean from them those bits of information which are vital to the success of a criminal lawyer. From time to time he would rise to their defence in courts where they were charged either with crimes or, as was more often the case, with breaches of the police discipline code.

Kantor intervened vigorously on behalf of his brother-in-law Harold Wolpe. He interviewed friends and senior officers in the police force. He lobbied, he used whatever influence he could. All to no avail.

For several weeks nothing was heard about Wolpe or Goldreich. Then suddenly one night, after they had been in jail for several weeks, a dramatic newsflash came across the air from the South African Broadcasting Corporation: Goldreich and Wolpe had escaped, accompanied by two young Indian men—Moosa Moola and Abdullai Jassat, both of whom had been held as political suspects under the 90-day Detention Law. It was towards midnight on Saturday, the 11th August, that the four men slipped out of Marshall Square and disappeared into the night.

This was the most dramatic jail-break in the history of the South African prison service. For several weeks the police, politicians, the Prime Minister and the Minister of Justice had been publicly crowing over the triumph of the police in capturing the Rivonia seven, and of the alleged key men in their subversive underground movement, Goldreich and Wolpe. There had been weeks of boasting of the revelations a trial would bring forth; of the fantastic plots, plans and adventures of Goldreich and Wolpe. And now both were gone. How they went was at first not clear. It became clear subsequently when a young warder by the name of Johannes Greef was charged with assisting their escape.

Greef was 18 years old, newly out of Police Training College. On that Saturday night he had been left in charge of the keys to the doors which stood between Goldreich and Wolpe, and freedom. Greef had unlocked one gate—Goldreich and Wolpe had released Moola and Jassat and all four had escaped.

By the following morning a tremendous hue and cry was under way. A £1,000 reward was offered by the police for information leading to the recapture of Goldreich and Wolpe. The public was exhorted by radio and press to assist the police in every way. Descriptions of the wanted men were broadcast throughout the day and their pictures published in the newspapers. Road blocks were set up all around Johannesburg and on all roads leading from Johannesburg to the border posts on the frontiers of the British Protectorates of Bechuanaland, Swaziland and Basutoland. Inevitably the hue and cry raised a thousand false trails and a thousand false alarms. Sightings of Goldreich's distinctive black beard and long black hair had been reported from a dozen different places. In the midst of rumour, all that was certain was that the two men had vanished.

Greef was under arrest. And by Saturday morning Mrs Wolpe and Mrs Moola were also taken in for questioning. Mrs Goldreich, who had been arrested with her husband on the day of the Rivonia raid, was still detained in Marshall Square. For a week an intensive hunt went on. None of the men were found. Finally, on the 23rd of August the news was flashed back to South Africa from Mbabane, capital of Swaziland—Goldreich and Wolpe had arrived in the capital of the British Protectorate, 50 miles outside the Republic of South Africa.

2 Escape, the Accused and the Defence Team

The story of the Goldreich–Wolpe escape falls into two parts. One part was told by Johannes Greef in the case in which he was charged with aiding and abetting the escape of prisoners in his custody. It seems that some time before he had borrowed a friend's car, and while driving it was involved in an accident. The damage amounted to some £50 which the friend was claiming from him. He was unable to pay. He had been going about his duties at Marshall Square looking morose and upset. During exercise period Goldreich had asked him what the trouble was. When Greef told Goldreich of the trouble he was in, Goldreich had offered to make good the £50 shortage. Greef had allowed Goldreich to use the Marshall Square telephone. And so Goldreich, theoretically held incommunicado, had phoned to his sister, a Mrs Arenstein, and arranged with her to pay £50 to Johannes Greef. Greef collected his £50.

Goldreich had read all the POW classics. And in the classic way he set to work to buy himself out of Marshall Square. Greef proved willing. Goldreich promised Greef £2,000 in exchange for the keys to the cells where he and Wolpe were held. The arrangement was that Goldreich was to simulate an assault on Greef and tie him up. Five minutes after they had escaped, Greef was to cosh himself into unconsciousness. When it came to the fatal night Greef unlocked the cell doors for Goldreich and Wolpe, who in turn released their friends Moola and Jassat and disappeared into the night. However, Greef lacked the resolution to carry through a cold blooded assault on himself and was duly arrested. He appeared in a Johannesburg court under extremely prejudicial conditions. The Government's anger and outrage at Goldreich and Wolpe's escape whipped up into a hysteria of vengeance against Greef, who had made it possible. He was still only 18. He had been tempted by a large promise and had fallen for temptation. He had never received a penny of the £2,000 promised. In more humane societies he would have been an object of pity. But here he became an object of hate and the victim of political frenzy. He had an unblemished record. It was his first appearance in court. But he was shown no mercy. After a brief trial he was sentenced to the maximum of six years' imprisonment.

The second instalment is the tale of the adventures of Goldreich and Wolpe. With the aid of Greef they had smuggled messages out of jail to friends outside. On the night of the break, at midnight, there was to be a car waiting for them outside. But something had gone wrong with the timing. The driver who had been waiting for them had waited 45 minutes. Then, convinced that the plan had failed, he had left, ten minutes before the escapees stepped out into the cold and deserted midnight streets of Johannesburg on that Saturday night. They turned their coat collars up and set out to walk, Moola and Jassat in one direction, Goldreich and Wolpe in another, for security reasons.

Goldreich and Wolpe walked for a long time. Finally, unexpectedly, in the early hours of the morning, when Johannesburgers are wary of stopping to pick up strangers for fear of assault, they were offered a lift in a car. By remarkable coincidence, the driver turned out to be a friend, who willingly drove them to safety. They went to a cottage which stood in the gardens of a house in the suburb of Mountainview, and there they stayed hidden for a week, the curtains drawn all day and all night. The electric light was extended on a piece of flex so that the naked bulb lay on the floor under a table so no light would be visible outside their room. For a week neither of them raised their voices above a whisper for fear that someone—a servant, a neighbour, a householder—might hear a noise in the cottage and come to investigate. During that week they made contact with those who had organised the mistimed car to carry them away from Marshall Square. At the end of the week, with a car which had been bought for cash during that period, the two men, dressed as priests, crossed the frontier into Swaziland by an unknown route and presented themselves at the home of Rev. Charles Hooper at Manzini. They claimed to be tourists, and Hooper agreed to give them accommodation for a few days. Hooper himself had fled the intolerance of South Africa. He had been the Anglican parson in charge of a mission station in an area in the Transvaal where some months before, tremendous tribal conflict had flared up over the Government displacement of the tribal chief, and the appointment of a new usurper, the story of which he himself had written in a book called *Brief Authority*. Hooper apparently had little doubt that these 'priests' were bogus. But in the atmosphere then existing in and around the Republic of South Africa, committed opponents of apartheid had already learned that knowledge could be dangerous. They had learned to ask few questions, to accept even patently false stories at face value and not to pry into the patent disguises, either physical or verbal, of people on the run.

Hooper gave them refuge. Within a week they chartered a light plane in Swaziland to fly them across South African territory to Bechuanaland from where they hoped to make their way by land, across friendly territory, to permanent safety.

But nothing that these two did could be done quietly. They were front page news, not only in Southern Africa, but all over the world. Their arrival in Bechuanaland was headlined by press and radio. Their movements inside the territory were covered by reporters, and recorded, commented on, gossiped over in Bechuanaland pubs and discussed among the local white citizens, most of whom hailed from the Union of South Africa, supported the Verwoerd Government and were extremely hostile to everything that Goldreich and Wolpe stood for. When they arrived in the northern Bechuanaland town of Francistown, from where they hoped to fly to Tanganyika, hostility from the local white population forced them to seek safety in the local prison. There they spent a week at their own request, passing the time playing cricket, chatting, sitting in the sun.

Finally, a Dakota plane organised by helpers outside the country arrived at the Francistown airport. It was due to leave the following morning for Tanganyika. But during the night a mysterious explosion wrecked the plane. There was little doubt in anyone's mind that the explosion was deliberately engineered by supporters of the South African Government, perhaps even by its agents.

For a time it began to appear that the two who had fled from Marshall Square would find themselves permanently lodged in the Francistown jail. But Goldreich and Wolpe had become a matter of international concern. Arrangements were made outside the country for another plane. This time a small plane arrived quietly, with less publicity, at a remote air-strip far from the main centre of white settlement in Francistown. Goldreich and Wolpe left Francistown in the middle of the night, stepped aboard the plane and flew quietly from Bechuanaland to Elizabethville, and finally to Dar-es-Salaam, Tanganyika. Mr Vorster, the Minister of Justice, described the escape as a great setback in the campaign against subversion. Asked how the escape of Goldreich would affect the trial of those arrested at Goldreich's house in Rivonia, he replied: 'It will be more or less like producing Hamlet without the Prince. But the show will go on just the same'.

The day after Wolpe's escape his wife, Ann-Marie, was taken into custody by the police and grilled. So was Moola's wife. When Jimmy Kantor heard of his sister's detention he was livid with rage. He stormed into the security police headquarters at The Greys Building, saw senior officials, blustered and threatened, demanding that his sister be released immediately. Twenty four hours later she was, in fact, released. But by then Kantor had blotted his copybook with the Security Police.

Shortly after Wolpe and Goldreich had reached safety in Bechuanaland, Security Branch police raided James Kantor's legal office, and removed hundreds of dockets and files dealing with criminal and civil cases, both past and present. Included amongst them were many confidential statements by accused persons and witnesses made in privileged circumstances to their attorney, for cases which were still proceeding before the courts.

Kantor was arrested and hustled off to Pretoria to join the other Rivonia detainees in 90-day detention. I took over what was left of the practice of James Kantor and Partners—a legal office stripped now of its two senior partners, and of almost all its files and financial records.

I shared the offices with Security Branch policemen who were ferreting, day after day, through all the papers and ledgers and account books and receipts, the bank statements, files and petty cash books which had accumulated over the years. I took over the shell of what had shortly before been a thriving and lucrative business, and set about the dreary task of burying the ashes and packing them into funeral urns. It was a sinister and cheerless task.

Though the press speculated and gossiped about the men of Rivonia there was no hard news, no solid information of what was happening to them or where they were. They had vanished into the silent tomb of imprisonment in isolation, incommunicado for at least 90 days, if not longer. Kantor occasionally appeared like a wraith, brought from the jails to help the Special Branch ferret through his office and unearth some document for which they were looking. For the rest, nobody knew or heard anything of the men who had been arrested.

I suppose 70 or 75 days had already passed when Hilda Bernstein came to my office to see me. Her husband had been one of those arrested at Rivonia. I had never met either of them. She introduced herself, and then asked me whether I would be prepared to act as attorney for her husband and others should they be charged at the end of their 90-day detention period or later.

Hilda Bernstein told me that she had seen the head of the Security Police. He had refused to tell her whether her husband would be charged or not. The authorities had refused her permission to visit him except on two occasions when the topic of conversation had been strictly limited to business and financial matters, prescribed by the Security Police, and checked by a listening Security Branch man armed with a list of permitted topics.

She didn't know, she said, whether he needed or wanted a lawyer.

But if he *was* in fact charged, and if he *did* need a lawyer, would I be prepared to take up his defence? She said that she knew I was preparing to leave South Africa, but she did not know where else to turn. She had tried other lawyers. Some were too busy to take the case. Others were too frightened. Or perhaps some of those who said they were too busy were also too frightened. There were some who claimed inexperience for this sort of case, and others who said that such a highly publicised appearance on behalf of such unpopular men would prejudice them in their profession. There was one at least who had said bluntly that 'it is against my principles to defend such people as these'.

She was asking that I should embark on a case of unknown duration in the defence of people I did not know, whose actions I knew nothing about, and on a charge which had not yet been formulated. I felt that even if I were to agree, it would be a waste of time. The trial would be a mere formality. Everything pointed clearly to a certain conviction for everybody involved. It was not just that there was a mountain of evidence, if the press leaks were to be believed, but the documents from Rivonia alone were sufficiently damning for everyone concerned to be sentenced with the utmost severity of the law.

For two months there had been an unprecedented media campaign against the Rivonia men and all their supporters. Ministers had inveighed steadily against the Rivonia men through the columns of the press and on radio. The tradition in South African law is that one does not comment publicly on any case which is pending in a way which might influence or prejudice the court. This tradition had been swept to the winds by everybody from the Minister of Justice to the Attorney General and the Deputy Attorney General of the Transvaal. The Chief of Police and the Head of the Security Branch had commented recklessly on the facts in the case, and proclaimed on the guilt of the accused.

Throughout the country, there was not a single voice raised against the flood. By the very nature of events there could be no rebuttal of the ex-parte statements, accusations and prejudgements made against the Rivonia men. The only people who knew or could answer the facts or the distortions that were being broadcast against them were held incommunicado, unable to answer or speak. Even had they been free, in such a time of hysteria where would they have found an editor brave enough to publish what they had to say?

It was a time when to be a non-conformist, to speak against the stream, even to think against the stream, was fraught with peril. Despite all the legal safeguards which were written into the law for the protection of an accused person, there was no longer any chance that this trial would be a fair trial. This I understood as a lawyer. I thought Mrs Bernstein should understand it as a politician.

She, like everyone else connected with the Rivonia men, had had her full share of publicity during the past two months. A member of the Communist Party up to its dissolution in 1950, she had been the only communist ever to have been elected to public office by the all-white vote of an all-white electorate and had been a member of the Johannesburg City Council at the end of the war.

I listened to what she had to say, perhaps less surprised than sickened by her account, of the reception she had had from others in the legal fraternity in Johannesburg. At one time Johannesburg's lawyers had claimed, probably with justification, to be the fighting liberal and progressive heart of the South African legal community. Not now, apparently.

I did not consider my decision for long and said I would take the case. But I went on to say what I felt had to be said, so that there should be no misunderstanding: 'Mrs Bernstein, I am a lawyer, not a politician. I will do the job as well as I am able. But public opinion is so heavily against your husband and the others that in the end this is likely to count heavily'. She looked at me in amazement. 'Public opinion,' she said, 'Public opinion, against the Rivonia prisoners?' I looked at her, surprised. Was it possible that anyone intelligent, adult, literate, and living in South Africa could doubt that the stream of public opinion was running heavily against the Rivonia accused? She looked at me again and said: 'Mr Joffe, I think we speak a different language. You're talking of white public opinion. I am talking of majority public opinion, which is not against, but *for* the Rivonia accused.'

It is so easy to go astray in South Africa. One lives in a society which is exclusively white, where all one's friends, neighbours and colleagues are white, where the only black men that one comes across are servants, or humble down-trodden men and women who have scraped together their life's earnings to come and beg a solicitor to appear in their defence. It is so easy to think that white society is all society, to forget that there is a black society in South Africa, four times as numerous. It was white opinion that was running heavily against the Rivonia accused. And they were going to appear, in a white court, with a white judge, white prosecutor, white magistrates, white witnesses, white assessors, white police-men, white court orderlies, white spectators, surrounded by white pressmen. So I took the case, thinking in advance that it was a lost cause. It was still a case without indictment and without charge.

Within the next few weeks several other people came to see me. There was Albertina Sisulu, wife of Walter Sisulu. And after her, Annie Goldberg, the frail mother of Dennis Goldberg. And then after a time, a new figure, Winnie Mandela, wife of Nelson Mandela.

This was a new element in the case. Nelson Mandela was per-haps the best known, the most significant figure in the African lib-eration movement in South Africa, after Chief Albert Luthuli. He had not been at Rivonia on the day of the arrest. He had, in fact, been in jail for a year. Since mid-1962 he had been serving a sen-tence of five years hard labour for the crime of inciting people to strike against the unilateral declaration of a Republic by the white government without any consultation with the black majority of South Africans, and for leaving South Africa without a passport. Official handouts, or perhaps they were leaks from the Attorney General's office to the press, had made it clear that Mandela was somehow involved with the Rivonia men, and that he would prob-ably be brought from the Robben Island penal prison to join the men of Rivonia in the forthcoming trial. If Mandela was to be charged jointly with the Rivonia men it could mean only one thing—the charge could not relate to the events of the day of the Rivonia raid, but must go back in time. This seemed to point to the so-called Sabotage Act, Act 37 of 1963.

If my assessment was accurate, the legal consequences were all unfavourable to the men to be tried. The Sabotage Act had many provisions which would militate against the accused, even more than the prejudicial and sinister sound of the Act itself. It provided, for example, that a summary trial could be held if the Attorney General so directed, dispensing with the normal South African procedure of a preparatory examination by a magistrate before committal to trial in front of a higher court. It removed a great deal of the onus of proof from the prosecution and placed it on the defence. It provided that an offence could be legally proved by a single witness, whereas in a charge of treason two witnesses are required for every overt act. It stipulated also a minimum penalty of five years for any offence and a maximum penalty of death.

Despite all this, it seemed to me that since I had been retained by four relations, I should at least attempt to find out whether any of my clients would be charged; if so, when and with what. I decided to see Colonel Klindt, the then-Head of the Johannesburg Security Police, and also Dr Percy Yutar, the Deputy Attorney General of the Transvaal, who had been appointed, so the press reported, to examine the evidence from Rivonia and to take charge of any legal proceedings arising from the Rivonia raid.

From my interview with them it became clear that secrecy had become a way of life in the government's conduct of South African affairs. When I asked them some straight and legitimate questions, everything they knew, thought and heard suddenly became official secrets. They said blandly that they didn't know if anyone would be charged. They didn't know when anyone would be charged, or what the charges would be if they were charged. They both appeared determined to be as unhelpful as they possibly could. This was a pointer of what was to come in the Rivonia trial.

Two things, however, did emerge from the interview. One was an unsolicited undertaking from both Klindt and Yutar that no harm would come to me if I undertook the defence of political prisoners. I thought they protested too much.

As I left Klindt's office, Yutar invited me into the room which he occupied temporarily in the Headquarters building of the Security Branch of the South African police. As soon as the door was closed he started off on a little song of praise for the police telling me that it was 'quite remarkable. I have been at The Grays for three weeks now, and in all that time I have not heard a single word of anti-Semitism from any of these people'. It didn't seem very remarkable to me. I would scarcely expect any senior police officer to vent his anti-Semitism in the presence of a Jewish collaborator, a 'good Jew' from their point of view. I told him I didn't think an absence of anti-Semitism was a cause for special praise. Yutar bridled, saying: 'If you were a policeman, Joffe, wouldn't it make you anti-Semitic to have people like Bernstein and Goldberg going around stirring up the Bantu?' I was beginning to get the idea that Yutar was not just prosecuting this case; he was entering into the politics of it—a thought that was to occur to me more and more often as the case proceeded.

I left The Grays, knowing little more than when I came in. But one thing was certain, and that was that Yutar was hard at work preparing a prosecution. There was obviously a limited time for me to assemble a defence.

It is not easy to organise a defence for a trial of unknown nature, of unknown duration, where even the accused are unknown. I was stumbling around in the dark. To add to my difficulties there was the special nature of the times. The atmosphere was filled with fear and hysteria. Men of no political record, and men whose politics had led them into varying channels of respectable, legal (if slightly radical) anti-government opinion, walked in daily fear lest their political record be closely examined, and some non-conformist behaviour revealed. Rumour fed on rumour. Who knew what step from the straight path of conformism could lead to disaster? It was a time when people vanished mysteriously without charge into 90-day detention. Amongst professional people, including lawyers, quiet intimidation had seeped through the ranks; the intimidation often took petty forms, such as the refusal of passports without explanation as retribution for political non-conformism.

Then again there was the problem of finance. None of the people who had approached me to take up the defence of their relations were in any position to meet the substantial costs which a long trial would run up in South African courts. They had all spoken to me of the possibility of getting assistance from the local Defence and Aid Fund, which had been set up some years before to help provide legal defence to people charged with political offences and also relief and maintenance for their families. I knew that the Fund was hesitant to foot the bill for cases where the charge arose from acts of violence deliberately committed by the accused, even for political and non-selfish reasons. I did not know what the Rivonia accused would be charged with, but certainly the rumours, the leaks and the official statements made up to that time pointed to a charge which would include the preparation of armed uprising or revolution. Funds for such a case were going to be hard to come by.

There was only one person to turn to for funds and that was Canon John Collins of St Paul's Cathedral, London, who had created the British Defence and Aid Fund which, together with his many other achievements, led to his being nominated for the Nobel Peace Prize. Canon Collins willingly assumed the responsibility for the difficult task of raising the £19,500 which was needed. That a trial stretching over a year could be run for only £19,500 was due solely to the four defence advocates charging rather less than one fifth of their normal fees; the minimum needed by them in order to survive during the trial when they could not afford the time to accept any properly paid briefs.

To lead the defence team there was one obvious starting point. All the families who had visited me had unhesitatingly proposed that I try to get the services of Bram Fischer for the defence. If they had not done so, I would still immediately have turned to him myself. Abram Fischer—Bram to everyone who knew him—was a remarkable man. As son of a Judge-President of the Orange Free State and grandson of a President of the former Orange River Republic (before the formation of the Union of South Africa) all doors in South African society were open to Bram. An outstanding lawyer, he could, had he so chosen, have been a judge, possible Chief Justice; or if he had chosen, as so many legal men in South Africa do, to devote his time and talents to politics rather to law, he could have been an MP and almost certainly a Cabinet Minister. He had a charm, a great gentleness and a personal sincerity which endeared him to everybody. But he had also the other qualities of outstanding men—a painstaking, conscientious mind, a clear insight, tremendous drive and ability, singleness of purpose, and immense courage and integrity. Bram was the most popular man at the Johannesburg Bar. Nobody had hard words to say about him though some, particularly amongst the Security Police, had harsh words for his politics. For Bram had chosen, not as a callow youth, but as a mature man, to identify himself with what has always been the most unpopular political creed amongst white South Africans: he joined the Communist Party.

He had spoken on Communist Party platforms and made no secret of his communist beliefs, thereby closing all those doors of personal advancement which would otherwise have stood open to him. His legal career had been one of the most remarkable of any lawyer anywhere. On the one hand he had appeared, usually without payment, in many of the most celebrated political trials in South Africa, throwing himself into the defence with a singleness of purpose and personal dedication only possible for a man devoted both to justice and to the triumph of the ideals which had led the accused to the dock. He had also appeared frequently on brief to the great financial institutions, especially the multimillion-aire mining corporations, in some of the most abstruse legal and financial cases in South African courts.

Some years ago, Bram had been the leader of the team of lawyers who had handled the history-making Treason Trial in which, over the course of three years, 156 white and non-white leaders of the movement for national equality in South Africa had stood trial, to emerge triumphant at the end.

Unlike me, Bram knew personally all the people involved; at one time or another he had worked with all of them in one aspect or another of the political movement. He accepted the case and the leadership of the defence team, knowing full well that in doing so, he was inviting on himself retribution byway of detention or house arrest or prosecution. Having accepted, he immediately raised the question which had been in my own mind. Would he be permitted by the police to conduct such a defence?

In the atmosphere then existing in South Africa it was not at all farfetched to imagine the arrest or detention—with or without charge—of Bram Fischer merely to embarrass the defence. We decided that we were in a situation where nice reckonings of this sort could not be permitted to sway our decision. We would go into the defence for better or for worse, and if the Government with its tremendous power of persecution were to interfere with the defence, we would meet that situation when it arose.

Nevertheless, we all felt that Bram might be whipped off at any moment. It was therefore necessary for us to assemble a team for the defence which would not be crippled should it be summarily removed. We discussed the people at the Johannesburg Bar. There were not many candidates for such a job who would be either willing or suitable. Finally we approached two men much junior to Bram.

George Bizos had been an advocate since 1954 and in his short legal career had handled more political cases than, I think, any other lawyer in Johannesburg. Why this should be so I do not know. Perhaps it was that he had been moved to a sympathy for radical causes, for under-dog causes, as a result of his own youth. In the midst of the second world war, he and his father had escaped from the Nazi occupation of his native Greece in a small rowing boat, drifting about in the Mediterranean for some days until picked up by a British destroyer. George was then twelve years old, but he seemed always in the back of his mind to remember Greece in the hands of the Nazi armies. He spent some war years in an orphanage, finally arriving in South Africa where he finished his schooling and later qualified as an advocate. All the Rivonia people, we felt sure, would know George—personally or by reputation—and be prepared to trust their defence to him.

What we did not know at the time, and which turned out in the conduct of the case to be of tremendous value to us all, was that

George with his pleasant, sociable personality, easy sense of humour and fund of humorous anecdotes and stories, would become not only a very valuable legal representative, but also a great public relations officer for the defence.

Arthur Chaskalson was younger than George. He had been an advocate for ten years and had built up an enviable reputation. Tall, good-looking, articulate, and a fine sportsman, had he stuck to his law, and in particular to the exclusive company and insurance law which was tending to come his way, wealth, status and the highest positions in the legal profession could have been his for the asking. He had no particular political associations or aspirations, nor had he ever been involved in any political organisation. But there was one thing we did know about Arthur. For some time he had felt it his duty as a lawyer to undertake the defence of people who would otherwise have gone undefended, such as people charged with political crimes during the 1960s in South Africa. He had done this as a lawyer, not as a politician, and as a personal duty, not as a protest against the state. We admired his legal ability and his legal brain and had little doubt that he would feel again that he had a duty to the people in need of a defence and accept a brief in the Rivonia case.

George and Arthur both accepted without hesitation, even though the brief was vague, the charge unknown, the defendants unstated. I had no doubt that we had assembled a legal team of quite exceptional ability.

I spent the next week or two trying to pick up bits of gossip around the legal profession, the small leads, the insubstantial threads and indications which were filtering into the press, in order to piece together some idea of what type of case we were facing. One thing was certain: in many ways this would be a case unprecedented in South African legal history. It would be the first time that the accused, prior to their appearance in court, would have been held for three months or more in solitary confinement, incommunicado and without charge, subject during the whole of that time to police interrogation under mental and physical pressure.

Until the Sabotage Act was passed, judges' rules had laid down that any person accused of an offence might not be compulsorily interrogated in connection with that offence by the police. That was now a closed chapter in history. For another thing, it had always been South African law that it is in contempt of court to comment on any offence or the facts surrounding it in any way which can prejudice the accused or influence the finding of the court. In better times the law had operated effectively to prevent trial by newspaper before the court case, and to curb public comment, gossip, innuendo and speculation about the persons involved in a trial or the facts surrounding the case. On this score, the Rivonia case was breaking new ground.

These accused had been 'detained', as the current euphemism had it, not arrested. Where the law required any arrested person to be formally charged within forty-eight hours of his arrest, the 90-day Detention Law permitted detention in the custody of the police for an unlimited period prior to any charge. For three months the press, and more blatantly departmental officials of the Ministry of Justice, officers in the police force and members of the South African Cabinet, had commented freely on the Rivonia case, made allegations, issued statements uniformly prejudicial to the defence and calculated to influence the court in its findings, sheltering behind the technicality that the accused had not yet been charged.

Thirdly, this case would break new legal ground in that witnesses who would appear for the State would in many cases be people whose evidence had been extracted from them while they were under detention by the police, subject to no-one-knew-what pressure, and to the threat—spoken or unspoken—that if their testimony was not wholly satisfactory to the police they would be returned to detention. We could not rely on the legal niceties to be applied in this case. The Rivonia people had been receiving pretty rough verbal treatment from the prosecutor elect, Dr Percy Yutar, from the Minister of Justice, from the police and from large sections of the press. There was little reason to expect that this would change to the nice politeness of the legal game as it had been played prior to 1963 in South Africa. The most we expected was that, in accordance with tradition, the defence would be able to operate without direct hindrance.

On 7 October 1963, we heard rumours through the legal grapevine that the Rivonia prisoners were to appear in court the following morning. I rang Dr Yutar and asked him if this was so. He said it was, and advised me to be in the Supreme Court, Pretoria, with my counsel, at ten o'clock. It didn't seem to me an appropriate time to suggest that he might have let us know in case the rumour did not reach us on the grapevine.

Bram was busy on another case that day, so Arthur, George and I drove off to Pretoria, thirty miles away. During the drive we discussed the fact that the trial was not being held in Johannesburg. After all, Rivonia lay in the magisterial area of Johannesburg. All the accused were resident either in Johannesburg or in the Cape Province. None of them came from Pretoria. The decision to hold the trial in Pretoria could not have been dictated by the convenience either of the accused or of the State, since the prosecutor and all the Security Police involved in the Rivonia raid were stationed in Johannesburg. We had been told by Yutar that all the documents and other evidence removed from Rivonia were kept in Johannesburg. There could be only one reason to hold the trial in Pretoria, and that was political. Pretoria was a civil servants' town. It was the headquarters of the South African bureaucracy where all the government offices of the country are stationed. Its white population was overwhelmingly made up of people on the government pay-roll, its black population also considerably dependent on the government. It was, accordingly, an extremely strong pro-government, pro-Verwoerd area, a centre of the most rabid and extreme Afrikaner nationalism.

Some years before, the Treason Trial of 156 anti-government whites and non-whites had also been shifted from Johannesburg to Pretoria because of the tremendous crowds of supporters of the accused who had gathered at the courts and staged anti-government demonstrations. In Pretoria, with its atmosphere hostile to everything progressive, radical or anti-government, the control of crowds and the subduing of demonstrations would be easier. The State, both before and during the trial, was at pains to insist that the Rivonia accused and their organisations had no support amongst the South African population, that the African population—or what they called the 'happy Bantu' of South Africa—were hostile to the accused and happy under the Nationalist Government. There seemed to us little doubt than the decision to hold the trial in Pretoria was to ensure that it was held in an atmosphere where public opinion would weigh heavily against the accused.

We arrived at the Pretoria Supreme Court—known as the 'Palace of Justice'—ahead of time. There was no sign of anything out of the ordinary, it seemed a normal working day, with the normal amount of traffic. Inside the building no sign of any excitement or anything dramatic. We looked wherever we could. The accused were not there and neither was Dr Yutar. The Registrar of the court said he knew nothing about the case and had heard nothing. The three of us waited impatiently for about an hour, growing more and more angry and frustrated. Finally we asked to see the Attorney-General.

We were ushered into his office. In the civil service hierarchy Mr Rhein was Dr Yutar's immediate superior. We told him that Dr Yutar had informed us the night before that our clients' case would begin that day. We had come from Johannesburg specially, and it now appeared that no one in the building knew anything about the case. Mr Rhein leaned back in his chair. 'I am afraid I can't help you,' he said bluntly. 'Although I am the Attorney-General, don't think that anyone, least of all the police or our Dr Yutar, bothers to keep me informed about this case. I can understand your annoyance gentlemen, but this is Yutar's case, not mine, and you'll have to take the matter up with him. Frankly, I am sick and tired of being blamed for Yutar's bungling. I cannot help you.'

When we had time outside to get over our own irritation, we realised that several pieces of useful information had slipped from Mr Rhein as he gave vent to his indignation. It seemed that a few days before, Yutar had brought him a draft indictment for the Rivonia accused, to be signed by Rhein in his capacity as Attorney-General of the Transvaal. Rhein had refused to do so. It was in his view a very poor piece of work and he had sent it back for re-drafting. Yutar must still be working on it. Rhein eventually agreed to phone Dr Yutar to find out what was happening with our case. Over the phone we heard him ask 'What is the charge, sabotage or high treason?' Pause. 'Who will be the accused?' Pause. When he rang off he said 'Dr Yutar says the case will begin tomorrow. The prisoners have all been released from 90-day detention. He wouldn't say what the charges would be, and he won't tell me who is to be charged. He says that when you go to the jail they will bring you whoever is to be charged in this case'. We asked if there had been any explanation of why we had been left standing at the court that day. Rhein said that Yutar had apparently not felt it necessary to convey any apology.

So we drove from the Pretoria Supreme Court to the local jail to discover who our clients were. We thought this at least would be smooth sailing. It proved to be far more difficult than expected. The jail authorities had prisoners for us to see. But the difficulty was that some of the prisoners were white and some were not white. And though they were kept in the same jail, they were in separate parts of the jail, since apartheid applies rigidly in South African jails, perhaps even more rigidly than outside. We were told that we would be allowed to see the prisoners, but first the whites and then the non-whites. No mixing!

We said that this was absolutely ridiculous. The prisoners, whoever they might be, would be charged together in court. They would sit together in court; they would have to consult together; it would be impossible for us to defend them if we had to see them separately. The chief warder would not be moved. We insisted. Finally he called the colonel in charge of the jail. He would not be moved either but referred the matter to 'head office', that is, to the Commissioner of South African prisons, somewhere in Pretoria. It turned out that somebody there had decided or been told that this Rivonia trial was to be a showpiece for South African justice. If necessary minor restrictions of apartheid could be relaxed, in order that it should not appear that the course of justice for the accused was being hampered. The colonel sighed at the thought of relaxing these apartheid regulations, but was forced to retreat. On this occasion we would be allowed to see all the prisoners together but we must understand clearly that this was an exception, and it was not to be regarded as a precedent either for future visits or future cases.

After all this, the wait while they found our clients was long and uncomfortable. We didn't know who we were waiting for, or even how many there would be. The papers had rumoured various numbers from seventeen downwards.

When they did arrive, Nelson Mandela was amongst them. The fact that he was ushered in made it certain, for the first time, that he would be charged together with the Rivonia seven.

Nelson was a remarkable man. I had met him on occasion before his arrest. In his middle forties, he gave the impression of being considerably younger, perhaps thirty, an impression created not by immaturity, but rather by youthful vigour of manner. He stood over 6 ft tall, heavily built and in former days had been an amateur boxer of some considerable ability. He had a natural charm, an easy smile, an infectious laugh, all adding up to an extremely friendly, outgoing personality. The Nelson Mandela now before me was somewhat different. He had withered during his year in a South African jail, and looked thin and miserably under-weight. His face, formerly well filled out and a rounded, deep-glistening brown, was now hollow-cheeked, a sickly pale, yellowish colour. The skin hung in bags under his eyes. His manner, however, was the same: friendly, easy going, jovial, confident. He alone, of all our clients, was in South African regulation prison garb—short trousers like a young boy's, made rather crudely of some heavy felt-like material, open-toed ill-made sandals, presumably manufactured somewhere in the inner catacombs of the prison, and a khaki open-necked shirt. That was all—the regulation prison dress for an African prisoner. Partly, no doubt, it must be what the powers-that-be and their Prison's Board of white social workers imagine to be 'suitable' for a black man; and partly, I have no doubt, this garb is a deliberate attempt to reduce the prisoner in his own mind from the stature of a man to the hesitations and doubts of a boy. White prisoners wear long trousers, African prisoners—shorts. Many African prisoners go barefoot. Nelson at least wore sandals.

Our other clients—not convicted prisoners—wore their own clothes. Since they were all new to me, I could not compare them feature by feature with the people they had been before. They fell into two groups—those that had been arrested at Rivonia on the day of the police raid, and those who had been arrested at some other time. The Rivonia men I could recognise from their photographs in the paper.

Walter Sisulu, short, and stockily built, was the former Secretary General of the African National Congress. Pale efface, calm, quietly spoken, Walter was then and throughout the trial one of the most impressive personalities amongst the accused. He was a man of deliberation and careful judgement. At no time during the whole of that period did I ever hear Walter make a hasty decision, or venture an appraisal of anybody or anything without first weighing it carefully, deliberately, generally against his own immediate, instinctive reactions. On every issue, the other prisoners gave the greatest weight to Walter's opinions. It seemed to me that throughout the case, neither Nelson nor anyone else made any decision without first seeking Walter's opinion. After a short time, we on the defence team found ourselves behaving in the same way. Walter proved to have a judgement of situations and people that, in my experience, was seldom wrong.

Govan Mbeki was an old man, his hair greyed. It seemed from the greetings of the others who were meeting for the first time since their arrest, that the grey had increased considerably during his 90-day detention. He had the softest voice and the quietest, calmest manner of any of the accused. Yet his temper flashed from time to time, revealing a steel-hard interior beneath the urbane and smooth exterior. Govan gravitated immediately towards Raymond Mhlaba, an old colleague from his home town of Port Elizabeth. They had worked together in the African National Congress for many years. Raymond was one of the largest amongst the accused, over 6 ft tall, heavily built, weighing, I would guess, well over 200 lbs. He was slow-moving, quiet, calm, with a stolid immovable determination which carried him, apparently undismayed, through all the vicissitudes of the trial. In the midst of a brief conversation a great shrieking laugh would boom out with flashing teeth and pink gums. That was Raymond's trademark.

Ahmed Kathrada—the only Indian—was younger than most of the others, still in his middle thirties. He had a sharp tongue and engaging personality. He struck me essentially as one of the doers, not the theorisers, of the movement. Whatever practical job had to be done in this trial, Kathrada was willing to do it. He seldom ventured an opinion, especially on a theoretical matter, unless pressed, and never took the lead in any discussion. Yet he held tenaciously to views in many respects at variance with those of the others. He stated these views quite uncompromisingly, defending them when pushed to do so, but always accepted and carried out a majority decision once it had been reached.

Dennis Goldberg, of about the same age as Kathrada, was the most talkative of them all, a man with a constant flow of puns, jokes and witticisms. Partly I think his nature was easy-going and good-humoured, and yet it seemed to me that this wisecracking was, in part, a nervous mechanism, some sort of tic so compulsive that when it was time for him to give evidence much later in the case, I feared that he would be unable to curb the wise-cracking even in the witness box. He started talking and making jokes with us from the minute he walked in and introduced himself. Yet running through these jokes, throughout the period of the trial, I sensed an undercurrent of awareness of the weight of the evidence which the police had against him, from which he shielded his inner self with laughter. The police, during interrogation, had convinced him that the evidence against him was overwhelming, that his chance of an acquittal was nil.

Rusty Bernstein—about the same age as Mandela—middle forties—seemed to be regarded all round as the scribe, the articulator. He was the one who put into writing the ideas and the opinions of the others. He was almost the exact opposite of Goldberg, speaking little, quiet almost to the point of being taciturn. He seldom ventured a joke or a witticism, and seemed only to sparkle in his writing, never in his speech. On the first day he struck me as the one most obviously affected by his detention. He seemed depressed, listless and nervous.

The seventh of the people arrested at Rivonia on 11 July was Bob Alexander Hepple, aged 29 but looking even younger, with a round pink-cheeked look which belied the sharp legal brain behind it. He had qualified at the University of the Witwatersrand, practised as an attorney, and subsequently been appointed to the staff of its Faculty of Law. After some years as a lecturer in Law he had resigned and started practice as an advocate. At the time of his arrest he had been in practice for 18 months. Hepple I knew slightly, professionally, in the way in Johannesburg a solicitor gets to know the counsel of the local Bar—a nodding acquaintance—nothing more. He looked tense and somewhat uneasy during the whole of that morning's consultation. He volunteered almost immediately the reason for it. During his detention he had been 'asked', as he put it, to give evidence against the others. At that moment he was, so he said, still considering what to do.

Bernstein and Goldberg had been confined in the same 'white' section of the prison as Hepple. They had managed during their period of solitary confinement to exchange a few surreptitious words with Hepple during exercise periods. They had been aware of Hepple's hesitations, but the others seemed stunned by the announcement. At that stage, Hepple did not seem very clear in his own mind whether he intended to give evidence or not, but he made it quite clear that he had not rejected the idea. This news put something of a damper on a meeting which in many ways was a rather excited reunion.

Amongst those present who had not been arrested at Rivonia was Jimmy Kantor. He had all the symptoms of shock, which I expected. I know that he had suffered something of a nervous breakdown during the period of his solitary confinement. He was pale and the usual effervescence of his extrovert personality had disappeared. He looked haggard and drawn and quite unlike himself.

The other two, both unknown to me, were Elias Motsoaledi, a short, vivacious and charming personality who seemed too young to be the father of a large family—which he was, and Andrew Mlangeni, a large solid man, who complained immediately that he had been tortured with electric shock treatment during his detention and demonstrated the still visible burns and scars. It seemed to us from the little we knew of Mlangeni that—even if it was not true—he was well characterised by the witness who said he was known in the national movement as 'Robot'. He certainly had the capacity to stick to his post to the bitter end, a man of single-minded loyalty to a cause. These two, Elias and Andrew, had, in fact, been arrested some weeks before the raid at Rivonia. They had been held in detention throughout this period, taken periodically to identification parades to be shown to various witnesses of acts of sabotage, and were now joined with the Rivonia accused on a basis which we did not then understand.

So there we were. Eleven accused, seven of whom had been taken in the raid on Rivonia; of those seven, one preparing to opt out; one, Mandela who had been in jail for 18 months before that; one, Kantor, arrested weeks after the Rivonia raid, in our view as hostage for his brother-in-law Wolpe; and two arrested weeks before the Rivonia raid in connection with unknown offences which did not seem likely to connect them with the others. None of these people had been able to talk to each other—except for a surreptitious word exchanged dangerously behind a warder's back—for the whole period of three months in which they had been in detention.

We had come on legal business to consult the accused. But it was clear that they were in no mood for consultation. They were rediscovering, it seemed to us, the joys of speech, not unlike people who had been dumb and had suddenly had the power of speech restored to them. They were miraculously wondering at the joy of it, turning it over on their tongues, feeling the taste of it on their lips; they were drunk with speech, with human communication and contact, with being able to talk, to meet with and touch other people, too involved in all these new sensations, too intoxicated with them to be prepared to consider serious problems of law. It was very obvious that our legal consultations on that day were not going to get very far. One problem, however, could not be delayed; that was the question of which of these men wanted us to represent them. We explained to them all how we came to be there and that it was necessary for each one to decide for himself whether he wished to be represented by us or not. They knew only that they were going to be charged, not the details of the charge.

The day before, without any warning whatsoever, they had all been hauled out of their cells and taken one at a time into a front office, finger-printed, formally charged with offences under three Acts of which they were given only the numbers, asked if they had anything to say, and told that they would be brought before a court within the statutory period of forty-eight hours from the time of arrest which was deemed to be that moment. At the same time, they were formally released from 90-day detention, and transferred to the category of awaiting trial prisoners—all, that is, except Mandela, who was then and throughout our association with him, in the category of convicted prisoner.

We did not expect that any of the accused would refuse our services. But what was necessary was to decide whether we could appear for all of them, and whether their interests would be served by a joint defence or separate defences. On this their opinions were all firm and unequivocal—they would stand together and enter a joint defence—except in the case of Kantor which they knew from the start could not be the same as that of the others. Neither the other accused, nor Kantor, nor we across the table, could see any merit even in suggesting that Kantor could possibly share in a single defence. He had never been part of whatever political causes it was that the others were striving for. He had never belonged to their organisations or worked with them. If they knew him, they knew him only as a lawyer. He had been dragged into the case, not because of any complicity in their political activities, but as proxy for his brother-in-law. We all advised Kantor that he should seek separate defence. Kantor himself felt, correctly, that his defence could have nothing in common with the defence of any of the others. On the basis that he would arrange to have a separate defence, he left us.

In relation to Hepple we were in difficulties. As a lawyer I could not try to dissuade him from giving evidence if this was what he wished to do, nor could I ask him to face the risks attendant on refusal to give evidence—a trial, a likely conviction, and the probability of spending the rest of his life in jail or possibly even of being hanged. This decision he had to make for himself.

I appreciated full well the agonies a man has to go through in making a decision such as this. Hepple had been alone under 90-day detention, subject to pressures from the authorities and the police. He had to decide for himself, in his loneliness, whether to face trial and the disastrous consequences which might flow from it, or to seek indemnification by giving evidence against his colleagues and friends. Nobody at that moment seemed prepared to give him any advice. We all felt then that it would be better for him not to participate in any consultation until he knew definitely where he stood—whether he was to be a witness or an accused. So he left the room, leaving us with the nine accused.

George Bizos put the position to them quite bluntly. The prison officials had restricted the time we could spend on this consultation and all that he had time for was to tell them how black the case against them looked from the outside. We were judging only from what had been said by Cabinet Ministers, by the police and by newspapers. It seemed that they would be tried on charges of attempting to overthrow the State by violent revolution, of organising armed rebellion and acts of sabotage. George told them that the penalty for any one offence charged, either as High Treason or under the Sabotage Act, could range from a minimum of five years to a maximum of death. It wasn't very cheerful news for men who had come out of three months of solitary confinement. None of them appeared either startled or chastened. I suppose in their own minds, with the knowledge they had, both of the law and the evidence which had been found at Rivonia, they must already have reached this conclusion for themselves. No one said anything for the moment. They seemed to be considering and weighing it up in their own minds. Finally Dennis Goldberg spoke up. He said that he had learned quite a lot from the police themselves during the sessions when they attempted to interrogate him. It was quite clear that the evidence against him was so strong that there could be no possible defence. He volunteered to take all the blame for any of the actions, and even to plead guilty if doing so would assist any of the others to go free. It was said, I am certain, with absolute sincerity, and was completely in line with Dennis' personality, and as I came to know later in the trial, typical of the man.

No one except Dennis, it seemed, really gave this offer serious consideration. None of them seemed then, nor did they ever seem later, the type of people to let others take the blame for anything they might have done. But in any case, it hardly seemed worth discussing at that moment. The offer was brushed aside and promptly forgotten.

It was in any case futile to discuss anything about the defence before we even knew what the charges would be. We made what arrangements we could about how to proceed in court the following day, when they were to be formally charged, keeping it all as short as possible, since most of them seemed utterly disorientated after their period in solitary confinement. They did not appear to be able to concentrate on any subject for any length of time, or to think too coherently. They seemed to have little interest in what we were discussing, and to be only really interested in news of their families and their welfare. We gave them what information we had, and chatted for a while about things not directly concerned with the morrow's court case.

From hints given by police interrogators they believed that other people would be charged with them. The name of Ruth Slovo, who was then detained at the women's prison nearby, had been specifically mentioned. We told them that the press had said something of the same sort, and that we were going from there to the women's jail to try to find out.

At the women's jail we were refused permission by the matron in charge to see Ruth Slovo. We were told that she was in solitary confinement and the police orders were that nobody was to see her. We explained that we were her lawyers, and as she was to be charged in court the following day, we were entitled to speak to her. The matron stuck to her opinion, we to ours. Finally we suggested that she telephone the Attorney-General and get his instructions. She refused. She never took orders, she said, from the Attorney-General. The Security Branch of the police had left Ruth in her care, and the Security Branch had said she was to see no one. She took orders from the Security Branch. We asked her to phone the Security Branch. She agreed grudgingly and returned triumphant. The Security Branch had ordered that no one—no one at all—was to see Ruth Slovo. We conceded the victory willingly. This could only mean one thing: whatever else was to happen to Ruth, she was not being charged with the Rivonia men the following day.

We went back to Johannesburg commenting on the remarkable fact that, in the middle of the year 1963, such secrecy surrounded political offences that the only information a lawyer could get about his clients was by piecing together the speculations in the newspapers, or by calling at the jail to learn from the jailers whether his client was still held incommunicado under the 90-day law, charged, discharged, or dead. The following morning we did, in fact, receive the only solid confirmation we ever had that the accused would appear in court that day—a report in the local newspapers. The newspapers always knew more than we did. Nobody had bothered to notify us officially that the case would be called, or tell us in which court, or at what time.

Dr Yutar, well aware that I was acting for the accused, had no time for such courtesies. He had managed, however, to find time to interview the press. Reporters had seen him at his house the previous day. Dr Yutar's picture appeared prominently in the morning papers and in exchange the newspapers were given advance copies of the indictment which they were not to print until it had been released in court later that morning. There was no copy of the indictment for us, and when we asked for a copy on the very morning of the court hearing, we were told that it was not yet available.

Percy Yutar had a passion for publicity. At first we found it extremely irritating. Later we found it so ludicrous that it became a topic for jokes between us. As the trial progressed, we began to understand that, come what may, dramatic evidence of some sort would be introduced in court late every Friday afternoon—late enough to be still newsworthy for the Sunday papers that have the largest circulation, and yet not early enough for the defence to have any time to rebut it or to cross-examine on it before the weekend.

On the opening day of the case we arrived at court well before the hour appointed. It was a remarkable scene. None of us had ever seen the Supreme Court in Pretoria so besieged by police. The rather fruity baroque building faces Pretoria's civic centre, Church Square. The Square was packed with police, as though for a passing-out parade. Inside the position was no different. The police were everywhere, in every lobby and corridor and doorway.

Perhaps the most remarkable sight of the day was the convoy of prisoners from the jail, about a mile away, to the court. There were three motor cars filled with prison dignitaries and high-ranking policemen; behind them, a lorry with a score of white policemen armed with Sten guns; behind that, the Black Maria in which the accused travelled, carefully segregated as South African police vans are—a small compartment at the front for white prisoners, and a large compartment at the rear for blacks. Behind this again a bevy of cars, policemen and warders and more policemen.

All the traffic pointsmen on duty between the jail and the Supreme Court had been alerted. The convoy swept through, while Pretoria's peak hour traffic stood stalled and angrily hooting at all intersections. The enormous convoy drove into the court building through great iron gates which clanged closed behind them, and the policemen with Sten guns jumped out and surrounded the prison yard as though on a military expedition. The prisoners had been handcuffed at the jail before being put into the van.

Two hours before the case was due to be called they were shepherded out and into the cells below the court. Inside the building police were spread around, all armed. At the main entrance of the building facing Church Square there was a contingent of men carrying satchels of tear-gas bombs in addition to service revolvers. They stood scowling at the members of the public who had been well-enough informed to know that the trial was on and brave enough to risk attending in the face of this show of force. Inside the courtroom itself, the white public benches were filled by plain-clothed policemen from the Security Branch and warders in civilian clothes, almost to the exclusion of any white spectators.

The court was rigidly divided down the centre, an aisle separating white seating from the non-white side; every seat was taken, filled with relations and friends of the accused.

The sight reinforced the contradiction between what one read and what one saw. One read daily the claims of the State representatives that the so-called 'subversive' organisations of the accused had been smashed and discredited, and that what little support they may have once enjoyed had now dissolved. And yet here one saw the other side—the panicky uneasiness with which the State faced the trial of the leaders of these 'unpopular' organisations, and the extraordinary steps which had been deemed necessary to prevent hostile, anti-government demonstrations inside or outside the court.

We waited anxiously to see who would be on the bench. We had heard rumours that the Judge-President of the Transvaal, Mr Quartus de Wet, might take the case himself and shortly after ten o'clock he entered. The court was in session.

Dr Yutar rose to call 'The case of the State versus the National High Command and others'. He then, for the first time, produced the indictment, handed a copy into court and passed a copy across for the defence. Bram Fischer rose immediately to apply for an adjournment. The accused, he said, were facing charges of the utmost gravity, where the death sentence could be imposed, and the indictment was an extremely complex document charging a large number of separate acts in almost every part of South Africa, citing co-conspirators and agents scattered throughout the country, many of them even abroad. Clearly, he argued, in a case where the issues were of such complexity, and the allegations so numerous, a long remand would be essential for the defence to prepare its case. He added that all the accused had been held in solitary confinement for three months. They were neither in a fit state to instruct counsel nor to consider their defence adequately before a period of recuperation. The State, he said, had had three months, since the arrest of the accused in which to prepare its case. It had been able to call on all the resources of the police force and of the Department of Justice to do so and yet two days before, when the trial had originally been scheduled to begin, the State itself had not been ready to proceed.

'There is an old saying' he added, 'that justice must not only be done, but must be seen to be done. The accused in this case are people who carry the deep respect of a very large proportion of the population, and for this reason alone justice should be seen to be done. There should be no urgency to bring them to trial. We want justice to be seen to be done. I ask therefore for a postponement provisionally for six weeks. By then we will be able to give the court an indication of when we hope to be ready. At this stage we are not even able to estimate how long the defence will require to prepare the case.'

Yutar jumped in to oppose the defence application for postponement. For the first time we had revealed to us the style of prosecution we were going to meet in the course of this case. He virtually ignored the arguments of the defence. Instead, with a voice which rose to a dramatic falsetto, he spoke of witnesses who had to be called before the end of that month: 'I fear for their safety,' he cried in a voice bordering on hysteria, fingers aloft in a dramatic Ciceronian gesture.

Whether it was this, or some other considerations not clearly in evidence that helped Mr Justice de Wet to make his mind up quickly, I do not know. He ruled that there would be a three-weeks' postponement and adjourned the case.

When we heard that de Wet was to sit in this case we had very mixed feelings. He had a strange reputation in South Africa. In legal circles he was not rated highly as a lawyer but was reputed rather to be one of those judges who dispense what they regard as rough justice, on a basis of common sense rather than law. And, as is so often the case, 'common sense' proves often to be a mixture of obstinacy and prejudice. In court he had always shown himself extremely self-willed, disliking interjections, interventions and procedural objections. We knew that on the broad general issue of white supremacy versus African freedom, we should expect all the prejudices of a typical white South African. On the other hand, Mr Justice de Wet did not have the reputation of being a puppet of the Nationalist Government who would take orders directly from politicians. We felt that while we could have done much better in the selection of a judge, we could also have done worse. The very short adjournment he allowed dismayed us. It seemed to us that before even entering the court he had made up his mind that the trial would proceed speedily. The reason could, of course, be personal convenience. But I felt fairly sure that the reason was political, dictated chiefly by the need to accommodate the case to the government's desires. I was becoming convinced that political considerations would play as big a part in this case as the law.

Immediately after the adjournment, the court reconvened to hear a bail application from James Kantor. Kantor's lawyers, who were not a part of our team, were so confident of his innocence and so certain that bail would be granted, that they voluntarily handed in to the court a copy of his statement to the police when he was interrogated in solitary confinement which could otherwise not have been used in evidence against him. The case against Kantor was threadbare. Kantor's counsel, believing that everyone must see, as he saw, that Kantor was clearly a victim of either persecution or a miscarriage of justice, based his pleas on the fact that Kantor had been at all times a hostage for his brother-in-law, Wolpe, that his legal practice had disintegrated during his detention, and he himself had suffered a nervous breakdown; and yet all the allegations contained in the indictment were of matters completely unknown to Kantor, and in which he could not possibly be shown to be involved.

At the end of an eloquent address the judge asked the prosecutor simply: were there any indications that Kantor had been involved in the acts of sabotage alleged against the accused? We were not then as accustomed to the recklessness of Dr Yutar as we were to become later. He jumped to his feet to assure the judge that there was no doubt whatsoever that Kantor was fully involved. Thus, on the unequivocal assurance of Dr Yutar, bail was refused, and Kantor returned to Pretoria Local jail, with the rest of the accused.

Kantor's counsel, Mr H C Nicholas QC, was thunderstruck. Immediately the court adjourned, he strode across to Dr Yutar to challenge his evidence of Kantor's complicity in any sabotage. Yutar gathered up his papers, in a hurry to leave. As he went out he said that he had an affidavit—in a tone of voice which implied that an affidavit was incapable of being false—that had been taken by a responsible *policeman*! It only occurred to us later that it was odd that he had not said 'made by a responsible witness'. The affidavit stated that Kantor had attempted to recruit Africans in the Johannesburg townships to undergo military training as guerrillas. Yutar bustled off. Nicholas was staggered. We were all staggered. Only Kantor seemed to see the funny side of it. He laughed. I thought that Yutar must surely be lying. I couldn't laugh. As it turned out, the affidavit was no laughing matter. We waited throughout the trial for the affidavit to be produced, but it never came. But as it turned out, I was wrong. Yutar was not lying. There was in fact such an affidavit. We learned about it by sheer coincidence quite outside the course of this case.

The coincidence arose in this way. An African from Cape Town who had been detained shortly after the Rivonia arrests, one Looksmart Ngudle, had been found dead in his cell in Pretoria Local jail. It was said he had hanged himself. At the inquest his wife had claimed that he had been driven to suicide to end the tortures which he suffered at the hands of the police. Another African who had been detained in Pretoria jail with Ngudle, one Isaac Tlale, was called as a witness. He was questioned about his interrogation sessions with the police. The record reads thus:

Advocate Berrange (for Ngudle): Now you say that you were hit on the head with a portion of a chair, that you were taken by the throat and that you were kicked.

Tlale: Yes.

And during this time what were they trying to get you to do?

They wanted me to admit that I am the person who organises the recruiting for the business. (The 'business' being Umkhonto we Sizwe, the para-military force set up by members of the African National Congress).

Thereafter were you taken anywhere else in the building?

They took me to another place. It is an office. I found three Europeans in that room. They asked me if I was still denying. I said I don't know anything. I was then asked to hop.

Indicate what you mean.

(Tlale then indicated)

Did you do that until you got tired?

I did that until I got tired.

And were you still denying?

I was still denying.

What were you told to do then?

I was told to undress.

Did you do so?

I did so.

And then where were you told to go?

I was handcuffed. There were two chairs joined together. I was asked to sit on those two chairs. I was sitting in this way. (He showed how he sat, knees up, with his hands clasped around them). My hands were handcuffed, and in between my knees they inserted a broom-handle.

Below your knees and above your arms?

Above my arms and below my knees.

So that you were pinioned then?

Yes.

What happened to your head?

My head was covered with a bag.

And what happened to your hands?

I could feel that something was tied to my two small fingers.

And during this time you were being addressed. Were they talking to you, asking you anything?

They were asking me continuously whether I was still denying.

Did you continue to deny?

I continued denying.

What was the next thing you felt?

I then felt my body was burning. I felt as if something was shocking me.

Have you ever had an electric shock?

Yes. I had it when I was repairing a motor car.

The same sort of thing?

Yes.

Can you remember how many times these shocks were put through you?

They did it twice.

And what happened ultimately?

Thereafter I lost my consciousness. The next thing I remember was standing next to a table signing a document.

Did anyone hold your hand?

One constable was holding my hand.

Was this a document that had any writing on it? Or was it blank, or what was it?

I could see, on this piece of paper, on top was written my name and address.

And the rest, was it blank, or had it writing on it?

It was blank.

And the sheet of paper on which you signed your name? Was that the same sheet of paper or can't you remember?

It was not the paper which had my name on.

And thereafter where did you go?

They said I should go and clean myself.

Why did you have to go and clean yourself?

I had messed myself up.

You defecated into your trousers?

Yes. I was taken to a latrine. I took a piece of paper and wiped out my trousers.

And then you were taken back to your room?

Yes.

That was the first instalment of the Tlale story. Sometime after the inquisition Tlale himself was charged with recruiting people for military training. I undertook his defence and he told me the rest of the story. After the interrogation and the electric shock treatment described at the inquest he had been left in his cell for three weeks and saw nothing of the police. One day a certain Captain Swanepoel appeared with a document in his hand. It was no longer blank. It was now a statement by Isaac Tlale. It read:

'During April 1963 Phineas Nene who is known to me came to my shop. He called me outside, pointed outside to his car, said there was a European in the car and we must go there. He introduced me to the European who was James Kantor, and I climbed into the car. We then drove out into the country. Kantor spoke to me in English and Phineas interpreted. He told me that I should not even repeat what he told me to my wife. He said I must get young unemployed Africans to be sent to Bechuanaland where they were to be trained as soldiers. He told me that when I got such recruits I must tell Phineas, then Phineas would tell Kantor.'

Captain Swanepoel said that now that they had his statement Tlale would have to be a State witness. He promised protection if he gave evidence. Tlale had denied the contents of the statement. Swanepoel told him that his signature was on it, and if he denied it in court he would be convicted of perjury. Tlale said it was their statement, not his; it was blank when he signed it. 'Swanepoel said that he would beat me up, as they had done. I told him that I was not prepared to be beaten up again and I would fight back and they could rather kill me. They then showed me the Sabotage Act and told me to read it for myself so that I could see what would happen to me. 'If you refuse to give evidence you will be hanged.' I still refused and he then left, after getting me to sign a statement that I had disclaimed my previous statement.' And so belatedly, long after it was too late to set Kantor at liberty, the basis of Yutar's glib assurance to the court which had led to refusal of Kantor's bail, came to light.

Captain Swanepoel was one of the key figures in the Security Branch side of the Rivonia case. Whether this affidavit was manufactured in order to implicate and convict Kantor, or merely in order to prevent him getting bail, I have never been able to establish. Perhaps both.

3 Quashing the Indictment

We spent the three weeks considering the indictment and the character of the case against the accused, and roughly deciding the line of defence. The indictment itself was a strange document. Seven of the accused, Mandela, Sisulu, Mbeki, Kathrada, Goldberg, Bernstein and Mhlaba were charged with being members of an association known as 'The National High Command, The National Liberation Movement, the National Executive Committee of the National Liberation Movement Umkhonto we Sizwe (The Spear of the Nation)'. They were also, like all the others, charged in their individual capacities; Kantor was charged personally in addition to his capacity as a partner in the firm of James Kantor and Partners.

Basically the offence charged was the planning of a conspiracy which 'envisaged a military basis and with hostile intent', violent revolution and an armed invasion of the country, and in preparation therefore the commission of more than 235 acts of sabotage. The indictment alleged that 'acting in concert and conspiring and making common purpose' with a list of some seventy people named and several organisations including the Communist Party of South Africa and the African National Congress, they had 'incited, instigated, commanded, aided, advised, encouraged or procured other persons to commit the aforementioned wrongful and wilful acts of sabotage, preparatory to and in facilitation of guerrilla warfare in the Republic of South Africa, coupled with an armed invasion and a violent revolution'; that they had solicited, accepted and received money from various persons or bodies both inside and outside the country in support of a campaign for the repeal or modification of certain laws, the modifications of which would 'further the achievement of one or more or all of the objects of communism as defined in Section 1 of Act No.44 of 1950'—the so-called Suppression of Communism Act. Communism is there defined so widely as to cover almost any social, economic or political change.

As a clear, legal statement of the precise charge the accused were required to answer, it was a shoddy and imprecise document. Its vague and general allegations made it impossible to discern precisely what the offence was, by whom the offence had been committed, and in what way the accused either individually or jointly were alleged to be connected with it. Our attitude to the indictment could follow one of three lines. We could accept it as a generalised allegation leaving the precise nature of the legal charge to emerge in the course of evidence, thus treating the indictment more as a statement of overall political allegation than as a criminal charge formulated in terms of the law. Alternatively, we could seek to clarify what was vague by a request to the court for an order that we be supplied with 'further particulars'. Or, finally, we could move to have the entire indictment rejected by the court, on the ground that its vagueness made it embarrassing and prejudicial to the defence.

We decided to make an approach to the prosecution for further particulars, and see how they reacted. The reaction was wilder and more ludicrous than we could ever have expected. We had asked, amongst other things, which of the accused or co-conspirators were alleged to have carried out each of the acts of sabotage listed in the indictment; how the conspiracy between the parties had been entered into, when and where and at what date it was alleged that each member of the National High Command became a member, for clearly no one could be responsible for actions of that body before he became a member of it. We asked for details of when it was alleged that the conspiracy between the Communist Party and the African National Congress was entered into, and who represented each of these organisations in deciding on their 'concert or common purpose'. There were several more questions of the same type. The replies were curt and repetitive. The almost invariable answer was either 'These facts are known', or 'These facts are peculiarly within the knowledge of the accused'. Occasionally facts were—more emphatically—'blatant and peculiarly within the knowledge of the accused'. The prosecution was clearly following a simple precept: 'You are guilty. Therefore you know what you did. Therefore we don't have to tell you'.

We decided to move in court for the dismissal of the indictment on the grounds that it did not comply with the law and inform the accused adequately and with reasonable clarity of the precise charges or allegations which they had to meet. We were quite determined that, guilty or not, our clients would get a trial in full accordance with the law. They would not be railroaded! Some people, I believe, took this attack of ours on the indictment as an indication that we intended to rely on legalistic 'point-finding' and obstruction for our defence. That misconception seems to have communicated itself to Dr Yutar and the prosecution. It is only in the light of this misconception that I can understand the peculiar tactics the prosecution adopted throughout this case.

From our very earliest discussions with the accused (again I stress that from here on wherever I speak of such discussions they were held without either Kantor or Hepple present) one thing stood out clearly. None of them were prepared to deny associations with the bodies to which they had belonged: those who had been associated with the African National Congress would under no circumstances deny the fact, nor would those who had been associated with the Communist Party, or Umkhonto we Sizwe. In their eyes, they made clear, this was less a trial in law than a confrontation in politics. They were all conscious of the fact that, in the eyes of their followers and supporters at least, they were public representatives of and spokesmen for organisations which were illegal, deprived of any public platform and banished from publicity in the columns of the South African press. They would be speaking in court as the defendants, almost the gladiators of their cause. And they intended to speak as they would expect representatives of such a cause to speak when they appeared in public outside a court—proudly in support of their ideals, defiant in the face of their enemies. This was their intention from the start, and the spirit of their general instruction to us.

Our attack on the indictment did not signify any qualification of that attitude. It signified simply our resolve that it be clear from the outset to the court and the prosecution that we would not be swayed by the hysteria in the country and the whipped-up witch-hunt against communism and subversion. We would not abandon any of the normal legal rights. We would insist that persons on trial for political offences, whatever the unpopularity of their cause or the needs of the government, be assured of their right to trial by the normal course of South African law. It was this combination of attitudes—on the one hand, tenacious upholding of their legal rights as citizens, and on the other hand, steady refusal to deny any political associations even with unlawful organisations—that Dr Yutar proved unable to understand, and thus unable to cope with.

We prepared our attack on the indictment as carefully as possible. We intended it to be a demonstration to the court that we would insist on the full requirements of the law being carried out, regardless of how extraordinary the circumstances of this case might be. However, on the day the case resumed, the court became the scene of a demonstration of a different type.

In the Supreme Court, Pretoria, prisoners in custody are lodged in cells in the basement of the court. They enter the court up a steep staircase which emerges in the centre of the court, immediately behind counsels' tables and immediately in front of the public gallery. For this case a special dock had been constructed alongside the staircase, so that the twelve accused sat side by side with their backs to the public. A few minutes before the hour when the judge would enter, the signal was given for the prisoners to be brought in. There were crowds of spectators on both the white and the non-white benches.

The first of the prisoners was Nelson Mandela. His head and shoulders appeared above the level of the dock as he climbed the staircase. There was a ripple of excitement amongst the public. He turned to face the public, and gave the thumbs up salute of the

African National Congress, with his right fist clenched. His deep voice boomed out the African National congress battle-cry 'Amandla' (Power). A large part of the audience, the African audience, replied immediately in chorus 'Ngawethu' (It shall be ours).

The demonstration took the police and prison staff by surprise. They had packed the courts in such numbers that they must have felt certain nothing could go wrong. The colonel in charge of the Pretoria jail and his head warder both arrived as daily escort to the Rivonia prisoners, as though all other duties were suspended during this period, to allow them to watch this group of men. Dozens of prison warders, all in plain clothes, filed in with the prisoners up the stairs; others took up places in all the seats immediately behind the prisoners, forming a cordon between them and the public. Each prisoner thus had one or two private warders sitting like footmen in attendance. This went on throughout the case. Security Branch policemen in 'civvies' packed the public benches and stood massed at all exits and entrances, surveying the crowd, watching the doors, waiting for what we did not know. None of this vast army was fast enough on their feet to cope with this unexpected demonstration. By the time the police and warders had recovered themselves, each of the accused in turn had filed in, repeated the salute, received the loud reply from the public benches and taken his place—each of the accused, that is, except Kantor and Hepple, who smiled at friends in the crowd, but remained silent. The orderly shouted 'Order in Court' and Mr Justice de Wet entered and took his seat. That round, I thought, had definitely gone to the accused. We weren't so sure about the next.

Bram Fischer handled the attack on the indictment. He is the complete lawyer. He is painstaking, clear, precise. Unlike the public concept of a lawyer, he is no orator. To listen to him is difficult, as he hesitates over a word, groping for precisely the right one before he uses it, thinking slowly and deliberately between sentences. His performance here might be crucial for the whole future, perhaps even for the lives of the people in the dock behind him. He was very conscious of the weight of it. The men in the dock were not just his clients. They were colleagues with whom he had worked for years, many of them close personal friends. He drove himself mercilessly in those three weeks, preparing his argument with thoroughness and meticulous care. He delivered his argument in that quiet, deliberate manner, so impressive to legal people, so unimpressive to the public who had come expecting, I suppose, dramatics, gestures, oratory. Patiently he traced every defect in the indictment—the lack of particularity, the confusion of allegation, the obscurity. Some of the acts of sabotage had been committed before any Sabotage Act existed in South Africa, and could not therefore be offences in terms of the Act under which they were charged. The indictment contained on the one hand extraneous and irrelevant matter, on the other, fatal deficiencies. It had patent anomalies, such as the fact that Nelson Mandela was charged with having committed 156 acts of sabotage which had taken place while he was in jail.

After a long and crushing exposure of the indictment, he turned to our request for further particulars: 'The acts of sabotage set out in the indictment may have been committed by other people and not by the accused. But the State refuses to tell us the names of the people who it alleges committed the acts. Unless the State says who carried out each of the acts, how is the defence to meet the charges? Either the State knows who committed the acts, or it does not. If it does not know, then it should not charge them with the acts. If it does know, it should tell us.' If the State with all the resources available to it was not able to furnish the accused with the necessary particulars of the allegations, how, he asked, was it possible that the accused with their strained resources should be expected to discover the necessary particulars and fill them in for themselves? There was only one explanation of an indictment such as this. With his voice rising to a rare passion and anger, Bram declared that the State had decided that the accused were guilty. It had further decided that since they were guilty a defence would be a waste of time. It was only in this light that one can understand the State's reply to our request for particulars, namely, that the facts in this matter are 'peculiarly within the knowledge of the accused'.

We watched Mr Justice de Wet while this was going on. He gave little indication that he had any particular interest in the argument, and yet he was following it, for as Bram developed one attack after another on one aspect after another of the indictment, he began to show signs of irritation and impatience. At one stage he closed the indictment and put his pencil on top of it, as though he was no longer interested in it and had made up his mind, as perhaps he had. Was his mind made up with us? Or against us?

This question was still unanswered when an advocate of a very different type, George Lowen, rose to attack the indictment on behalf of Jimmy Kantor. Bram is the epitome of the British lawyer. George had a continental background. He learned his law in Germany and appeared for the defence in several important and dramatic trials of opponents of the Hitler regime. He had left Germany as a refugee. To this court he brought both his continental background and a very considerable oratory. He was a very able advocate who could be relied on to inject drama and emotion into his arguments and pleas in a way quite foreign to lawyers trained in the Anglo-Saxon tradition, as most of ours had been. In this case there was a real emotional basis for his intervention. He was particularly affected by Jimmy Kantor's position, partly because he had known Kantor as a lawyer before the trial, and partly because Kantor's position reminded him too closely of innocent men he had defended against political frame-ups in Nazi Germany.

George thundered into the attack. He poured scorn on it with tremendous rhetoric. The adjectives rolled out. The State behaviour was 'presumptuous, nay ludicrous' in its reply to the request for further particulars. Kantor's request had not been the same as ours, nor had the replies. In many ways his replies had been less informative even than ours. He had been told, for instance, that in order to understand the allegation, 'the count is to be read in conjunction with Section 12 of the Act'. Lowen took this and reduced it to the verbal nonsense it was. 'Kantor,' he said, 'is an awaiting trial prisoner. He has no legal library at his disposal. To tell him in reply to a question that he must read this count together with a section of the Act does not comply with the requirements of the law, which is to inform him what case he has to meet.' He had a further and even more telling objection to the indictment. Kantor was charged not only personally for acts which he was said to have committed himself, but also vicariously in his capacity as Wolpe's partner for Wolpe's acts. For him to defend himself against a charge based on Wolpe's acts, it was essential that he be told precisely what Wolpe was alleged to have done. The indictment gave him only the vaguest generality of Wolpe's part in the conspiracy.

Lowen's sarcasm thundered out as he read one reply after another from the prosecutor: 'These facts are not known; these facts are peculiarly within the knowledge of your client'. And finally, in a flourish of rhetoric, he said 'Take for example question 5. The answer given by the State is dash, dash, dash, exclamation mark!'

At this stage Mr Justice de Wet looked up and remarked cynically 'In my copy there are four dashes, Mr Lowen'. George read the judge's feelings well enough. He cut short his argument, and wound up with a short impassioned harangue in which ill-concealed contempt and scorn poured further on the indictment. By the time he had finished, Yutar was red and writhing.

Mr Justice de Wet then asked Hepple whether he too, wished to attack the indictment. Hepple at this stage was unrepresented. As a lawyer, he should have been prepared for this. But he appeared to hesitate. Before he could frame a reply, Dr Yutar sprang to his feet. He announced that the State was withdrawing the charge against Hepple, adding in a voice of triumph that Hepple would be the first witness for the State against the accused.

There was consternation in the public galleries of the court. The accused, who had known something of this beforehand, sat deadpan, looking utterly unmoved. I think that their poker-faces rather robbed Dr Yutar of his moment of triumph. His bombshell, if bombshell it was intended to be, proved something of a damp squib as far as the prisoners were concerned. Hepple rose, deathly pale. He muttered something as he left the dock—I was told later he said 'Good luck'—and walked out.

After that day's session, we sat over a coffee table discussing the reasons for Dr Yutar's sudden move. He could have withdrawn the charge against Hepple earlier. Why did he wait until the judge forced Hepple into a position of speaking up? There was only one possible explanation. At the time it seemed far-fetched, but it proved to be so completely in keeping with Yutar's character as the case went on, that I have no doubt it is the right one. Yutar, on the one hand, hated Hepple with the kind of passionate hatred which he bore against all the accused and everybody connected with them. It was as though he had been personally wronged by them, and was determined to bring them all to what he regarded as justice. He wanted Hepple as a witness, and was determined to use him, but he would punish him by leaving him in jail as long as he possibly could. The announcement of Hepple's defection was to be a master stroke of publicity. I don't know at what stage of the case he had originally intended to announce it, but he had been faced with a crisis. Bram had virtually demolished the indictment. George Lowen had scorned it. The sentiment in court was running strongly against him. It was at this moment, when he knew that nothing he could say by way of reply could rehabilitate his indictment, that he decided the moment had come to save the face of the prosecution—and also his own face—and in doing so to steal some of the headlines from the evening newspapers if the indictment was rejected by the court.

In defending his own indictment, Yutar ignored all the legal arguments we had raised, and dealt with none of the legal authority we had cited in support of our contention. When I had been listening to Bram's argument, I had been wondering how Yutar would attempt to rebut. In fact, he made no attempt at all. Neither then nor at any other time did he try to argue law with our team. He turned rather to attack as the best means of defence. He attacked our application on the grounds that it had not been genuine and sincere. We had not applied genuinely and sincerely for further particulars, we had merely tried to harass and embarrass the State. He seemed to think that if these allegations were true, they would, by some mysterious process, render his unsatisfactory indictment satisfactory. Finally he produced his ace. If we were so anxious to know not merely the generality of the Crown case, but the precise details of the allegations against the accused, he would be prepared to hand over a copy of his opening address which would serve in lieu of further particulars. This, he said, would be the real test of our sincerity.

We could not believe our ears. Was the man serious? Dr Yutar was said to be the most qualified prosecution lawyer in South Africa. He was a Doctor of Law; we had very few such. He surely knew that an opening address is not a charge, it is a speech. In it the prosecution may summarise any evidence which it intends to lead against the accused; it gives the prosecutor free rein to make as wide a statement as he cares of what he thinks he is going to prove at some time in the case. It is intended to inform the court of the manner in which the State will seek to prove its allegations. Such a speech is so far removed from an indictment that we could not believe that the offer was seriously made. In an indictment no reference to the evidence itself is permitted. What the State has to set out in the indictment is not the evidence it will lead or the argument of guilt which will be based on that evidence. It has to set out precisely only what it says the accused has done in transgression of the law.

Bram was rising to his feet to protest. But Mr Justice de Wet was as amazed as we were. He said: 'I can see no reason why I should allow you to hand that in, Mr Yutar. Have you any authority that I can do that? Your opening address is not a document that you are entitled to hand in'.

Dr Yutar was not a man to retreat gracefully. He fawned on the judge. He said that he was only concerned to accommodate our wishes, and that in reality he was doing us a favour. By some curious line of reasoning he came to the conclusion that our refusal of this favour 'I make bold to say, My Lord, obviously illustrates quite clearly that the defence do not want further particulars'. To which Mr Justice de Wet snapped: 'That piece of advice is quite irrelevant. This is a legal argument as to what particulars the defence may be entitled to, and the matter is irrelevant'.

Dr Yutar abandoned the offer of his opening address with obvious reluctance; once again, avoiding the legal issues, he began to catalogue for the judge the evidence he intended to lead. Bram objected.

Mr Justice de Wet. 'I regret I must uphold that objection, Mr Yutar. This is not a political meeting. This is a legal argument, and this is a Court of Law. I don't know anything about any of these organisations you have mentioned. If the State wishes to make allegations like that they should be made in the proper manner'.

Yutar pleaded with the judge. He begged the judge not to reject his indictment. His voice was beginning to crack as it did in moments of high strain; he was 'begging' and 'imploring' in a falsetto note as the court adjourned for lunch. He gave the impression of being close to tears, stricken by the fate that seemed to have overtaken this most important and publicised indictment of his career. After lunch he started again on a statement of the evidence, cataloguing the documents he would hand in, explaining what the experts would say of the handwriting on the documents, recording what Nelson Mandela was alleged to have done when he was in hiding and how he had later planned to escape from prison. We could have made another objection but decided to let him speak on. Perhaps we could learn from this despairing ramble something we were not able to learn from the indictment. In a short time the judge himself lost patience: 'I am very doubtful how far I can allow you to give these facts at this stage. The whole basis of your argument as I understand it, Mr Yutar, is that you are satisfied that the accused are guilty. And you are arguing the case on the assumption that they are guilty and that they had known of all these documents. You cannot beg the question and say that you have got the proof and ask the court to decide on the preliminary matter on the basis that the accused are guilty. A preliminary matter like this must be approached on the assumption that the accused are not guilty. I know nothing about any of these papers. That is the correct approach and once you adopt the correct approach you are in difficulty with your argument'.

Yutar saw that he had lost. He tried bargaining with the judge, to save something of his indictment. He offered to give us whatever further particulars the judge wanted. All the judge had to do was to say what he wanted and the State would co-operate. Mr Justice de Wet seemed to be getting riled. He pointed out rather testily—and correctly—that it was not his responsibility to tell the State what particulars were required to make a good indictment. The State must draw the indictment and then he would say whether it was good. Yutar, getting increasingly rattled, began to cast about for sudden inspirational solutions. One aspect of our attack on the indictment was that the National High Command was cited as the first accused. In our view, this alone rendered the indictment fatally defective. To meet this, Yutar, off the cuff, proposed that he change the form of the indictment to eliminate this defect. In so doing, he sank his own ship. He realised, too late, that under the law there was only one way to do this, by filing a new indictment. It was now becoming apparent that this showpiece trial, opening with tremendous international attention focused upon it, was not going to go quite as Yutar or the government wished it should. The judge was almost certain to quash the indictment. If that were so, the case would be postponed until probably sometime the following year. The hysteria and witch-hunt atmosphere could not be sustained that long at white heat. We knew that and Yutar knew it. Such a postponement might well alter the whole complexion of the case.

Dr Yutar begged the judge not to quash—or as he called it 'squash', the indictment. He would do whatever the judge wanted him to do. He would give the defence summaries of all the evidence and copies of all the documents in the hands of the State. He would deal with all the complaints that had been raised. He would take the National High Command out of the indictment entirely. 'I would earnestly beg your Lordship, nay crave your Lordship, not to squash the indictment, but to order that the State does what it undertakes to do, that is to supply further particulars. And I undertake to do this within a week from to-day.' The judge appeared unmoved by this plea from the heart. He heard our counsel in the briefest of brief replies, and immediately delivered his decision. He said very little about the arguments that had been made on either side. It was fairly obvious, he said, that the indictment was defective. 'When details are required of the date, when and place and manner in which each of the accused was alleged to have commenced acting in concert with the alleged co-conspirators, the reply is that this is 'peculiarly within the knowledge of the accused' and is a matter of evidence. I have never come across a criminal case where a reply of this nature has been given to a question of this nature. The accused are assumed to be innocent until they are proved to be guilty. And it is most improper in my opinion, when the accused ask for particulars in regard to an offence which is alleged to have been committed, to say to them:

'This is a matter which you know all about'. That presupposes that he is guilty and he will not be told anything about the offence.'

In the circumstances the proper order was to quash the indictment, which he then did. He rose and left the court.

Theoretically, the accused were now free. But freedom surrounded by an army of police, detectives and warders is an empty phrase, as they all discovered. Dennis Goldberg leaned down to kiss his wife. Warrant Officer Dirker, of the Security Police, grabbed hold of him and hauled him off to the underground cells. Dennis appeared to be struggling to get out of his embrace. I hurried across to get between them. Dirker was a rather fat, heavy man with a dark porcine face reminiscent of Adolf Hitler, the carefully cultivated little black tooth-brush moustache, the hang-dog lock of hair across his forehead—all-in-all an overripe, overblown 200 pound version of the late dictator.

He roared at me: 'Joffe if you ever interfere with me again while I am performing my duties, I'll arrest you'.

I told him that he had better learn first of all what his duty was. I told him that my clients had been discharged from arrest, and he had better keep his hands off them. Captain Swanepoel entered the fray. He leaped into the dock and thumped each of the accused on the shoulder: 'I am arresting you on a charge of sabotage' he said. That was that. The warders and police regained their wits, and the re-arrested prisoners were roughly shepherded down the stairs back to their cells. Freedom had flickered briefly for a moment, and died.

The law required that people arrested be brought to court and formally charged within forty-eight hours. The accused were, but nobody bothered to inform the defence. They were taken out of their cells without warning two days later, rushed off to court, formally charged without any possibility of any appearance being entered in their defence, and before we even knew of it, they were back in their cells in Pretoria jail. So much for Dr Yutar's promises in court to do anything, but anything to assist the defence so that the case could go ahead without delay.

In the legal profession, Dr Yutar had a reputation for unpredictable behaviour. We had an example of this immediately after his indictment was quashed. We had prepared an application for bail on behalf of Bernstein; Kantor's lawyers had prepared a similar application for him. Shortly after the accused were re-arrested, we arranged for the court to reconvene to hear these bail applications. This certainly did not suit Dr Yutar's book. The newspaper headlines for the day had already been weighted against the prosecution. The main story of the day was bound to be the news that Dr Yutar's indictment had been quashed. Another favourable news item for us would be very damaging for his reputation.

The court reconvened to hear the bail applications. Dr Yutar jumped up before anyone else could speak. Would the court formally remand the accused to a date some weeks hence? Mr Justice de Wet looked stunned. He curtly reminded Dr Yutar that the indictment had been quashed. There was therefore no charge against the accused, and since there was no charge, there was no case to be brought before his court for remand. Dr Yutar struck out on another tack, once again arguing off the cuff—a habit which invariably led him into disaster. This new argument was that if the court was unable to remand in the absence of a charge, it was equally unable to hear applications for bail. Mr Justice de Wet, with an unmistakable note of contempt in his voice, this time reminded 'Mr Yutar' that under the South African Criminal Code, a judge had jurisdiction to hear bail applications for any person at any time. From this time on, the judge persisted in ignoring the title 'Dr' when addressing Yutar.

Bail applications from Kantor and Bernstein were taken separately. Immediately Kantor's counsel began arguing his case, it was apparent that the judge was sympathetic and intending to grant bail. At one stage the judge asked defence counsel what he considered would be a reasonable sum for bail in the circumstances. We were all delighted. Jimmy himself was obviously quite satisfied that he was finally going to leave jail, even though the trial still lay before him. The discussion on his bail was nearly at an end, when there was a bustle of whispering and consultation between the prosecution team and some of the surrounding coterie of police officers. Major van Niekerk had just come in, importantly. We saw him take a scrap of paper from his pocket, and hand it with a flourish to Dr Yutar. Yutar began to whisper excitedly to his colleagues, ignoring what was being said by Kantor's counsel. As soon as counsel sat down, Yutar jumped to his feet: 'My Lord, I want to take the court into my confidence. I want the court to believe what I am going to say from the bar. Before your Lordship gave final judgement I had arranged with Major van Niekerk to try and meet the demands, the request of Kantor and his counsel to release him on bail, subject to certain conditions, in view of the delay that will now follow as a result of the quashing of the indictment. Almost immediately after that I was handed this confidential secret document'. He waved van Niekerk's scrap of paper in the air. 'I cannot, I dare not read the whole of it. It is to this effect, my Lord: that there is a movement afoot to get Kantor and whatever other accused who gets bail out to Lobatsi (Bechuanaland), and if bail is not granted, to make arrangements and take certain steps to get the accused out of custody, or out of this country before 9 November 1963. My Lord, in the light of that, I stand by my original opposition and must oppose bail.'

The whole application, so nearly settled minutes before, was now wide open. Kantor's counsel argued forcibly that there was no evidence at all before the court. The State had merely produced a slip of paper; no one knew what was on it, or where it came from. Dr Yutar had summarised its contents, but he was not on oath, or subject to cross-examination. The court could not rely on information of this nature. He therefore asked to be allowed to cross-examine the police officer who had produced the document. The judge refused. He expressed the off-hand opinion that a responsible police officer would only put such information before the court if there was good justification for it. Instead of allowing the officer to be called to the witness stand, he would adjourn the court to enable Dr Yutar to set out in affidavit form what he had just said in court. There was another brief adjournment. Kantor, it seemed fairly sure, had lost, after bail had been so close to his grasp. But Yutar was going to make the most of his triumph. As soon as the court reassembled he started off with righteous indignation in his voice: 'My Lord, I gave an undertaking to the court that the State would honourably abide by any decision the court made, and I have stood by this undertaking.' In fact he had given no such undertaking. Had he done so it would have been ridiculous. The State could not pick and choose whether to abide by any decision of the court and an undertaking to do so was utterly meaningless. Yutar swung round dramatically and pointed an accusing finger at Kantor's junior counsel, Denis Kuny. His voice shook with indignation. A policeman, he said, had heard Kuny comment to Kantor about van Niekerk's slip of paper. Kuny had said that 'they'—that is the State—would 'stop at nothing. They would perjure any amount of evidence.' Yutar protested. He took the strongest objection to it, he said. He felt it a duty to tell the court about it. He wanted Mr Kuny to know he didn't propose to let the matter rest there.

Denis, a devotee of karate and normally the mildest of men, had been incensed at the dramatic—and he thought stage-managed—eleventh hour intervention of van Niekerk against Kantor. Yutar's pious indignation incensed him further. In a short, angry statement to the judge, he denied that he had said what Yutar had reported. But when he sat down, he said to us that perhaps he should have said it, because it was exactly what most of us were thinking.

This little exchange simmered down. Yutar presented his affidavit, as uninformative and undetailed as his earlier statement. He once again strongly opposed any bail for Kantor under any conditions, and finished off with a statement which he was to regret. 'May I just observe here, my Lord, with all the emphasis and deliberation at my command that never, my Lord, have I been presented by the police with a more powerful case against each and every accused than in this case.' He repeated these words, quoting himself with evident admiration, some time towards the end of the trial. George Bizos leant across and said in a loud aside 'Where is Jimmy Kantor?' By that time, the case against Kantor had collapsed and Kantor had been acquitted without even being called on to enter a defence. But now at this stage, Kantor was well and truly in the police grip, and they were not letting go. The judge accepted Captain van Niekerk's affidavit at its face value, and bail for Kantor was refused. In the light of this, Bernstein's bail application was the merest formality. Kantor, in his application, claimed his complete innocence on all charges. Bernstein did not. His application mentioned neither guilt nor innocence. It was based only on the fact that if granted bail, he would stand his trial. He cited by way of proof his own long record. He had stood trial, or faced imprisonment and arrest knowingly in many different situations over the course of many years. He had never sought to evade arrest or run away at any time. He argued that the court should recognise this as a consistent course of conduct. If it did so, he claimed, he was entitled to bail, as the only reasonable ground for refusing bail would be a reasonable fear that he would not stand trial. It was a good argument, and this public statement of his history, I think, did something to impress his personal standards on the judge. But with van Niekerk's affidavit about plots to release the accused, and smuggle them out to Bechuanaland, he didn't stand a chance. The court refused bail and Kantor and Bernstein went back to jail.

4 The Trial Begins

With all our clients back in jail, we again set about preparing the defence. It was not as easy as it sounded. We had only a general idea of what the charge would be, assuming that it would follow the broad lines of the first, defunct indictment. But that was not the only difficulty. Our real problem was to prepare any sort of a defence in a case like this in a South African jail. After our insistence on our right to interview white and non-white accused together, a special office on the ground floor had been set aside for our consultations. The prison officials were not indifferent to us, the accused or the political issues in the trial. The air of the jail was heavy with their antagonism. We suspected that the office was probably bugged and that everything we were saying was being listened in to. We couldn't take a chance on that in a case of this nature, and we had to devise a complex system of communications. We learned to speak and write in a kind of code throughout the period of our preparations. People were all known as A or B— and key words in sentences were omitted. Key concepts were never spoken, only written down. We gradually built up a type of slang, a coded language of South African politics. It was not an elaborate code; de-coding experts could have cracked it quite easily, but it served at least the simple need for all of the prisoners to feel that they were not giving away in consultation information they were not prepared to give in court.

The result of the code was that the consultations moved excruciatingly slowly, and were often somewhat obscure even to us. Much of what we wanted to say we had to commit to writing. The prison warders watched us constantly through the door of the office where we sat, and though they were out of hearing they seemed to be distressed to see us write notes, pass them around and then burn them carefully in the ashtrays before our daily sessions were over. No doubt, this sinister behaviour was faithfully reported to the Security Police and after a few days we found Captain Swanepoel pacing up and down the corridor. He was trying rather obviously to be unostentatious, but his great red neck swelled ominously whenever he passed our door, and shot sidelong glances at us, attempting presumably to 'detect'.

One day he seemed to have found what he was waiting for. We had suspected for some time he wanted to catch one of those pieces of paper before it had been consumed by fire. That day he had been snorting about like a cat on hot bricks. Govan Mbeki decided to put him out of his misery. On a piece of paper he wrote: 'Isn't Swanepoel a fine looking chap' and waiting for Swanepoel to pass he ostentatiously handed it to Nelson. Swanepoel saw it—as he was intended to do. Nelson studied the sinister message for some time and whispered in a conspiratorial manner to Govan and the others. Then he prepared to light the paper, dropping it into the empty tin which served us as an ashtray. Swanepoel dashed into the room, his face turkey-red, breathing heavily: 'I think I left my ashtray here,' he said. 'I always have the same ashtray with me in this place.' He grabbed up the tin with the paper still unburned in it, and was out of the room as quickly as he had come. At the time he seemed pleased with his coup, but we didn't see him again outside the door of our consultations for a long time after that.

The tactics of our defence case proved a knottier problem than I had at first expected. We didn't know how the State would approach its case, who its witnesses would be, what evidence they had extracted from other 90-day detainees, or what documents they had in their possession. There was little specific we could do until we had a new indictment and further particulars. In the meantime we set the accused to work, listing those witnesses whom they thought the police might have, and preparing memoranda for us about these people, what they might say, and what their background was. This raised new problems. The prison authorities could well raid the prisoners' cells and confiscate anything that they had written. With things as they were, this would pass rapidly from the prison, to the police, to the prosecution and perhaps become evidence against the writers themselves. It would have been unethical, even unheard of behaviour, and yet our fears were not completely wild. When the police had raided Jimmy Kantor's office shortly after his arrest, they had taken away all his office records and had refused to return them. In his files were many copies of statements made to him in confidence by his clients—lawyer's privileged communications in better times. We knew that people whose confidential statements were in Kantor's files had subsequently been prosecuted by the police. We challenged the police right to take such files. They promised that, in going through the files, they would not read the statements of persons who had been charged. I might be forgiven for being cynical about this.

I took the whole matter to the Law Society. Perhaps they would do something to protect the inviolability of an accused person's statement made in confidence to his attorney. But even the august Law Society had fallen prey to the atmosphere of hysteria, and of 'State worship' then current in South Africa. They advised me coldly that there was nothing they could do about the matter. And so the prisoners wrote in their cells, censoring themselves. Statements about witnesses had to be coded and organisations began to have elaborate code names and abbreviations proliferated. Gradually the preparations for the Rivonia defence began to have much of the atmosphere of an underground conspiracy within the confines of Pretoria Local jail.

We decided to ask Yutar for copies of the documents which the State planned to introduce in evidence at the trial, especially those found at Rivonia. The day before in open court, when arguing for a short postponement, he had put his hand on his heart and said that he was 'prepared to assist the defence all along the line'. We had asked for copies then, and we now asked again. Until we had those copies, we had to do what we could with what some of the accused thought would have been amongst the papers found at Rivonia.

It seemed to us from what they told us that it was quite possible that there might be conflicts of interest between some accused and others. Such conflicts would make it difficult if they were all represented by the same counsel. A line of enquiry, or cross-examination of a witness, might be to the advantage of one accused and yet to the disadvantage of another, for from what they told us they were far from being all in identical positions in relation to the activities charge. We tentatively suggested separate representation for some, but they rejected the suggestion out of hand. There was a real and deep band of unity amongst them. They had spent too many years working together, thinking together, debating together, discussing together and reaching agreement together to be prepared to drop it now for some temporary legal advantage. They could not visualise any of them being prepared to improve his own case at the expense of another, regardless of the circumstances. At the time, before the full weight of the evidence was known, and before their lives were clearly in jeopardy, this could have been a bold boast. But when the acid test came where lives were in jeopardy, they all lived up to it.

We had a short wait of two weeks before the new indictment was forthcoming. On the day it was served, Mr Justice Galgut heard argument from us on the need for a lengthy postponement to allow us to prepare our defence. He took it on himself to defend our clients from us. It was in the interests of the accused, he said, that the case should go on as quickly as possible since they were all waiting in jail. We knew this. So did the accused. But they felt even more strongly that every delay allowed the atmosphere of panic and hysteria in the country to wane, and thus time was on the side of justice. They were sweating it out patiently, seven months after their arrest. The judge ruled that two weeks would be sufficient time for us to start the trial.

The new indictment dismayed us, not so much for its content as for its length. Yutar had made considerable changes. We now had a nine-page document to which were attached nineteen pages of further particulars and twenty-one pages of annexures detailing all the acts of sabotage. On the surface, it looked very impressive. The National High Command as one of the accused, had disappeared. But in essence, the State case was unchanged. The three charges in the original indictment had matured to four, with a new charge of having prepared for the commission of further acts of violence in the future. There were 193 acts of sabotage listed, committed by one or other of the 122 named people who were alleged to be agents of the accused, but in no case was it specifically stated which of these 122 agents had committed which specific act of sabotage.

In a request for further particulars we asked which of the acts was alleged to have been committed by which agent, to which the reply was: 'The acts particularised in the annexure were committed by the said agents and servants in their respective areas'. The rest of the replies were of a similar uninformative, patently evasive character. For all its size, the new indictment was as slovenly and badly drawn as the first. We thought it so lacking in particularity as not to comply with the requirements of the law. We again drew up notices of complaint, listing about forty major errors in the indictment. On this basis, at the first sitting of the court, we moved that the indictment be again rejected by the court as insufficient to inform the accused of the charge before them and to enable them to prepare their defence. By this time it was 25 November; the atmosphere in court had changed radically. There were fewer spectators, and everybody seemed much calmer than they had been some weeks before. Partly, no doubt, this reflected a decline in the general hysteria in the country. But partly it was due to the fact that an artificial fever-interest had been developed by police and politicians, who predicted spectacular 'revelations' in this case. Such an atmosphere could not be held for long periods between adjournments.

Almost from the beginning of his argument, it was clear that Mr Justice de Wet was not going to treat Bram Fischer's application sympathetically. He gazed vacantly at the ceiling while Bram was talking, made pointed gestures of putting his pencil down and closing his book, and made no further notes. He gave all the appearance of a man with his mind made up long before he came into court.

De Wet's reputation was that of a man unsympathetic to anything that smacked of delaying tactics. He was always impatient to get on with the job without any legal niceties, and this time it seemed that he was certainly going to do so. Bram presented a devastating argument. We all knew he was talking into thin air.

Mr Harold Hanson, QC, followed up with an attack on the indictment from Kantor's particular point of view. The basic allegation by the State was that Kantor's office had handled funds through the firm's trust account, some of which had been used amongst other things for the purchase of the Rivonia Farm. Kantor's defence had asked for further particulars, and Hanson took each answer to this request, analysed it and characterised it, with great oratory, as being nothing at all, 'absolutely nil'. The judge seemed unimpressed. He pointed out that though individual allegations might not be particularly weighty, their cumulative effect might well be significant.

Mr Harold Hanson: My Lord, the cumulative effect of seven noughts is nought.

Mr Justice de Wet: You will have great difficulty in convincing me that this indictment does not implicate Kantor.

Hanson: Is your Lordship inviting me then to sit down? My application is made seriously and I am not here to play the fool.

Hanson is one of the most senior counsel in South Africa. He was obviously beginning to fray at the edges under the rather brusque and off-hand treatment that he was getting from Mr Justice de Wet. The judge, attempting to rectify matters, said it was quite obvious that something was *implied* by the indictment.

Hanson snapped back: 'I've yet to hear my Lord that an indictment is made good by *implication*'.

After a short while his argument ended. Without ceremony Mr Justice de Wet dismissed the application without any reasons.

We asked again for a postponement. We based our application on the State promise to make available to us documents that would be given in evidence, a promise they had not fulfilled; on the fact that we had to track down 122 alleged agents of the accused for whom no addresses were given in the indictment; and that we had to interview persons and take statements in regard to 200 acts of sabotage, in none of which was it alleged that the accused had participated in person. All the facts therefore would have to be ascertained from other people. We would have to interview and consult co-conspirators, many of whom were not even in South Africa by that time, but were living abroad. The judge was unimpressed. He suggested what turned out in the long run to be quite useful—that since the State was anxious to lead their case without delay, he would let them do so, but he would allow us to reserve cross-examination if he felt it necessary, to allow us to take instruction on the evidence of any particular witness.

Percy Yutar did not like this. He argued that postponement was unnecessary and that the defence application was not bona fide. It was clear, he said, that we had had several weeks since our clients were first charged in which to make preparations for their defence. We had not used that time seriously or efficiently. And then, like a conjurer producing a rabbit from a hat, he pulled out a piece of paper, which he said was a schedule showing how many hours a day had been spent by each counsel in consultation with the accused at Pretoria Local jail on every day since they were first charged.

I don't think I have ever heard of another prosecutor stooping to spying on defence counsel and enlisting the prison staff to record and tot up the hours spent by them closeted with their clients. And even if any did, only Yutar would have had the gall to use that as argument against a postponement in court. It seemed to me outrageous that the prison authorities should lend themselves to such a procedure, and outrageous that the judge should sit there in silence, listen and accept the piece of paper. Yutar argued that, from the paper, it was clear that not every possible available hour had been spent by every possible counsel in consultation at Pretoria Local jail. He was right. We had had lots to do that couldn't be done in Pretoria Local jail.

Yutar passed on to a dramatic wail that we were to hear repeated over and over throughout the trial—'The State cannot guarantee the security of witnesses if the case were postponed'. This was untrue as all the State witnesses of any importance in this case were either police officers or in custody, and would remain in custody until they had given evidence. And finally, timed carefully to make the afternoon editions of the newspapers, Yutar announced in his most dramatic falsetto, that his intended first witness, 'Advocate Bob Alexander Hepple' had been threatened by the accused or their supporters, and fled the country.

This was the first day any of us knew of Hepple's defection. He arrived, I think, that very day in Dar-es-Salaam. He told a somewhat different story from Yutar's. It was not the accused or their supporters who had threatened him but the police. They had made promises and given undertakings which they had broken. He said that he had no intention of testifying against the accused whom he admired and supported.

The judge ruled that the case proceed the following day. Although we had known of his reputation as a temperamental, moody character, his attitude that day caused us great concern. At the earlier hearings when the first indictment had been rejected, he had been remote, cold, taking no side, impatient with everyone and especially with Yutar, who I think merited this impatience. But on this day he had seemed clearly antagonistic to the defence. He had been deliberately rude to Bram during his address; he had been rude and impatient with Hanson; he had tolerated outrageous antics from Yutar with indifference, even with a grin on his face, and at times had seemed to encourage those antics by nodding agreement when no agreement was called for. The most disturbing thing, however, had been his attitude to postponement. We recalled, even if he didn't, that when the first indictment had been quashed he had said that a trial with a new indictment could not possibly begin before the 1964 session of the courts, that is to say, next February. We had taken that statement as correct and based all our arrangements on it. Now, in November, for no apparent reason, he had changed his mind and was going ahead immediately.

I do not think there is any simple explanation for Mr Justice de Wet's behaviour at any time. He was not a simple man, but an extraordinarily complicated character. Yutar, I feel sure, took instructions quite definitely and without question from the political authorities of the State—and in this case, from the senior officials of the police. He quite obviously fashioned his case and his tactics to suit the political requirements of the government. I do not believe Mr Justice de Wet took or would take instructions from anybody, nor do I account for his behaviour by the popular idea that he was 'told'. He was a rather arrogant man, proud of his position as judge and of the family tradition which had made his father a noted South African judge before him. Yet he seemed at the same time aware that, as a lawyer, he was unable to measure up to the very high standards of many of the counsel who appeared before him. This might have made some men rather pliant or deferential to counsel. But it had made de Wet an obstinate and self-willed man, who would not, I think, have taken kindly to either direct government or even indirect political intervention in his domain.

On the other hand, he showed throughout this trial that he was a typical white South African, with all the prejudices that that implies, with all the ready-made attitudes of white superiority and 'knowing the Bantu' that goes with white South Africanism. He was unquestionably sensitive to the needs of the white society which he believed in and upheld, and also of the government which was its foremost protagonist. He acted out their role, I think, unconsciously, in the firm conviction of his own judicial impartiality, and without any need for a direct word or intervention from any source whatsoever.

We had a hurried consultation with the accused after court that day. We had made our preparations in the belief that Hepple was to be the first witness. Knowing him, we expected that he would tell the truth. We were, therefore, preparing to cross-examine him with a view to establishing, through this State witness, many of the facts about the accused, their organisations and their policies which had been completely distorted in the prosecutor's opening address and in the indictment. Now Hepple had disappeared. We were going to be faced immediately the following morning with a witness unknown to us, probably hostile.

Yutar was keeping the identity of the witness up his sleeve, but we had up our sleeves an ace with which to trump his. As soon as we saw the indictment, we had realised that there was likely to be some pretty outrageous lying on the part of State witnesses, for otherwise none of the false allegations in the indictment and the prosecutor's opening address could possibly be sustained. Unless the accused were themselves misleading us, there could be no truthful evidence or documentary proof, for example, that any of them or their organisations had at any time prepared for, asked for or even favoured foreign military intervention to solve South Africa's internal conflicts. Yet exactly that was charged in the indictment. There must, therefore, be witnesses who would tell blatant lies.

To deal with this problem, we had taken steps to recruit Mr Vernon Berrange for the defence. Vernon was known, both in the courts and outside them, as the most devastating cross-examiner in South Africa. He had been in London on holiday at the time we decided to ask him to join the defence. He was then 65 years old, though he looked a young and handsome 50, and was still an immaculate dresser. In his younger days he had been a driver of racing cars, a big game hunter, and a fighter pilot during the first world war. Vernon was always against authority; he revelled in danger and fighting. He cross-examined witnesses with a steely cold manner, which, coupled with devastating insight into their psychology, seemed to strike terror even into the most belligerent of policemen. He was the most sought-after criminal lawyer of the time, and had also appeared in almost every major political trial in the country, including the Treason Trial.

When we approached him, he was anxious not to become involved in a long and tiring trial for reasons of his health, but he accepted unhesitatingly when we explained to him why we would need him. Berrange had been named as a member of the long outlawed party on the list compiled by the government in terms of the Suppression of Communism Act. At the time we approached him, he knew, as we did, that the government was drafting legislation which would permit them to debar any listed person from practising law in South Africa. In accepting this brief, Vernon knew that he was signing the warrant of his excommunication from the legal profession. He accepted.

We were all relieved, not just because we needed his courtroom skill, but also because we thought that he was just the man to deal with Dr Yutar on the level which would be required if this case were to go on as it had started. Bram would never be able to do it. Bram was too much of a gentleman. He never quite understood Percy Yutar and even if he had, he would have been quite unable to descend to the levels of infighting which Yutar was driving us to use. Vernon was different. In Berrange, Yutar would surely find more than his match. We had said nothing to the court of his coming appearance in the case, believing that when Vernon walked into court unexpectedly and unannounced, Yutar, at any rate, would be put off balance.

We arrived in court next morning anxious to see who the first witness would be. Instead we were thrown off balance. Dr Yutar came across before the court was seated to tell us that 'in order to help Kantor's counsel', he was about to apply to the judge for a week's postponement. We were stunned. The day before it had seemed that the security of the State and all its witnesses had rested on immediate commencement. Today everything could readily be postponed for a week. We suspected something sinister in that scheming mind of his. He was fawning on Kantor's counsel and being fairly rude and off-hand with us. Exactly what he was plotting, we only appreciated later.

Hepple had been his star witness, the dramatic witness who would speak as a former colleague of the accused to reveal all the internal secrets of their organisation. Now Hepple had vanished. Yutar was looking for a substitute—and in his mind had picked James Kantor. The week's adjournment was granted. And during that week, a suggestion filtered down through devious channels to James Kantor: if he told the police everything that Bernstein and Goldberg discussed during exercise periods which all three had together, the case against him would be dropped. The offer was known to us—there is a fruitful grapevine of rumour and gossip both in legal circles and in prison, but we were not worried. We knew James Kantor as a man with no political beliefs, perhaps very little political conviction, but with a great deal of personal integrity. We were quite confident that the kind of deal which would foment in the mind of Dr Yutar would find no answering echo in James Kantor.

5 The Case for the Prosecution

The accused spent that week putting us in the picture, trying to explain to us—as they saw it—what they had been doing in political terms, what their organisations stood for, how they had all come to be at Rivonia on the day of their arrest, and what part Rivonia had played in their plans. For the rest, we spent the week drawing up an application on behalf of Govan Mbeki for the Government party's official newspaper, Die Vaderland, to be cited for contempt of court. That newspaper had published a number of reports of statements made by the Minister of Justice, the Commissioner of Police and even the prosecutor in this very case, Dr Percy Yutar. These reports were all to the effect that the accused were guilty, their crimes enormous. They were, we said, calculated to prejudice the courts.

We were not playing a game of private legal warfare, but the contemptuous disregard of our clients' rights had gone too far. By this application to court we served notice on the prosecution and on the Government, that we would not allow illegal and prejudicial comment to go unchallenged, no matter who made the comment. We could have made the application in the first place against Dr Yutar, and in fact we considered doing so. Had we done so, it may have had a salutary effect on him. But in the end we decided against it, lest we appear petty and perhaps vindictive. His statements had been no worse than those of people senior to him—the

Minister of Justice, the Commissioner of Police—and certainly his offence had been inspired in part by the willingness of the newspaper concerned to publish prejudicial material.

On the other hand, he at least, as 'the most qualified lawyer' in South Africa, must have known that the statements he gave to the press were in contempt of court. We made the application against Die Vaderland and in the event we won an order citing them for contempt. Some months later, during the trial, when the matter had been all but forgotten, Die Vaderland had the judgment upset on appeal.

We had several important matters to settle before the case got under way. How, we asked, were our clients going to plead to this charge? This opened up a discussion amongst them which was, I think, an eye-opener to our whole legal team. They did not appear to be much concerned with the legalities of the charge. They were concerned with the politics of it. They readily admitted that the organisations cited in the indictment, and almost all of the accused themselves, had taken part in a political campaign which was designed to bring about the overthrow of the government, and that in the course of that campaign they had, to varying degrees, known about or taken part in preparations for military and paramilitary action, such as sabotage. They had no intention whatsoever of denying these facts in the witness box. In fact, they welcomed the opportunity to use the court as a platform from which to clarify to the country and to the world their position on the matter they considered to be in the very forefront of South African politics.

Should they then plead guilty? If they did so, would their followers and supporters understand? Should they plead guilty and take the consequences for a legal transgression against laws so unjust that in their own eyes their behaviour had been no offence at all, but rather a patriotic duty? Or should they plead not guilty, even though they would admit the truth of much of the State charge?

We lawyers participated in some of the sessions in which this question was debated. There were others held in private. Finally we were told that they would all enter a plea of not guilty. That is what we expected them to do when we came into court after the recess. What happened was not what we expected.

The court assembled in a rather unusual fashion that morning. The traditional procedure is that the public are allowed in first, the accused are then brought in, and finally, when everyone is present and ready for action, the judge enters. But on this particular occasion the orderly called 'Silence in Court' before the accused were brought in, and the judge entered and took his seat. Only then were the accused brought in. This was clearly a manoeuvre to prevent the accused and their supporters amongst the public repeating their demonstration of salutes, and the shouting of the cry 'Amandla' and the reply 'Ngawethu'. Whose hand devised this arrangement we never discovered. It seemed too subtle for the mind of a South African policeman or court orderly, and probably too subtle also for Dr Yutar. For the rest of this trial this procedure was followed rigorously: first the judge, then the accused.

On this first occasion, immediately the accused were seated, the registrar of the court read the charge. He asked in the traditional phrase 'Accused Number 1 (Nelson Mandela) how do you plead to the indictment served upon you?'.

Nelson stood up and said clearly: 'The government should be in the dock, not me. I plead not guilty.'

This caused some consternation. The police muttered angrily. Mr Justice de Wet looked somewhat annoyed, Dr Yutar absolutely horrified. Mr Justice de Wet made no comment, and the question was put to Walter Sisulu. How did he plead?

'It is the government which is guilty, not me.'

Mr Justice de Wet had to take notice. He said sternly: 'I don't want any political speeches here. You may plead guilty, or not guilty. But nothing else'.

Walter went on calmly, unmoved by the judge's remarks. 'It is the government which is responsible for what is happening in this country,' he said. 'I plead not guilty.'

Dennis Goldberg, how do you plead? 'I associate myself with the statements of Mr Mandela and Mr Sisulu. I plead not guilty.'

And so it went, except for Kantor who said firmly 'I am not guilty my Lord.' Each of the accused in turn, in one phrase or another, pleaded not guilty, and charged the government with responsibility for whatever crimes were charged.

After his initial attempt with Sisulu, Mr Justice de Wet did not intervene.

If Yutar had been a more thoughtful or perspicacious man, he would have realised perhaps that in opening their defence in this way, the accused had revealed the line of defence that they would enter throughout the case. But Dr Yutar is not a thoughtful man, and at that moment his thoughts were probably not on them but on himself. The long awaited moment for his opening address had come, and nothing, I think, could have been more gratifying to his ego than this dramatic moment, when he held the star role and all eyes were upon him, and on the dramatic revelations which had been promised so often by him and his Minister in the months before. Here was a group of men who had steadfastly refused, through three months of solitary confinement, to make any statement at all to the police (with minor exceptions in the case of Goldberg and Mlangeni). How would they answer the allegations? This was the key to the whole case, and should decide the tactics and conduct of the prosecution. Yet Yutar seemed never to have grappled with the question of how the accused would defend themselves, or if so, had never come to understand their defence, and thus failed to rise superior to it.

He rose to his feet with printed copies of his opening address, all beautifully bound and tied up in green tape. This slightly obsessional concern for presenting the evidence in beautiful bindings became a hallmark of his conduct of this case. Everything tended to appear in beautifully printed covers, as though in this way the evidence grew more weighty. I think the reason for this obsession was that throughout he was conscious that this case could become part of the country's history, and thus in part a monument to himself also. He wanted that history treated with due pomp and ceremony.

He handed copies of his address to the judge and to us—the press had had theirs earlier—and opened his copy to start reading his address. At that crucial moment Bram Fischer stood up. He pointed at a small black microphone which had grown up overnight on the desk in front of Dr Yutar. It hadn't been there before, but while we had been waiting for the case to start we had noticed some technicians of the South African Broadcasting Corporation tinkering around and doing tests on this microphone. It appeared to us that someone had decided to broadcast the prosecution's opening address. This may be normal in some countries, but broadcasting any part of a court case was utterly unknown in South Africa. It had never happened at any time in history.

The SABC was not an impartial body. State controlled, it had become a blatant spokesman at this time for government policy, and a vehicle for some most vicious, slanted and smearing attacks on opponents of the government. We had no doubt whatsoever that the broadcast of this opening address was designed with only one purpose—to inflame public opinion against the accused and everything they stood for. We were certain that no facilities whatsoever, not even mention in the news bulletins would be given to any rebuttal by the defence or to any part of the defence case.

Bram asked whether it was in order for this opening address to be broadcast in this way. Mr Justice de Wet looked uncomfortable. He said that at a previous hearing he had been asked if the SABC could have permission to record the opening address 'in order to inform the public'. At that stage he had no objection and had given that permission. But he said, the position had now changed—though he made no explanation of how it had changed. For this reason, he said, the previous permission had lapsed, and since no further permission had been sought, he was not at the present moment prepared to allow the broadcast, particularly if objection was taken by the defence. He asked Dr Yutar whether he had any comments. Yutar ran for cover, and declared that he had had no share in the matter at all. There was a recess. The man with the South African Broadcasting Corporation suitcase came back, dismantled the apparatus and took it away. Up to that moment all the victories had been ours. It was now Dr Yutar's turn.

I suppose that the opening address was his most effective piece of work of the whole trial. Perhaps it was that in the writing of it he was helped or advised by his colleagues, who certainly got almost no share in the affair in court. Or perhaps in writing he got less emotional and carried away than in speaking. Here, for the only time in this case, we had a controlled, unhysterical presentation of what the State would set out to prove, and some indications of how. It was really the first occasion on which we in the defence team had any indication of the line the trial would take. Amongst other things, the address said that 'the accused deliberately and maliciously plotted and engineered the commission of acts of violence and destruction throughout the country, directed against the offices and homes of municipal officials as well as against all lines and manner of communications. The planned purpose thereof was to bring about in the Republic of South Africa chaos, disorder and turmoil which would be aggravated, according to their plan, by the operation of thousands of trained guerrilla warfare units deployed throughout the country at various vantage points. These would be joined in various areas by local inhabitants as well as specially selected men posted to such areas. Their combined operations were planned to lead to confusion, violent insurrection and rebellion, followed at the appropriate juncture by armed invasion of the country by military units of foreign powers. In the midst of the resulting chaos, turmoil and disorder it was planned by the accused to set up a provisional revolutionary government to take over the administration and control of this country'.

The address went on to say that by mid-1961 the African National Congress had decided to embark on a policy of violence and destruction and for this purpose had formed the Umkhonto we Sizwe (the Spear of the Nation) which was to be the military wing of the African National Congress. The Umkhonto we Sizwe had placed itself under the political guidance of the National Liberation Committee and the national executive of such committee representing all the banned organisations in the country, including in particular the African National Congress and the South African Communist Party. Umkhonto received its instructions from the so-called National High Command.

The farm at Rivonia, it was said, had been bought in order to provide headquarters for this underground conspiracy, and Goldreich and his family had gone there to live and to provide a cover for secret operations. In the buildings of the farm, Nelson

Mandela had lived for a time going by the name of David, and later Sisulu and Kathrada had done the same, Kathrada being disguised to look like a Portuguese calling himself Pedro. At another time Mbeki had lived there under the pseudonym of Dlamini, and also Mhlaba. There had been many visitors to the house including Lionel Bernstein and most of those cited as co-conspirators, and also on occasions Dennis Goldberg. Goldberg it was said had conducted various operations under various assumed names, sometimes Williams and at other times Barnard.

From its headquarters the National High Command had planned its campaign of guerrilla warfare, sabotage and violence. It had installed a radio transmitter, known as Radio Liberation, and had made a study of armaments and explosives and produced plans for large-scale production of grenades, time-bombs and other explosives. Experts had been sent throughout the country to train young men in the art of manufacturing explosives and also to recruit young Africans who would be sent abroad to Tanganyika, Nigeria, Egypt and Ethiopia for military training, and training in sabotage and guerrilla warfare.

Sabotage had taken place on a large scale, and so, in fact, had military training of young men sent abroad. In this comprehensive task the accused were promised military and financial aid from several African states and even by countries across the sea.

In order to carry out their objectives they bought a further property at a place called Travellyn, which was to be the site of manufacturing explosives. They had also hired a cottage in the Johannesburg suburb of Mountainview, to use as a temporary hiding place as and when they needed it. Thus, said Yutar, 'the accused hoped that the Republic of South Africa would find itself in a chaotic condition with widespread disorder and turmoil, and as a result of which the accused further hoped they might bring the present Government to its knees and thus violently overthrow it. In these conditions and circumstances the accused in the final stage of their campaign planned to set up a provisional revolutionary government to take over the administrative control of this country.

'In conclusion it remains only to be said that the documents and witnesses will reveal to the court that the accused together with the other persons and associations named in the indictment had so planned their campaign that the present year, 1963, was to be the year of their liberation from the so-called yoke of the white man's domination.'

We had no way of knowing what impression Yutar's address was making on the accused, but on counsel it was producing an atmosphere of considerable gloom. Had our clients told us the whole truth? And if there were any truth in Yutar's promises of overwhelming documentary and verbal evidence, was there any hope whatever that any of the accused would escape the death sentence?

Our instructions from the accused were that they had considered the question of guerrilla warfare, that no agreement to embark upon it at any specific time had been reached, and that at no time had consideration been given to inviting military units of foreign countries to participate in South Africa's troubles. And finally, they said, in their view the liberation of South Africa was a long-term project, and certainly no one had ever imagined that the end would be seen in 1963.

From that moment on we saw the case in a very simple light. For most of the accused the only possible verdict was 'guilty'. The case was therefore, as far as we were concerned, a battle to prevent the death sentence being carried out. As it turned out, the aims of the accused were somewhat wider, but this we only learned when we came to consider in greater detail the way the defence was to be conducted. At this stage we were concerned with the State's case.

Dr Yutar chose to lead off with a series of apparently minor witnesses—the domestic servants and farm labourers who had been employed at the Rivonia property, and who had been held in custody since the day of the raid five months before. I think he probably decided on this order of witnesses in order that his witnesses should not compete with his own opening address in the newspaper headlines of the day. These witnesses did not really bother us at all. They told a very simple tale of how they had come to be employed at Rivonia. Some of them had been in Goldreich's employ for many years before he moved to Rivonia and others had been hired in a normal way. They had worked there. They described the cottage which came to be known by everybody as the 'thatched cottage', a self-contained flat which stood in the grounds some fifty yards from the main house. They described how they had seen various of the accused there, living or visiting. There was little else that any of them had to say.

The first of these servants, a middle-aged woman Edith Ngopani, was rather frightened and not very educated. I doubt whether she was aware that she was participating in one of the historic trials of South Africa. Her evidence was quite straightforward. We decided to cross-examine only to find out what had happened to her in the five months of her detention by the police.

She said 'I was arrested on the 11th of July, the date of the Rivonia raid. I am still locked up. I have not been told why I have been kept locked up. I have requested them to let me go so that I can see my children, but was refused. Just now I have been brought from Marshall Square (Johannesburg police headquarters). Since the 8th October I have been with somebody else in a cell. Before the 8th I was alone for three months. They said that if they were satisfied with the answers that I gave they would release me. I told them what I knew. What I didn't know I couldn't tell them.'

We knew this was what was going on. We wanted from the outset to underline that witnesses were being held in jail for five months, being told that they would only be released after they had given evidence *'to the satisfaction of the State'*. It was our contention then, and it is my contention to this day, that evidence obtained in this way is evidence given under duress, and cannot be taken seriously by any responsible court. Edith Ngopani testified that she had made a statement to the police immediately after her arrest. For at least three months they had kept her in prison and continued to badger her, and clearly the promise had been made that she would only be released after she had given her evidence to *the satisfaction of the State*.

We immediately challenged the legality of such detention. Dr Yutar in one of those off-the-cuff statements that he was so prone to make—and later to regret—jumped up to explain that she was not 'in detention', she was in 'protective custody'. There is no procedure in South African law for 'protective custody', as he should have known, and so this explanation merely made the illegal nature of the detention more blatant. Mr Justice de Wet decided to ignore this aspect. And so we had a procession of Rivonia farm employees giving the same type of evidence. One was Thomas Mashifane who had been foreman at Rivonia and told of having once seen Arthur Goldreich and Nelson Mandela shooting at a target with an air rifle. The public galleries buzzed. It sounded dramatic, but why the prosecution considered it significant enough to their case to elicit it by questioning, we did not understand.

Joseph Mashifane, Thomas's son, gave evidence about the erection of some radio masts at the property, and amongst others identified Lionel Bernstein as one of those he had seen working on the erection of the mast. The State alleged that these masts had been erected for the illegal 'Radio Liberation' broadcasts. Bernstein denied that he had anything to do with this operation, and Arthur Chaskalson accordingly took Joseph through a most careful cross-examination. It soon became apparent that his testimony was false. We were here faced with the difficulty that he could be making a genuine mistake in identification. There had, in fact, been a fair-haired man involved in this work—this the accused told us. But not Bernstein. Was Joseph making a genuine error? Had he been shown a few photographs of suspects by the police and selected Bernstein because he alone was fair? Or had he been deliberately lying? Had he been told what to say as the price for his freedom after five months in jail? Whichever explanation was correct, one vital factor had been overlooked. All the evidence showed that the erection of the radio masts was done on a Saturday afternoon. Bernstein, as one of the terms of his house arrest order, had to be at home from 2 p.m. on Saturdays. It was scarcely credible that he would have taken the grave risk of a random police check—which were made fairly frequently—revealing his absence, in order to do what was not much more than lend a semi-skilled labourer's help to the radio mast erection. This vital flaw in Joseph's evidence we did not reveal at that stage. That was reserved for a later time.

As time wore on, we began to understand that Dr Yutar's procedure was dictated by two attitudes to which we were unaccustomed in our courts of law. One was the constant desire to inject some drama into what would otherwise become a rather dull hearing; his method was to produce either a surprise witness, or a revolutionary-sounding document, every few days, usually with due pre-arrangement with the press to ensure dramatic headlines.

The other was to keep the defence constantly guessing what was coming next. Now this, it might be said, is a legitimate tactic of the prosecution. In my view, in this case it was deliberately calculated to hamper the accused's defence. It seemed to me then, as it does now, grossly unfair to charge a large number of people with conspiracy, and to base a large part of that conspiracy on documentary evidence which might be unknown to all except one of the accused, or possibly unknown to all of them but known only to co-conspirators named in the indictment but not present in court. The danger of prejudice to the accused can only be mitigated if they are provided in advance with copies of all documents which are going to be used, so that they can acquaint themselves with the contents and prepare an adequate defence.

To do this cannot possibly prejudice the State case. It might, however, remove the element of drama and of newspaper-headline snatching which became so important to the prosecution in this case. Despite all the promises made by Dr Yutar in court, we were never provided with copies of the documents prior to their introduction. In fact, a special procedure was adopted. Normally the witness who would testify to the finding of the documents in a certain place would then hand them all in, identifying them as he did so, and if necessary reading them. In this case, documents were read into the record, piecemeal, as and when it suited Dr Yutar, a novel procedure to which we objected, but our objection was overruled by the judge. And so, between witnesses, we were constantly having reading sessions of documents unconnected with the last or the next witness and irrelevant to the particular point of the preceding or succeeding evidence.

Even the order in which Dr Yutar introduced witnesses puzzled us at first. The farm servants we ascribed to the fact that he did not want to top his own dramatic act, the opening address, with a scene-stealing piece of verbal evidence. After some ten days of the farm servants, we thought we would really get down to the solid evidence. But this was not Dr Yutar's way. We had a further succession of witnesses who had very little of interest to say.

We had, for instance, Mrs Anne Ezra, wife of one of the men named as co-conspirator. Her husband, it seemed, had been the nominal purchaser of the farm at Rivonia and the sole director of the purchasing company. He had left the country shortly after the Rivonia raid. His wife testified only that she had been unaware of the purchase and that he did not have the financial resources to purchase the farm on his own behalf.

Looking back it is clear that even at this stage Dr Yutar failed to understand both the character of the accused and the nature of their 'defence'—if defence it was. He set out to prove every trivial aspect of the State case apparently on the assumption that the accused were going to deny everything from beginning to end. Had he been a more astute student of psychology, and devoted more time to trying to understand the accused and less to the publicity angles of this case, he would have seen from our cross-examination of the farm servants, that we were not denying any of the story of what had been going on at Rivonia. We were not disputing that the accused had visited and some of them had lived there. We were not disputing that some had been there in disguise or under pseudonyms. We were not disputing that they had used the place both for duplicating documents and for operating a radio transmitter. We were not disputing that the place had been bought specifically for these purposes and that the accused were more than Goldreich's visitors, being if not co-proprietors, at least in some control of the property and its administration.

All this Dr Yutar failed to appreciate. As a result he burdened the case and the record with reams and reams of evidence on matters which were not in dispute, which we did not intend to dispute, and which we had made clear right from the beginning would not be disputed.

Mrs Ezra was followed by a Mr Ismail Makda, who had been a clerk in the offices of James Kantor and Partners for many years. His evidence, led by Dr Yutar in great detail and at great length, was intended only to nail home the case against Kantor. As far as we were concerned his most damaging statement—if it was damaging at all—was that Wolpe had the habit of using his office to meet with people who were prohibited from communicating with him.

This should perhaps be explained. Some people who had been listed as members, supporters or sympathizers of the former Communist Party of South Africa had been served with Ministerial orders in the 1960s, denying them all manner of civil rights, including the right to communicate with any other persons who were listed.

Wolpe himself, though listed, had not been served with such a banning notice. But most of the accused had, and so had several other people in Johannesburg. Makda testified that these people would meet Wolpe in James Kantor's legal offices, and when they did so, Wolpe would borrow Makda's office, draw the blinds and close the doors. Kantor, seemingly, was being accused of guilt by association twice removed. He was in court, not Wolpe. And whatever offence was being committed by these meetings was not by Wolpe—who was not banned—but by others. Makda's evidence did not specify a single name of these others, or a single date or specific occasion.

The rest of his evidence consisted of information about the workings of Kantor's office, and particularly the finances of it. He explained how the finances were handled and how the bookkeeping system worked. He told the court of one occasion when Wolpe had asked him to take a parcel to deliver to another attorney. This attorney had taken over the legal formalities connected with the purchase of the Rivonia property by Ezra in the middle of the transaction, when Kantor's firm had apparently refused to carry on with it. Makda told the court that the parcel had been opened in his presence, and the other attorney had counted out £2,500 in bank notes. A receipt had been given to him for the amount which was an instalment of the balance payable on the Rivonia property. This was one year after the purchase.

Much sinister innuendo seemed to be inferred by the prosecution from Makda's evidence, but there was not much solid fact. In evidence he explained that in Kantor's office files the normal procedure was to note all interviews and instructions on the outside cover of the manuscript. The prosecutor introduced several files in evidence, particularly those dealing with the Rivonia transaction and associated financial matters, on which no notation at all had been made on the cover. The court was asked to believe that this revealed that a deliberate effort had been made by Kantor and his staff to conceal the facts about Rivonia. Since James Kantor was the senior partner and usually, though not always, one of the signatories to the cheques, no such transaction as the Rivonia purchase could have taken place in the office without his knowledge.

Kantor's counsel made a rather devastating job of the cross-examination of Makda. Makda was not after all a hostile witness. He had worked for Kantor for many years. In South Africa it is rare that a white attorney would take an Indian into his employ and give him the seniority, responsibility and status in the firm which Makda had clearly enjoyed in Kantor's office. Gradually as Kantor's counsel, Mr John Coaker, developed his cross-examination, Makda relapsed into a stereotyped answer: 'That is so,' 'That is so,' 'That is so.' Finally, the entire statement of Kantor's behaviour and responsibility in the firm as put by Mr John Coaker had been fully confirmed by this State witness.

It was apparent that Dr Yutar was in a towering rage. He seemed to take it as a personal affront that his witness had agreed with defence counsel, and had not even tried to fight for the State version of the facts. He began to brow-beat Makda. Why had he agreed with certain suggestions put by counsel for Kantor? Makda gave the obvious answer—the suggestions were correct, that was why he had agreed. Yutar snapped 'I know you agreed with him. You agreed with a lot of things. You said 'Yes, that is so. That is so, that is so' so often that I thought I was listening to a gramophone record'.

At this stage Mr Justice de Wet intervened to remind the prosecutor that he could not cross-examine his own witness. The Deputy Attorney-General sat down in a huff. The case against Kantor, phoney as it obviously was, had not been improved by the first and main State witness to it.

For the public at least the State case needed to be reburnished. So Makda was followed by a dramatised reading of documents by

Dr Yutar. No one handed the documents in or identified them. The prosecutor read them into the record, announcing only that they would be formally identified and handed in at a later stage.

The particular document chosen to undo the Makda debacle was marked 'Top Secret'. It was alleged by Dr Yutar—no evidence led at this stage—that it was in the handwriting of Arthur Goldreich and had been found in his private study at Rivonia. It seemed very clear that Goldreich had thought extensively on problems of sabotage and of guerrilla warfare. He had kept written notes on methods and tactics, and on techniques for the manufacture and handling of explosives. He had apparently discussed and recorded various possibilities of obtaining outside assistance, and of commencing internal guerrilla activity. He had what must be regarded as unfortunate for a revolutionary—a habit of filing these documents carefully in his own home. Throughout the case we were confronted with letters and documents which Goldreich had collected. His house must have been a small library of information and opinion on guerrilla warfare.

Dr Yutar read this 'Top Secret' document with his greatest histrionic ploys. He would start quietly, but his voice rose to a high-pitched crescendo of indignation as he came to what he regarded as damning phrases. His voice shook over 'revolution' or 'uprising' or 'overthrow of the authority of State'. In this particular document there was much scope for shaking. It appeared to be the notes of extensive discussions on tactics and prospects of guerrilla warfare, which had been held by or perhaps with—it was not clear—people in various countries including China, the USSR, Germany and Yugoslavia. In general they had said little about guerrilla warfare which is not readily obtainable from the published books of Mao Tse-Tung and others. But they did apparently discuss methods of obtaining arms and explosives for use in South Africa. It was also clear that, in part at least, whoever had taken part in these discussions had been concerned to relate them to Umkhonto we Sizwe in South Africa.

For the press, perhaps even for the public, this document was the shocker that Dr Yutar seemed to think it was. The accused took it with comparative indifference. They had a simple view.

Umkhonto had spoken openly of sabotage and military struggle. What then was surprising in this document? In this reaction, again, they both mystified and disappointed Yutar, who seemed to expect them to be devastated that their 'top secrets' had been revealed, and anxious to deny the truth of the contents of the document. Yutar never came to understand the accused, or their reaction, and so never really knew or was able to distinguish the really damaging evidence from the chaff.

After this, we were shown another method of introducing documents. Dr Yutar called as witness Mr Ralph Sepel, the attorney who had received £2,500 in notes from Wolpe via Ismail Makda. Mr Sepel told the court how Goldreich had come to his office, and requested that his firm act as attorneys in the transfer of the property to a company, from which Goldreich would lease. Dr Yutar clearly distrusted Sepel, even though he had called him as a State witness. Sepel had been in detention for some six weeks prior to his evidence. Unless it was claimed that receiving £2,500 in cash and paying an instalment due on a property was itself subversive, there was no apparent reason for his distrust.

On the face of it, nothing Sepel had done seemed to me either suspect or unlawful. He was asked to identify Goldreich's handwriting on a document which had been found in his office. It was a routine instruction in connection with the Rivonia account. Sepel did so. He was then shown the 'Top Secret' document and asked to identify the handwriting as Goldreich's. Sepel was an attorney. He refused to do so. All he would say was that the document *might have been* in Goldreich's handwriting, and even then, he prefaced his statement with a disclaimer of any expert knowledge of handwriting. Yutar, undeterred, put six other documents to him for identification, and got the same answer every time. On this flimsy basis six more documents were before the court and Yutar began to read them.

Bram immediately objected. Never in his experience, he said, had he come across such a procedure. The defence insisted that all documents be introduced in this court in an ordinary manner, and proved before they were read. Yutar's reply was a bit hesitant: 'My Lord,' he said, 'I do not want to spend days on end on my feet reading dull and uninteresting documents one after another which I have no doubt your Lordship would find both tedious and boring. In order to spare your Lordship this tedium, I had in mind reading the documents piecemeal. I assure your Lordship that there is no ulterior or improper motive. I am doing it solely for your Lordship's convenience'.

We expected Yutar to receive a rather indignant blast from Mr Justice de Wet. Instead the judge replied coolly 'I can see no objection Mr Yutar. Proceed'.

This then was the procedure until the end of the trial. Documents unproved, or of unproved authorship, whose place of discovery was 'testified to' only by Dr Yutar, were handed in, described by Yutar and read into the record. We could, the judge assured us, object to any of the evidence at the end of the case.

After dramatised readings of documents for several days, Yutar announced his intention of calling his next witness, whose evidence, he said, would cover a wide field.

He asked the court to order that the evidence of the next witness be heard in camera. 'He is definitely in mortal danger,' he cried, with breaking voice. 'I assure this court the State fears for the safety of this witness!' He would not object to the presence of the press provided reporters did not identify the witness. The judge asked our attitude.

We certainly wanted all the witnesses to be heard in public. But to insist on this in the face of the unsubstantiated statement of the witness's dire danger, might well persuade the Judge that Yutar's fears were well founded and might lead both court and public to believe that our clients or their friends were terrorising witnesses. Vernon Berrange was forced to take a quick decision. He said that the defence would make no objection to the witness giving evidence in a cleared court, if the prosecutor so desired, although we would certainly prefer all evidence to be heard in public.

While on his feet, however, he took the opportunity to object to a new procedure which had been introduced at this stage—namely that the witness box had been moved from its usual place in front of the defence counsel, to the opposite side of the court where the prosecution team were seated. The witness thus would stand surrounded on all sides by the prosecution and the Security Branch policemen who were part of the prosecution team. He would face directly towards what in normal cases was the jury box. Our objection was not to this change, but to its obvious purpose, for sitting alone in the unused jury box was the large and formidable figure of a gorilla-like Security Branch policeman, Detective Sergeant van Rensburg. Van Rensburg had the face of a Gestapo man, and the reputation of a thug who, it was alleged, regularly assaulted prisoners in his hands. The effect of this brute, alone in the middle of the jury box, glaring menacingly directly at the witness on the witness stand could only be intimidatory and calculated to remind the witness not to say anything that he was not supposed to say. We objected to the presence of van Rensburg. The judge agreed with our objection. The court was cleared of the public, and the jury box was cleared of Sergeant van Rensburg. The first substantial witness took the stand.

His name was Bruno Mtolo. The court ordered the press to refer to him as Mr X. He was a tall, well-built man with considerable self confidence. He appeared to feel quite at home in the witness box, very casual, very self-possessed. We had been expecting him. Rumour had come down the prison grapevine weeks before that he was 'talking'—that is, informing. We had seen him that very morning sitting in the passage outside the courtroom where witnesses waited, chatting to the Special Branch policemen— white Special Branch policemen—who had been plying him with cigarettes and treating him as a celebrity, almost as though he was not black. We knew in advance that he would be a very valuable witness for the State.

In the absence of a public, Dr Yutar had to play to the press gallery. His opening gambit, a rather bogus piece of rhetoric which I think he imagined to be Perry Mason stuff was: 'Bruno, are you a saboteur?'.

Bruno had been well drilled. He was quite confident, at ease, as he replied: 'Yes, I was!'

'Did you blow up pylons and other Government property in Durban?'

'Yes, I did.'

Bruno Mtolo spent three days in the witness box. He said he had carried out many acts of sabotage on the instructions of the Durban Regional Command of Umkhonto we Sizwe which, he said, had taken its orders from the National High Command at Rivonia. He described how various co-conspirators—Jack Hodgson, Harold Strachan and Ronnie Kasrils—had taken part in establishing the Durban branch of Umkhonto.

Mtolo was the first witness to directly implicate Nelson Mandela with Umkhonto. He described a meeting of the Natal Regional Command in Durban in August 1962 attended by Mandela who told them he had been abroad and had met the leaders of African states. They had all expressed sympathy with the movement in South Africa and their satisfaction with what was being done in the battle against the government. Mandela said he had met the Prime Minister of Algeria Ben Bella and Emperor Haile Selassi of Ethiopia. The Ethiopians said they were not only prepared to train men from South Africa but also to assist with funds. At a conference in Addis Ababa African leaders had agreed that the only way to gain freedom was to fight for it.

Mandela told the meeting that the campaign in South Africa amounted to a military operation, but that this would expand to guerilla warfare. He advised them to study their own history so they could tell the people that the struggle dated back to the time of Dingaan.

According to Mtolo the name Umkhonto we Sizwe was then given to the sabotage organisation by Mandela. Mtolo then moved on to testify that shortly after the Natal meeting Mandela himself was arrested. After his conviction, but before sentence was passed, the Regional Command decided on a wave of sabotage by way of protest. These acts of sabotage took place three days after Mandela was sentenced. Having implicated Mandela, Mtolo then went on to implicate almost all the accused and many whom the State had named as co-conspirators.

He had been trained by Ronnie Kasrils, and he had been sent by Leon Levy to Jack Hodgson, who had instructed him in the use of dynamite and gelignite. Joe Modise had given him twenty detonators, and he had met Andrew Mlangeni, who was known as 'Robot'.

He had been given this name because when he set out to complete a task nothing deterred him. He had met Motsoaledi, who had taught him how to make use of black powder and thermite. But he felt that Motsoaledi could teach him very little because of the extensive knowledge of sabotage and explosives that he already had.

He described a visit to Johannesburg where he was sent to see Advocate Joe Slovo, who was his contact man and gained him entry to the Rivonia Headquarters of the National High Command. There he met four men in a room who were Walter Sisulu, Govan Mbeki, Ahmed Kathrada and an unidentified fourth man, an African. He also saw Rusty Bernstein there.

Dr Yutar then led him in great detail through the twenty three acts of sabotage in which he had participated, ranging from blowing up pylons and government offices to the homes of informers and collaborators. The police net had eventually closed around him and he was arrested.

Naturally, Dr Yutar was inordinately pleased with his witness Mtolo, as well he might be. We, on the other hand, were puzzled by several aspects of his evidence. There were many features of the acts of sabotage which he claimed to have committed on the instructions of and under the guidance of the Natal Regional Command of Umkhonto we Sizwe. He described, for instance, several occasions where bombs had been put in places where they were either calculated to endanger human life or very likely to do so. He had placed bombs on railway tracks at the time when passenger trains were likely to pass. He had placed bombs in passenger trains, in apparently unoccupied coaches. Bombs, he said, had been placed in the doorways of homes of pro-government Africans in KwaMashu Township outside Durban. Bombs had been placed in the doorway of a certain 'Induna' (that is to say, boss-boy or charge-hand) of the African labourers employed by a Durban hospital.

The accused had told us that Umkhonto had set out deliberately to commit acts of sabotage against Government property and installations. But their instructions had at all times been that under no circumstances should human life be endangered. In fact, Mtolo himself had testified that this was the instruction. The accused found it difficult to explain to us how such actions as Mtolo described could possibly have been decided upon by the Natal Regional Command. We found it equally difficult to understand. Was the witness lying? Were the accused misleading us? Or had the Natal Regional Command gone off on a frolic of their own? Nobody in Johannesburg could answer these questions, so it was necessary for me to go to Natal to ascertain the answer. Another aspect of his evidence which puzzled us had come right at the end. Mtolo had described how he himself had come into the trade union movement, and later become a trade union organiser and full-time official; how he had joined the African National Congress, and later the South African Communist Party, and had been an active member of both; and how he had come into Umkhonto we Sizwe and become a full-time saboteur, employed by the Natal Regional Command. Then, at the very end of his evidence, he was asked by Dr Yutar why he now volunteered evidence for the State against the members of Umkhonto, and was prepared to reveal all their secrets to the police.

His reply, if it could be believed, was that some time in June 1963, he had been sent by the Natal Regional Command to a place called Bergville, an area high in the Drakensberg mountains. His mission was to contact the local chief and discuss with him the formation of armed Umkhonto units amongst his tribesmen. He had gone to Bergville.

Question from Dr Yutar: Did you train them in the arts taught to you?

Answer: I did not put myself out to teach them for a particular reason.

And what was that reason?

Because I did not at that time feel that—in literal language—my heart was not with the Umkhonto we Sizwe anymore.

Why not?

Because as I have already said, since April I was in hiding. I was taken out of my fixed employment, my Lord. I was promised that I would receive a monthly payment. And since June 1961 until the date of my arrest the only money I was given by Umkhonto we Sizwe for that whole period was £10.00, although they kept on promising me that my money would come. Also the people, these recruits, that were arrested—they didn't care about them.

Yutar: Who didn't care about them?

Mtolo: The High Command. But they, when they ran away from South Africa, they were not arrested. But they didn't care of the security of those groups of recruits.

It sounded plausible to the clique around the police benches. But not to us. It did not ring true. The only members of the High Command known to Mtolo were those he had met at Rivonia. They were all sitting in the dock in front of him. Not one of them had run away. Was he voicing his ideas? Or Yutar's, picked up from the prosecutor's repeated references to the 'so-called leaders' who had 'run away?' Yutar felt that this so-called 'running away' was important enough to get into his opening address, though whether he intended to blame the accused for the others who had gone, or for their own failure to do likewise, was never clear to me.

Question: How did the so-called leaders of the High Command live?

Answer: Well it so happened that while I was at the party at Pafeni (which is in Orlando in Johannesburg) one of them took me and showed me the house of Walter Sisulu. The house and its furniture inside, everything was like that of Europeans. In Joe Modise's house there is a telephone in the house and furniture that I don't possess. The room in which I stayed in Durban I paid £1.10 rent, but when I left there was not a single person who paid that £1.10 for me apart from the fact that they did not see what my children had to eat.

Question: In regard to these leaders, what was the position as far as money was concerned? Can you tell us whether or not they had money?

Answer: Mlangeni had a motor car.

Yes, and the others? Did you see whether they had money or not?

Answer: Walter Sisulu paid bail of £3,000. Over and above that when he came out on bail he had a motor car. Bail for £3,000!

And so, on the basis of disillusion about the Umkhonto leaders—if he could be believed—Mtolo, who had spent three years as perhaps the most active saboteur in the country and one of the most energetic members of Umkhonto we Sizwe, turned evidence for the State and incriminated everybody who had ever worked with him or who was ever known to him either in the African National Congress or Umkhonto we Sizwe. The list of those fingered included his own brother, whom he identified in court as one of the young men who had been recruited by Umkhonto to be sent abroad for military training. We asked the accused about Sisulu's house. We were told that the furnishing, if anything, was below average for an urban resident of Johannesburg African Township. The motor car was a lie. Sisulu could not even drive, and had never owned a car. Mlangeni's car was to be shown over and over again, in the evidence in this very case, to be the property of Umkhonto we Sizwe. Mlangeni used it for official business only. So much for Mtolo's 'reasons'.

I went off to Pietermaritzburg to interview members of the Natal Regional Command to find something more about this mysterious character and his testimony. It was not easy. All those still available were in jail, themselves awaiting trial. They were hesitant to speak to me in the prison, and they were doubtful how much they should tell me without first consulting their own counsel. When I returned from the interview, I knew little more than when I went down. I had learnt, however, that Mtolo had been a saboteur for three years as he claimed. He had been perhaps the most active saboteur in Natal, had always egged them on to greater daring and greater activity, and he had shown an almost demented passion for violence and a singular disregard for his own safety. Though he was all of this, I learned that he was also a convicted criminal, with a record which could be checked.

When I learnt this, Mtolo's character began to fall into place for me. In the witness box he had shown the sort of swaggering arrogance and self-confidence which I had seen from the old lags who know it all, the ones who 'know the ropes', and even what sentence is going to be given before the case is even called to court— the recidivist criminal who knows what job he is going to angle to get in prison, and what branch of crime he is going to turn to when he comes out. It is a type one gets to know in the courts and prisons. That knowledge should have warned me what we would be up against in the cross-examination of this man. He had shown that he had a phenomenal memory, and a very quick mind, of a peculiar lying criminal type. I realised that we would be meeting a formidable opponent in our cross-examination of Mtolo. We had a three weeks' adjournment in which to prepare our cross-examination.

So far as his testimony against the Natal Regional Command was concerned, there was little we could or wanted to say. We could not admit that the people he named as members of the Regional Command were members—they were all themselves accused and awaiting trial on that very charge in Natal. Nor could we deny that they were members, for reasons of truth and because we did not know what they themselves would say in their own trial. We could not question Mtolo's details of the precise acts of sabotage carried out, or the names of the persons who he said had accompanied him or given him instructions, because we did not know the facts.

We were left then with only two aspects of his evidence: a meeting of the Natal Regional Command which he said Mandela had attended and addressed on behalf of the National High Command, and the red-baiting and smearing which, led by Dr Yutar, he had used against all the organisations, their leaders and the accused in the dock.

Mandela, as always, was quite decisive in his attitude. He told us he would freely admit that he had attended a meeting of the Natal Regional Command of Umkhonto, that he had reported to them on his trip abroad and the arrangements he had made for the training of military personnel. But he would not under any circumstances testify as to who was present nor would he admit that those named by Mtolo were members of the Regional Command. He would deny and challenge Mtolo's version of many of the things he was alleged to have said at that meeting. Mtolo, he said, had deliberately tried to smear Umkhonto we Sizwe with communist slanders, and to equate the African National Congress with communism in a deliberate attempt to discredit all three organisations. Mtolo was lying, and Mandela was determined that our cross-examination should indicate that he was lying and slandering organisations, even though we admitted that he did attend the meeting at which Mandela had in fact reported.

Nelson was a lawyer. He understood fully the implication of what he was saying. Nevertheless, we felt it necessary to warn him of it, and even tried to argue him out of his position. Cross-examination such as he was suggesting amounted to an admission of all the main charges against him. It would be an implicit admission that he had belonged to Umkhonto and had held a senior position in it, and that he had canvassed and obtained the aid of foreign countries to train military personnel for the struggle against the South African government. We pointed out that in doing this, he might well be signing his death warrant, for there could not thereafter be any possible denials of guilt or attempts to evade conviction because the full proof of the offence had not been given in court.

Nelson was unmoved. This much, he said, he had understood ever since he had taken a position of responsibility in the political movement. A leader who holds a responsible position, he said, must accept the responsibilities that go with it. On this occasion the responsibility on him was to explain to the country and the world where Umkhonto we Sizwe stood, and why, and to clarify its aims and policy, to reveal the true facts from the half-truths and distortions of the State case. If in doing this his life should be at stake, so be it. As he saw it, that was his responsibility derived from the position he held in the national movement. Walter and Govan, both of whom were said by Mtolo to have had discussions about Umkhonto we Sizwe with him at Rivonia, took the same attitude. They would admit having discussions there with Mtolo with reference to Umkhonto we Sizwe, but they would certainly deny Mtolo's version of many aspects of this conversation. Thus our difficulties in cross-examining Mtolo would be multiplied by the stature we would give to his credibility by freely admitting that parts of his evidence were true. Any lawyer will know that the most difficult witness to attack is not the outright liar, but the one who is telling 90% of the truth, but slipping in 10% of lies in places where the really vital issues are at stake.

Our investigation in Natal revealed that Mtolo was telling lies not only about facts known to our clients, but even more about the events which had taken place there, of which our clients knew nothing. We were faced with the challenge that we would have to destroy his version of events and establish the version which was given us by members of the Natal Regional Command. We had to do this without admitting that the people from whom he said he took instructions were in fact the members of the Natal Regional Command, for to name other persons was something none of the accused would do. Under no circumstances were they prepared to say or admit anything which might incriminate any of the Natal men then awaiting trial in Pietermaritzburg jail. This was like fighting with one hand tied behind one's back.

We returned to court to cross-examine Mtolo with a whole field of cross-examination closed to us. We restricted our attack to a few issues, our cross-examination to be handled by Vernon Berrange. I know of nobody who could do it better. Vernon is at his best in such a contest, where it is necessary to have an understanding of the witness' psychology and seize on his every weakness. A tremendous quickness and agility of mind is required to capitalise on every false step made by the witness, and to lead from it along unexpected tracks until a gross lie is drawn out into the open, logically, irresistibly, from a slight initial mistake. Vernon had the delicacy of an artist with the finest of rapiers, but he also had the necessary ruthlessness to hammer destructively and mercilessly once advantage turned his way. He opened his cross-examination by referring to the witness as 'Mister Mtolo'.

Outside South Africa this might not seem strange. But here it was a calculated move of enquiry. Was there any last spark of manhood or pride in this witness which might be awakened, as once the ANC had awakened it, and started him on the path that led to Umkhonto we Sizwe? If there was, he would react. Up to now, he had not been 'Mister' or even 'Mtolo'. He had been 'boy'. Dr Yutar in typical white South African fashion called him 'Bruno'.

Mtolo did not respond at all to the courtesy of Berrange's address. It seemed that it meant nothing to him that he was being treated by one side as a man, and by the other side as a boy. This was what we had expected. He had sold himself to the prosecution, and with that sale he had sold whatever pride he might once have had in himself.

Gradually, under cross-examination, he became increasingly the 'old lag'. I suppose once, during the period he had spent in the national movement and became a figure to be reckoned with in Durban, he must have been a man with some dignity, some pride. But now he was just another lag, without dignity, quite shamelessly going over to the side of his enemies, tolerating their insulting patronage without even resentment, and so desperately anxious to please that he would almost certainly finish up either as a cringing stool-pigeon or as a brutal bully-boy. Mtolo had started off by giving an impression that he revelled in his role of chief witness for the prosecution.

Mr Berrange started his cross-examination on the very question of why, or perhaps how, Mtolo had come to make this volte-face, from leader of Umkhonto to police informer. He recalled Mtolo's evidence that he was arrested on the 3rd August.

Berrange: You thought matters over?

Mtolo: Yes

And, therefore, at the most within twenty four hours, you had decided to tell the police all you knew?

Yes.

And the reasons that you have given us were that you weren't getting the money which you were promised?

Yes.

And that the higher-ups did not seem to care for the security of the recruits?

Yes.

That Nelson Mandela and Sisulu seemed to be well off?

Yes.

That the leaders had left the country?

Yes.

Berrange referred back to Mtolo's career in the African National Congress and the trade union movement before returning to this line of questioning:

And then you became disillusioned for the reason you have given us?

Yes.

Did you become disillusioned because you no longer thought that what the ANC and the liberation movement were struggling for was the right thing?

I will say this: that I thought all the time that what the ANC was working for was good and I still say so now, that it was good and is good. But what made me feel disillusioned was the action of the leaders.

And because you became disillusioned with the leaders you were prepared, within twenty four hours of your arrest, to go and make a statement, to expose the whole of this movement which you believe to be to the benefit of the black man?

Mtolo sidestepped rapidly, expertly. 'If I talk about the African National Congress, it must be known that I talk about the ANC and not this thing about the communists.'

Berrange was not easily thrown off balance. He kept to his line of questioning, seemingly ignoring the feint.

What about the Spear of the Nation?

The Spear is connected with the communists.

Did you agree with what The Spear was doing?

I agreed with it when it was doing it for the ANC.

So you say you became disillusioned with The Spear when it was doing it for the communists?

Yes, my Lord, in the way in which they were deceiving the people.

How were they deceiving the people?

Because the majority of the members of the ANC were not aware of the fact that the leaders were communists.

Now, do you mind telling this court what difference it made to you whether the leaders were communists, or whether they were members of the Liberal Party, or whether they were members of any sort of party, so long as they were doing something which you agreed to and thought was good?

The deception, the deceiving was the thing.

What deceiving?

Because they are holding the people under the impression that they are members of the ANC, whereas in fact the leaders are members of the Communists.

You still have not answered my question. What difference did it make to you?

Because they were not doing it for the ANC, but they were doing it for themselves.

Were you a member of the Communist Party?

Yes.

Did you agree with what they were doing?

Yes.

You did. You knew what they were doing?

Yes.

They were doing the very things which you are now objecting to?

Yes.

And you went along with them wholeheartedly?

Yes.

Why?

Mtolo appeared to pause to think, for the first time. 'As I have already said, I was in agreement with it. I was a member of the Communist Party. But what we were doing at the time was all being done for the ANC.'

Berrange: That is my whole point!

Mtolo: But then afterwards in recent times, particularly from the beginning of 1963 up to now, it has been quite clear that what is being done is not done for the ANC. It's being done for the Communist Party.

How did that become clear to you?

Because the members of the ANC, it became clear to them afterwards that the leaders were communists. In other words, the genuine ANC people, members—it became clear to them and they realised that the leaders were now the heads of the organisation and they were not working for the ANC any more, but were working for the Communist Party.

How did that become clear to you?

Because in the beginning of 1963 we were receiving directives that were coming from the Communist Party. According to those directives we were advised that because the ANC members are dissatisfied and don't agree with The Spear of the Nation, that we who were members of the Communist Party must get into the ANC organisation and get into the different branches so that we can get hold of the leadership in those branches.

Mr Justice de Wet: just a minute. Can you explain to me? Is there any difference between the aims and objectives of the Communist Party and the aims and objectives of the ANC?

Mtolo: Yes, there is a difference, my Lord.

De Wet: That is what counsel wants you to explain. What is the difference?

Mtolo: Because the policy of the ANC is not that the wealth of the country and the government should go to the workers, my Lord. The difference between the ideas of the ANC and the Communist Party is that the communist says that the wealth of the country must come to the workers, in other words, the workers will rule this country. It is the worker who will then have to decide how this wealth is shared and distributed. The difference is that the policy of the ANC—the way they looked at things—was that the wealth of the country should be divided and shared by the people of the country, not the workers.

Berrange: So you draw the distinction between the people and the workers?

Answer: Yes.

And you were prepared, therefore if your evidence is true, to betray these members of the ANC for whom you had such a soft feeling, because they were being deceived—merely because of the fact that members of the Communist Party had infiltrated into the ranks of the ANC?

Mtolo: As I am standing here I am satisfied in my own mind that I did not harm the members of the ANC. As a matter of fact I have done them a favour.

Berrange: Are you serious?

Yes.

Well, who have you betrayed?

I have told to the ANC people that these people who are leading in this way were deceiving them.

But what about those members of the ANC who have been arrested and sent to jail, and those who will still be arrested and sent to jail because of the fact that you have exposed them—if your evidence is true. You have exposed, if your evidence is true, the whole of the set up. What about them?

Those who have been already convicted because they were furthering the objects of the movement and the ANC are prepared to go to jail for their cause, and I am still prepared to go for that cause, but not to go to jail through being deceived.

Now you gave evidence for many days last year (prior to the adjournment)?

Yes.

And you gave us then a reason for your disillusion—a number of reasons which I read out to you this morning.

Yes.

You never at that stage mentioned at all any of the reasons you have given me today. You mentioned then the fact that you weren't getting any money, the recruits were not being cared for, the leaders seemed to have a lot of money and the leaders have left the country. And I want to indicate to you in due course that all those reasons are false. When did you think of the reasons that you have given us today?

When I was giving evidence in chief I was not questioned about the ANC as I am questioned by you now.

You were questioned.

But those reasons which you have just mentioned now were in regard to Umkhonto we Sizwe.

You were questioned as to the reasons for your becoming disillusioned and never gave this as one of your reasons.

I was questioned then, when I gave my evidence in chief in regard to Umkhonto we Sizwe. There are many other things I can say. The more you question me the more I can bring out that I haven't said before.

I am sure. Is this the first time you have ever been in a court?

No.

In this court?

I was here last year.

Is this the only case you have appeared in?

Do you mean one that is not concerned with politics?

I am just asking you. Is this the only case that you have appeared in?

I have given evidence in other courts.

It was at this stage that the court adjourned for the day. When it resumed next morning, Berrange did not immediately return to this topic. He turned instead to various specific acts of sabotage to which Mtolo had testified during his evidence in chief. After one or two clashes with the witness on this, he returned without warning to the previous day's question.

Berrange: I return now to the question I was asking you before the interval. You say you have given evidence in other cases before?

Mtolo: Yes. But not political cases.

Cases in which you yourself have been involved?

Yes. One.

Well, what sort of cases?

Attempted murder.

Who was the accused?

Joseph Nduli.

You say that that was not a political case?

No, that was an attempted murder charge.

Wasn't that a case where a bomb was put in the Induna's room?

Yes.

One of the acts of sabotage that you have related here? (And one of the acts charged in the indictment!)

Yes. But the difference is that that person did not attempt to murder this person for the . . . he had no connection with the organisation.

Berrange: It wasn't a political crime? It was a personal crime?

Mtolo: Yes.

It was a personal grudge?

Yes.

You made the bomb though, didn't you?

Yes.

And you gave evidence about it?

In that case, yes.

And one of the witnesses gave evidence to the effect that he had received a bomb?

When the witnesses gave evidence in court we were not listening.

But you must have been questioned by the police?

Well, whether I handled the bomb.

No, but you must have been questioned about this incident by the police?

Yes, I was.

You actually gave evidence for the State?

Yes.

And did you tell the police that you had made this bomb?

No, I did not.

You hid that from them?

Yes.

Any other cases in which you have been involved?

When you say I hid it from the police, you mean at that time?

Yes.

Yes, that is so.

And you didn't give any evidence about it? Although you knew all about it?

I did not give evidence.

Tell me, have you ever been to a reformatory?

No.

Is that truthful?

Yes.

Have you even been in jail?

Many times when I was still a youngster, but not a reformatory.

How many sentences have you served?

In 1950 there were several charges that were taken as one. I am sorry, my Lord, all the sentences taken together amounted to four years, four and a half?

Four and a half is what you served. Six is what you were sentenced to.

Mtolo: I served actually four and a half years. Two years of that, I am not certain whether it was consecutive or not.

Berrange: We are not worrying whether it was for four years and a half or six. What was the offence for which you were sent to jail, for six years?

It was for taking articles, parcels from a goods train, a truck.

Stealing?

Yes.

That was in 1952?

1950.

How many convictions have you got? I am only talking about convictions in regard to dishonesty.

I would say, three.

Have you been in jail on every occasion?

Yes.

And they were all for dishonesty or theft?

For theft.

And yet you broke from the Communist Party and its ideology because you were a respecter of property?

Yes, and the reason for that is serving in jail in 1950 taught me to respect other people's property.

And it taught you so well that you were not prepared to serve in the Communist Party when they said that the property was to go to the workers and not the people?

Yes.

You were still blowing up other people's property though, weren't you?

Yes, I was doing that.

And that was because you were completely satisfied that the policy of the African National Congress was the only policy which would enable the African people to achieve what you felt they would be able to achieve?

Yes, and the reason for that is serving in jail in 1950 taught me to respect other people's property.

They can only achieve this by violence?

The word violence is rather . . .

Berrange: Yes, by acts of sabotage and that sort of thing.

Mtolo: I would say yes.

And so from Mtolo's record back to his reasons for giving evidence.

Question: One of the reasons that you gave was the fact that you said that the leaders had run away.

Yes.

Was that true?

Yes.

Who had run away? Who had left the country?

Jack Hodgson. Johnnie Makatini.

Why do you call him a leader?

He went on military training. He is in Morocco. He was a leader.

A leader of what?

Of the ANC.

And he is in Morocco now?

Yes.

And what happened to him?

He is staying there.

Anybody else?

Many of them. Joe Slovo.

Give us the leaders who had run away at the time when you decided to give evidence for the State, over that 24-hour period when you got arrested. What leaders had left the country at that stage?

I am not only referring to what happened in June. I am referring to what was happening all the time. The people as soon as they were faced with particular difficulties, they fled.

You said that the leaders had left the country and that was why, when you were arrested, during that night, you decided that you were going to give evidence for the State. I am asking you what leaders had left the country at the time when you came to that decision?

Joe Slovo, Michael Harmel, Jack Hodgson.

They all left the country at that time?

They had left.

Really? And Nelson Mandela?

Talking about Nelson Mandela, I want to tell you that he is the only one of the leaders that I have respect for.

But you were talking about a lot of leaders leaving the country. You see a lot of men in the dock here, don't you?

Yes.

Tell me, other than going to jail for theft, breaking into railway coaches and that sort of thing, have you ever been banned? Have you ever been put under house arrest?

No.

Have you ever been prohibited from attending meetings?

No.

Have you ever been sent to jail for your political beliefs?

No.

Well, that is what happened to most of these men here.

That I admit.

But you, Mr Mtolo, prefer to give evidence against these men because you say the leaders had left.

I said one of the reasons. But these people, referring to these people sitting here, there are some of these also that I realised were playing the fool with us. I haven't suffered the suffering they have suffered, but the deeds they have done are almost the same as the deeds of those who have fled.

Berrange then referred to the allegations that the leaders were not looking after the recruits.

Question: So in order to ensure the safety of the ANC you decided to make the statement.

Answer: In the interests of the ANC. Not the ANC alone, all the people in South Africa.

They would all benefit? And you regarded yourself as a benefactor?

Every person on this earth ought to think of other people.

Don't you think that that is just a bit of sheer hypocrisy?

No, I am saying that for it is true, from the bottom of my heart, my Lord.

Dr Yutar continued to smirk throughout the whole of this cross-examination. He felt, probably correctly, that while we might be tearing holes in the motives of the witness, we were not really destroying his testimony about the sabotage which he had committed or the people with whom he had co-operated. I suppose he was right. We knew that the reasons Mtolo was giving for becoming a turncoat were not valid.

We were intrigued particularly by his statement that he knew how Sisulu lived and that Sisulu had a house almost as good as that occupied by white people. Sisulu insisted that Mtolo had never, to his knowledge, been near his house. Berrange questioned Mtolo about this. He said that it happened that when he was once in Johannesburg, a certain Levy Seloro took him to Sisulu's house.

Berrange: Did you go inside the house?

Mtolo: Yes.

Who was there?

There were some children sitting in the door. We went in a and enquired for his wife. She was not there.

His story was that he had left a party in the area specially to make this inspection of Sisulu's house.

Question: Why should Seloro want to show you Sisulu's house?

He was just going to show me the house of one of the leaders. He was one of the leaders.

But why?

So that I should just know.

Know what?

Know my leader's house.

But why?

It was just incidental.

What parts of the house did you go into?

We went through the kitchen, we went to the dining room.

Yes. Anywhere else?

We sat down in the dining room.

In the absence of Sisulu or his wife. What for?

Seloro then asked where Mrs Sisulu was and the boy said she was not at home. Then Seloro said it was alright, we would see him at the party in any case because he would be there.

So that was your only reason for going to his house?

That is all.

When was this?

Towards the end of April 1963.

But by that time you had already become disillusioned with your leaders?

Mtolo did not faze easily. The best he could manage was: 'That does not mean to say that I would not agree to go to their house'.

Berrange fired another broadside. Mtolo's tale was that, at that time, he was hiding from the police. 'Did you think it a very safe thing for you to go to Sisulu's house under the circumstances when you were supposed to be in hiding?'

Mtolo shrugged. Yutar smirked. The police smirked. De Wet looked bored.

We were more certain than ever that this part of Mtolo's evidence was a put up job. This was the first of a number of such attempted smearing of the accused which we were to be subjected to by either the police investigators or the prosecution. They were not designed to secure a conviction but rather to undermine the public standing and reputation of the accused and the organisation to which they belonged. The general tenor of them all was that these leaders lived well, while their followers suffered and sacrificed. How Yutar imagined Mtolo's indemnity and Sisulu's long persecution and trial squared with this, only he could say.

Eventually, cross-examination returned to what was for us an important matter. This was the question of precisely what Mandela had said when he met the Natal Regional Command. It was not important legally. The admission that he had met the Natal Regional Command in his capacity as a leader of Umkhonto we Sizwe was enough to convict him. But Mtolo was deliberately distorting what Mandela had said in order to smear Mandela, Umkhonto and the African National Congress. We decided to tackle some of the specific distortions to show that Mtolo was lying. He had said that, at the Regional Command meeting in Durban, Mandela had told them what had happened to a certain Eric Mtshali who had gone abroad for military training. Mtshali, he said, had broadcast the fact that he was a Communist, with the result that he had received the cold shoulder from a number of African states. On the strength of this, Mandela had warned them against revealing their communist affiliations—so Mtolo said. They must pose as genuine ANC people. Mtolo also said that Mandela reported that a large number of African States had agreed to give 1% of their annual budget to help the cause of the South African liberation struggle. We knew that both these allegations had to be false.

Evidence had been given in another political trial of the exact date when Mtshali had left South Africa. He could not possibly have had time to do anything in any African state before Mandela attended the Durban meeting. He certainly could not have been abroad for long enough for his communist opinions to have come to the attention of the authorities or for this fact to be reported to Mandela when he was abroad, as Mtolo had said. So far as the 1% allocation from budgets was concerned, we had the published record of a conference of the Organisation of African Unity which had been held at Addis Ababa one year after Nelson's return. It was at this conference that, for the first time, a resolution had been proposed and adopted urging 1% contributions. Mtolo was either assisting his memory with bits and pieces from his imagination coloured by his own reading, or he was being told what to say.

Berrange put Mandela's version of his address to the witness. Had he not said that communists who join Umkhonto and are sent abroad for military training must not use their position in Umkhonto to make communist propaganda, or to seek to advance the partisan cause of the Communist Party? They were welcome to hold communist opinions if they chose, but they must understand that any attempt to spread communist propaganda in foreign countries would lead not only to their personal unpopularity with the authorities, but also to the discrediting of Umkhonto we Sizwe.

Mtolo insisted he was right. He would not admit to any lapse of memory on anything. His version was absolutely correct, and Mandela's was wrong. Berrange turned to certain acts of sabotage which Mtolo had given evidence about. He questioned him about his evidence that certain acts of sabotage had been planned by the Natal Regional Command in 1962 as part of a campaign of protest against Mandela's arrest, which had just taken place. He insisted on this under cross-examination. He said that when the Regional Command had read of Mandela's conviction in court, they decided to show the government how strongly they protested by committing a series of acts of sabotage. The particular acts were enumerated and charged in the indictment. But again, there had been some lack of care, either by Mtolo or his prompters, because as Berrange showed, the acts of sabotage said by Mtolo to be in protest against Mandela's conviction had taken place on the 14th October, whereas the official record showed that Mandela's conviction and sentence both took place on the 7th November. Mtolo disputed this strenuously and stubbornly. Perhaps he realised he was out on a limb. He would not accept the facts.

If what Berrange said was proved to be correct, then it could only be, he said, that the facts set out in the newspaper reports on which the Natal Regional Command based their decision, must have been different—and wrong. It was quite impossible that he was wrong about the reasons for the decision to commit these acts. The Mandela trial court record, or the press, or the dates in the indictment in this case must be wrong. He was right.

Berrange seized on another curious quirk in Mtolo's memory. 'Do you remember saying to his Lordship that the Rivonia arrests were hard on Billy Nair? Those were the exact words used. You went on to say that you did not care.'

Answer: That is correct.

Do you remember saying that?

Yes, I do.

Did you discuss those arrests with Billy Nair?

Yes, we did.

Berrange: The Rivonia arrests. I see, well that's rather interesting. Because at the time the Rivonia arrests took place, Billy Nair had already been arrested for some time . . .

At this moment there was an interruption by the interpreter who said 'My Lord, the witness is now deep in thought. He is still thinking very hard while counsel was putting that question'.

Berrange: I am sure.

Interpreter: He was softly whispering 'Billy Nair, Billy Nair', he was evidently thinking very hard.

At this point Mtolo recovered himself with the agility of a top-class acrobat. 'My Lord,' he said, 'I think that I should say that in my evidence I said—I think what I meant to convey was that the arrests at Rivonia were a sore point to people like Billy Nair'.

Berrange: Oh, no! You said that the Rivonia arrests were hard on people like Billy Nair, but you did not care. And you also said only a few moments ago that you actually discussed the Rivonia arrests with Billy Nair.

Mtolo: No, that I did not say.

Oh, yes, you did.

No. Then it would be a mistake.

Oh, no it is not, I am sorry. Now what did you mean when you said that the Rivonia arrests were hard on people like Billy Nair, seeing that he was already arrested?

What I . . . I may have expressed it in those words, but what I meant to convey was that the arrests at Rivonia was something that was a sore point. It hurt people like Billy Nair.

Is that what you meant to convey, although he had been arrested before Rivonia?

Yes, he was arrested before Rivonia.

Although you did say a few moments ago that you discussed it with Billy Nair?

No, not discussed.

In this type of passage—and there were others of the same kind—Mtolo showed he was an old hand in court. He appeared to have no nerves. He was prepared to wriggle and talk his way out of any difficult situation with a speed of shift which challenged the ability of experienced counsel. We were to experience more of this side of Mtolo as our cross-examination dug deeper. But at this stage we merely informed the court that we had been unable to get adequate briefing on all the events in Natal, and we might at some later stage wish to recall this witness.

We left him well pleased with himself. The prosecutor seemed equally pleased with him and the court impressed. On our side, our own case had taken a knock, and our chief accused, Nelson Mandela, had admitted the main burden of the charge.

6 Unreliable Prosecution Witnesses

I have dealt with Mtolo at length because in a way he was unique. As a witness he had a lot of inside evidence of Umkhonto and the ANC, but his evidence was an interwoven mixture of fact and fiction, moments of truth in between downright lies. The lies were so neatly tailored to suit the State case that I do not believe Mtolo could have invented them for himself.

The difference between Mtolo's evidence and that of most of the other accomplice witnesses was that while his knowledge of the real facts was more extensive than most, his interlarding of fiction was more extensive too. His evidence, covering a broader span, a longer period of time, and a wider number of incidents than that of any other witness, gave us a clear understanding of what we were up against in dealing with witnesses who had been in solitary confinement for a considerable length of time. They had all been grilled under conditions of varying pressure and intimidation, and held totally incommunicado before being brought to court to give evidence.

All of them were aware that the police would hold them in solitary confinement until they had 'answered questions to the satisfaction of their interrogating officer'. All of them knew that their only chance of liberty depended not only on giving evidence to the satisfaction of the court, but even more, on giving evidence to the satisfaction of the police, who had only recently been given the power to detain people indefinitely, even where an absolution from prosecution had been given in court by a judge after satisfactory testimony under oath. Such witnesses, we expected, would lean over backwards to please the prosecution. They did. Most of them lied shamelessly, purposefully and apparently to order.

The first such witness was a coloured man from Cape Town called Cyril Davids. His testimony was only relevant against Dennis Goldberg. Unlike the others, who had all worked in Johannesburg for many years, Goldberg was from Cape Town. He had come to Johannesburg only a few months before his arrest. The evidence which related to his activities in Cape Town was against him alone and, like so much in this case, became relevant against the others only because a conspiracy had been charged.

The prosecution would attempt to show that Goldberg had joined the conspiracy while he was in Johannesburg for some weeks and that his actions in Cape Town for a period of some years before were also connected with Umkhonto. Davids' story was, on the face of it, fairly simple.

He said that in December 1962 a camp had been held for young men on a farm at a place called Mamre, outside Cape Town. Goldberg had been the organiser of this camp, and had approached him to give a series of lectures on electricity and judo at the camp. The young men were all, according to his testimony, members of either the African National Congress Youth League or of the Coloured People's Congress. He had come prepared to talk about basic electrical circuits, the operation of the telephone and other every-day electrical devices. He was not, he said, a politician, but an expert in electrical installations.

The fact that this camp had taken place was already a matter of public record. At the camp, dispute had arisen with the local Church Mission Society, which claimed that it owned the land on which the campers had pitched their tents. The campers on their part claimed that they had received permission to camp there from a man in Cape Town who they believed was the owner of the land. The upshot of the dispute was that the secretary of the Mission called the police. The police, who had come to turn the campers off the land, had found that all the campers were not white—which in

South Africa in itself was suspicious, if not criminal. So they in turn had called in the Security Police and there had been an extensive raid. All the documents and books they could find were confiscated, and the names and addresses of everyone present had been noted. The camp had been formally closed down and everybody ordered off the land. Goldberg and other suspected ringleaders in the camp had been ordered to report to the police the following day in Cape Town, which they had done. Statements had been taken from them all. No prosecution of any sort had followed, nor had there, at that time, been any suggestion of any offence other than a possible accidental trespass on the Mission Society's ground.

Cyril Davids was one of those who had reported to the police at the time. He had been arrested later, after the Rivonia arrest of Goldberg, and held in solitary detention. He told the court of the activities at the camp during the two days for which it had survived before the police closed it down. There had been lectures on first aid, on simple electrical circuits and the telephone. There had been talks on news of the day. There had been a demonstration on how to operate a duplicating machine and how the process of duplicating worked. There had been a preliminary lecture on elementary judo tactics, and on how a motor car engine worked. All this was common cause.

But into this factual account, Dr Yutar repeatedly put the question: 'What was the purpose of this lecture?' And the answer came back, pat and prompt—'For use in guerrilla warfare.'

Question: Why were you learning to handle a duplicating machine?

Answer: Because in guerrilla warfare we might need to hand out leaflets.

Why were you being taught judo?

Because in guerrilla warfare it would be used for unarmed combat.

Why to use a telephone?

Because in guerrilla warfare we might need field telephones.

And so on.

If Davids was to be believed, Goldberg ended every talk on the day's news, every discussion about a motor car engine or first aid or the workings of a telephone by telling them all loud and clear that they were learning all this as part of their preparation as guerrilla fighters. Such evidence was hardly credible. Could one believe that Goldberg was the sort of idiot who would gather together some 30 young men, most of whom the evidence showed were quite unknown to him, selected by the organisations which had sent them, and announce to them over and over again that they were there to learn to be guerrilla fighters. At this time, as later evidence showed, there was in fact no intention amongst the accused or any of their organisations to launch guerrilla warfare. Would Goldberg recklessly place his whole future at the mercy of these 30 men, and rely on their silence to protect him? Was it feasible that of the 30, all interviewed by the police at the camp, not one at that time had said a word to give the police an inkling of the real purpose of the camp?

Davids, by his own account, was not interested in politics. He said he had never taken part in any of the political movements in Cape Town, but had attended an occasional house party organised to raise funds for the Coloured People's Congress. At one such party, he said, he was approached by Goldberg to lecture on electrical circuits, because Goldberg had seen him erecting the electric light and loud-speaker system. Was it feasible that Goldberg would have selected such a non-political outsider as this for the task of training youths to become guerrillas, and to listen to guerrilla warfare training by others? Yet this was the story we were asked to believe.

Davids had been in solitary confinement for a long time. He was first arrested some nine months after the camp. When the police had asked him what the purpose of the camp was, he had told them that it was for 'health and spiritual purposes.'

Question by Berrange: How long was it after you were first arrested that you were interrogated?

Davids: Five days.

And you persisted with your assertion that this camp was for health and spiritual purposes?

Yes.

And I suppose you were laughed at?

Yes.

You were told that you weren't telling the truth?

Yes.

You were told that unless you did tell the truth you would be kept there for 90 days and a further 90 days and a further 90 days?

Yes, I realised that.

You were told that?

Yes.

But despite that fact you insisted that the camp had been run for health and spiritual purposes?

Yes.

So, thereafter, when were you next interrogated?

A week after that.

And I take it that you again insisted that the camp was run for health and spiritual purposes?

Yes, I did.

And again you were told that they didn't believe you? And they told you that unless you came out with a different story you were going to be kept there?

Yes.

When was your next interrogation?

Three weeks after that.

And did you again persist in your statement?

Yes, I did.

We come then to the fourth interrogation. How long was that after your third?

I can't remember the exact period, but it must have been about two weeks.

Did you again persist in your attitude?

Yes, I did.

And again you were told, 'Well, you will be kept here indefinitely'?

Yes.

Not told that you would be charged, or could be charged?

I realised that. I can't remember having been told.

Is it possible?

It is possible that I could have been told that.

But you had a distinct feeling that you might be charged?

Yes, I had an idea that I might be.

And the fifth interrogation—how long was that after?

It was about three weeks afterwards.

Who interviewed then?

Lt. Sauerman.

I suppose he was friendly again?

Not exactly.

Well, what was he, if he was 'not exactly friendly'. Was he angry with you?

Yes, he was. That time he must have been very angry with me.

He now got to the stage of threatening you?

Yes.

What did he threaten you with?

A further 90 days.

Yes, but you had been told that before. On every previous occasion as I understand it, you had been told that you would be kept for a further 90 days, as you said on previous occasions. On this occasion you say he was very angry and threatened you. How did he show his anger?

He only threatened to leave me in prison for a further 90 days.

Well, then how did his anger show itself on this fifth occasion?

Because he refused to see me again.

Did he call you a liar?

Yes. He did that often.

What was going to happen if he didn't see you again?

I would stay for another 90 days, I should imagine.

Now, you would just be kept there for the rest of the time by yourself without even having the privilege of visitors from the Special Branch, from the Security Police. Is that the idea?

Yes.

What did you do on this occasion? Again adopt your earlier attitude?

Yes.

Were you interrogated again?

Yes, I was, another three or four weeks—possibly four weeks after.

Now, did you still persist?

No.

Who came to you on this occasion?

Lt. Sauerman.

That was the occasion on which three weeks had elapsed between that and the earlier occasion?

Yes.

What did he ask you?

He asked me what the camp was all about.

Did you say for health and spiritual purposes?

No, I did not.

What did you say?

I told him it was a camp where young guerrillas would be trained.

Now you were prepared to assist in the training of young guerrillas?

Which Lt. Sauerman knew.

Did he tell you that?

Yes. No.

Now, please, why did you say 'yes'?

It slipped actually.

A very significant slip. I want to suggest to you Mr Davids that Lt. Sauerman came to you and said to you: 'I know that you were one of those training young guerrillas, because I got that evidence from other people'. And that was why you said 'yes' when I asked you the question?

No.

Well, why did you say so?

It was a slip.

I see. Now, Mr Davids, you said that you weren't particularly affected by this 90 day imprisonment. You weren't feeling lonely. You weren't feeling depressed. You had been well fed. You didn't miss your wife, though you had missed your children. You did not mind being alone, because you are not a man who likes a lot of people around you. And you had adamantly persisted in what you say was a lie on at least five earlier occasions—there were actually six including the occasion when this matter was discussed with you three weeks after the camp. What made you change your mind?

I felt that I had had enough of 90 day detention.

Were you by that time getting very depressed?

Yes, I was.

At this point Davids had forgotten his earlier attempts to convince us that his confinement had been something of a lark. Earlier on, he had been asked: 'You weren't feeling lonely?'

Davids: No.

Were you enjoying yourself?

To an extent, yes.

You like being alone?

If it is possible.

You welcomed this 90-day imprisonment?

To an extent.

But by this stage, Vernon's questions were exposing the witness's real feelings—not those so carefully prepared to prove his bona fides to his police captors, which were trotted out somewhat earlier.

Question: You told us on the last occasion that the reason why you told your interrogators on so many occasions what you now say is not the truth was because you were concerned to save your own skin, and to a lesser extent to protect your companions. You remember telling us that?

Yes, I do.

And that was why you kept telling your interrogators that the object of this camp was quite an innocent one?

Yes.

You say you did that to save your own skin?

Yes.

I am therefore asking you what made you decide that you were no longer interested in saving your own skin?

Because I was getting fed up with the 90-day detention.

Yes, but you might have done more than that. You might have had not only 90 days detention, but you might have had years and years and years in jail. You realised that didn't you?

Yes, I did.

So what was it that decided you to risk these years in jail?

I wanted to get the whole thing over with.

Was it that you preferred jail to 90-days detention?

That's one way of putting it.

No, no. I don't want to put words into your mouth. Is that what you really felt?

Yes.

You felt that jail as a hard labour prisoner would be a very much easier life to you than to be detained as a 90-day detainee?

That is correct.

Had the police told you that you won't be prosecuted?

No, they did not.

Never?

Never.

Had they told you that you would be released from your 90-day detention as soon as you had given your evidence?

Yes.

You are still under 90-day detention? You are still in custody?

No ... Yes, I am.

And have you been told that when you have given your evidence you would be let go?

Yes.

So you don't expect to be charged, do you?

Yes, there is a charge against me in Cape Town.

But you have been told that you would be released as soon as you have given evidence here?

That's right.

You realise perfectly well that if now you were to go back to the statement you had made to the police and to tell this court what you had originally told the police, namely, that this was an innocent camp, you would again be detained. You realise that?

Yes, I do.

How should a judge weigh such evidence? First, it was on record from the witness himself that considerable pressure had been put on him by the police to make him change his statement. Second, even in giving evidence on the basis of that changed statement, he was acting under duress, with the constant threat of re-imprisonment if his evidence did not suit the police. Third, even under duress of solitary confinement for a long time, he had five or six times repeated that this was a 'health and spiritual' camp, as he called it, with no guerrilla aspects whatsoever. He had only changed his mind after completing his first 90-day detention period and being re-arrested for a further 90-days. Fourth, his evidence was, on the face of it, inherently improbable. People in an underground and illegal conspiracy would be unlikely to broadcast intentions of starting guerrilla warfare to such non-political people as Davids, or to employ such people as instructors of young guerrilla trainees. All these factors taken together led us to assume that this evidence at least, would not be accepted. As it turned out, we were wrong. Mr Justice de Wet found Davids completely credible and accepted his testimony in all respects.

As far as Dennis Goldberg was concerned, Davids' evidence wasn't the main part of the evidence against him. Other testimony of his participation in preparations for sabotage and guerrilla warfare was overwhelming. The story which was unfolded against him in court was that since he arrived in Johannesburg a month or two before his arrest, he had taken various identities. He was known at some times as Mr Williams, at others as Mr Barnard, and yet others by other names. He had made a series of visits to manufacturers with requests for quotations for the casting of certain iron mouldings, which were shown to be the components of hand grenades to a design found in Umkhonto documents at a place called Travellyn. He had made enquiries also for wooden boxes which fitted a design for landmines made in accordance with drawings found at Rivonia. He had hired a farm house in the district called Travellyn, where the police had found the fingerprints of Mbeki and Mhlaba, together with a large number of documents belonging to the African National Congress and Umkhonto we Sizwe. The farm exactly matched a description contained in a document found on the premises in which Goldberg suggested that the 'National High Command' should purchase just such a place for the production of vast quantities of hand grenades, landmines and other military equipment.

There was little point in our cross-examining all the various merchants and businessmen who testified to one aspect or another of the vast investigation Goldberg had undertaken. Most of what they said was true. And even if we had eliminated the false, we would still have been left with a case capable only of two explanations—either, as the prosecution sought to explain it, that a decision had already been taken to embark upon such production and Goldberg was in charge of the actual operation, or, as Goldberg himself explained it, that he had only been asked to investigate the feasibility, the costs and the logistics of such production, and to report back so that a decision on what to do could be reached on the basis of proper information. Whichever way the court interpreted this evidence, and whichever version it accepted as correct, Goldberg had little chance of acquittal.

But the interpretation could be vital both to his sentence and to that of the others. Their evidence, they said, would be that they had indeed planned that if all else failed they would pass from a campaign of sabotage to guerrilla warfare. They had indeed asked Goldberg to investigate the practical problems, so as to enable them to assess the practicability of guerrilla warfare for themselves. The conspiracy charged in this case was a conspiracy to prepare acts of guerrilla warfare. If Goldberg had fallen in with any part of that preparation, he could be found guilty of the offence, so whether Davids was believed or not was not really material to Goldberg's future. But it was perhaps the best pointer in the case to the attitude of the judge in relation to evidence given under duress. The process by which evidence had been extracted from Davids, in my view patently false evidence, was the process which had been used against each and every one of the many accomplice witnesses called in the case. Mtolo was, I think, the only exception—a willing accomplice. The other accomplices were all unwilling. They had all been held for long periods in solitary confinement. They had all made statements to the police which the police did not find satisfactory, and they had stuck to those statements despite months of brow-beating and threats, until finally they agreed to amend their statements to satisfy the police and thus provide a possible route to their own freedom. The duress was naked and shameless. And in addition, most of those forced testimonies were to facts which, on the face of it, were not themselves credible.

Let me take the case of two witnesses from Port Elizabeth. They were called only to testify to a conference of the African National Congress which had been held in Bechuanaland in December 1962, two years after the organisation was outlawed. Once again, the fact that such a conference was held was not disputed by us. Because the African National Congress was illegal, its national conference had been held in Bechuanaland in order to avoid the legal restrictions in South Africa. Delegates had crossed the border secretly, sent from South Africa. But some leading figures in the African National Congress had also come to the conference from ANC offices abroad. The holding of the conference was widely publicised in the press after it was over. The South African police had certainly known that it had been held, and the British police had in fact insisted on attending throughout as the condition for permission to hold the conference. No one had been prosecuted for participating in this illegal conference, presumably because up to the time of this case the police had no direct evidence of the participants except for those who had come from and returned to other countries—Tanganyika or Britain—and had there made public statements about the conference. So these two Port Elizabeth witnesses were the first to testify in public to the proceedings twelve months before.

The one man spoke Xhosa and understood no English. The other spoke and understood both Xhosa and English. Both said that the conference lasted for two whole days. Both said that Oliver Tambo opened the conference and that Mbeki was the first of the main speakers. Both remembered of Tambo's speech only two things—that he said the African National Congress had opened offices abroad, and that he said that delegates should go back to their own areas and organise groups for military training and for guerrilla action. Nothing else. Neither witness could remember the name of any other person at that conference—only Mbeki and Tambo. Neither of them could remember a single other word of the full two days' discussion.

Both agreed that the conference had been conducted entirely in English. The one witness thus understood everything said from the platform and in the discussion; the other witness had a precis given him by a man who sat alongside, listening to the English discussion and summarising it for him in Xhosa. If this testimony was to be believed, here was an identity of memory so singular as to be striking. Out of a two-day conference attended by a large number of people, both witnesses remembered precisely the same two statements, the same two speakers, in precisely the same order.

To us, an even more interesting thing was that Mbeki absolutely denied that it was Tambo who had opened the conference and he himself who had made the speech. Mbeki insisted that he had been the chairman, and opened the conference, and had called on Tambo to speak. And he insisted further that Tambo had not said anything whatsoever about either military training or guerrilla warfare for the simple reason that the Bechuanaland police were present throughout all sessions. Nobody at the conference had been foolhardy enough to even mention violence, military preparations or military training.

The evidence of these two witnesses didn't matter at all in itself. No one was interested in disputing what they had to say. But there were two other witnesses whose stories were equally remarkable. And their testimony did matter.

These two were also from Port Elizabeth. The first owned a car which he hired out from time to time—what is known in South Africa as a 'pirate' taxi, which means it is unlicensed and unregistered. He told a story of a long involved journey which he had taken, he said, after being hired by Mbeki. It was Christmas day 1961. The journey was most remarkable. It started early in the morning, and it meandered backwards and forwards from New Brighton, the African township on the outskirts of Port Elizabeth where Mbeki lived, into the centre of town to Mbeki's office, back again to New Brighton, out along a main road, back again, in and out, backwards and forwards, from early morning until late in the afternoon. The gist of the story was that Mbeki had first gone to his office in town, several miles from New Brighton. At his office, he had fetched only a paper carrier bag, empty. They had then travelled around, picking up several other people most of whom were named as co-conspirators in the case. Finally they had driven out along the main road from Port Elizabeth to Uitenhage, with four or five passengers in the car talking all the way. The drive lasted over an hour.

During the course of this drive, the driver heard conversation relating to electric pylons. That was all he remembered of the whole day's conversation. After talking about pylons, they turned round, returned to New Brighton, and then started a new series of elaborate movements from one house to another. In the course of these wanderings the brown paper bag was gradually filled with bombs or with the material for making bombs, picked up from various places. This elaborate tale linked Mbeki directly with some dynamite attacks on electric power pylons in the district on the day after Christmas.

Mbeki denied the whole story. At that stage he had told us very definitely that he would admit to membership of Umkhonto we Sizwe and its National High Command. There could therefore be no purpose whatsoever in his denying this story if there was any truth in it. Yet he denied it absolutely. He admitted that he knew the witness, and that from time to time he and other members of the African National Congress had in fact hired his car for Congress work. But this whole string of events on Christmas day 1961 he described as a complete fabrication.

Vernon Berrange went to work on this witness. He cross-examined him very carefully, going over every detail of his trip, making sure that the order and the places were absolutely correct. The witness did not deviate one inch from any aspect of his story. He had that journey memorised better than any AA route map. It involved complicated doubling back on itself, and re-crossing tracks, but he had it in such order and in such detail that no matter how we cross-examined and in what way we approached the question, he stuck to the story in every detail. When we added together the mileage of all the journeys of that day, and with a car we generously allowed to move at ten miles an hour, we could find not more than one and a half hours' travelling time. Yet in his evidence he said that he had spent seven to eight hours over it. Obviously there was something seriously wrong with his evidence.

The basic facts were in themselves inherently improbable. Would Mbeki go from his home in an area surrounded by small shops, all the way to his office several miles away in order to get of all things a brown paper bag, empty, on Christmas morning? Would anyone do this sort of thing and, if he did, draw attention to the fact by calling at this unlikely time at an office well known to the Security Police, in a building which police evidence showed to be directly overlooked by Security Police Headquarters in Port Elizabeth? Could one credit that from a whole day's conversation, a witness giving evidence a year and a half later would remember not one single item except the discussion about the electric pylons?

The story, I was certain, was false. Yet it had obviously been concocted on a foundation of truth. At some time, for some reason, this man had in fact made precisely the journey that he described to us. It had not been December 1961, or if it had been, the passenger certainly was not Mbeki. The conversation had perhaps not turned on electric pylons, and the parcels that had been picked up had perhaps not been bombs. But the journey must have been done in precisely the manner he described it to us, for if it had not been, Berrange's cross-examination would surely have revealed flaws. I do not think that even the most skilled liar can stand up to a detailed cross-examination of this sort without putting a foot wrong. And yet he was lying, and in a way which implicated Mbeki fully in sabotage at a time when the prosecution couldn't know that he was going to admit membership of the High Command.

Mhlaba was the victim of a more serious and yet strangely similar lie told by another Port Elizabeth witness, also the owner of a private taxi, who hired himself out on occasions to members of the African National Congress. This witness told how on December 16th, 1961, he had been hired in the evening. His journey consisted of loading up three or four men in various parts of Port Elizabeth, driving out to a place where they picked up parcels, again from an unidentified man, and then driving with the parcels to a lonely spot where there was an electricity sub-station some distance from the road. There his passengers got out and walked off into the dark while he waited there. They came back some minutes later. As they drove away he saw a flash far behind him and heard a dull explosion. That was the night that Umkhonto we Sizwe launched its sabotage campaign throughout the country.

December 16th is celebrated annually in South Africa as the anniversary of the white Voortrekkers' military triumph over the Zulu armies at a place which has come to be known as Blood River. Here the Zulu armies with assegais were decimated by firearm and gun powder. It is an occasion commemorated every year by white South Africans with political and religious gatherings, as the climax of their ascendancy, finally and forever, over the Africans of South Africa.

On December 16th, 1961, Umkhonto had gone into action. Along with many other targets, the transformer station which the witness described was blown to smithereens. Possibly the witness actually drove the saboteurs to the site. But one fact, the vital one, was a lie. That was that amongst his passengers was Raymond Mhlaba. It had to be a lie. Mhlaba had left the country in October 1961. This all the accused knew and swore to, and as events proved later, the prosecution knew it too. So they knew their witness was lying when they led him. It was on the strength of this evidence more than any other that Mhlaba was directly implicated in the activities of Umkhonto we Sizwe. There was practically no other evidence telling against him. And this damaging evidence was wholly false.

Again cross-examination, skilful though it was, failed to reveal the lie. For again, it would appear, the witness was probably telling the truth in every particular save that he put Mhlaba in the car at a time when Mhlaba had been abroad.

Such lying as this could not be the instinctive, self-protective lying of a man in trouble. Like the lies about Mbeki it was purposeful, calculated to fill an obvious weakness in the State case. It was not voluntary—of that I am sure. It was evidence proposed by the police to the witness in custody.

The large number of witnesses called by the State added little to the real evidence against the accused. What they did was lend atmosphere. They gave an air of drama and apparent depth to a case that really, except for documentary evidence, was remarkably thin in evidence. Apart from the police witnesses whose testimony was mainly formal, about the finding of documents, or the scene of sabotage occurrences, the witnesses had little to add to what had already been recounted. Yet, Dr Yutar relentlessly insisted on their adding that little bit.

An elderly lady, so sick that she shuffled slowly from the door of the court to the witness box and found the effort of climbing the one step up to the stand almost too much for her, was summoned from Ladysmith, Natal, some 300 miles away. Her evidence was that some two or three years before, Walter Sisulu had passed through Ladysmith. She had attended a meeting of the African National Congress members in her area, at which Sisulu spoke. She remembered from three years back that he said something about turning to violence. That is all. Every word seemed to be costing her her last reserves of energy. She had, she told us, an extremely severe heart condition. To extract this meagre piece of evidence from a woman whose memory was obviously extremely shaky, she had been held in solitary confinement in a police cell for a long time, and finally, when her heart condition had become so serious that the authorities apparently feared she might die on their hands, she had been released, told to stay in her house, virtually a prisoner under house arrest, until brought to court to testify.

There were others who came, some willing but most unwilling, to add their little piece of gossip, their vaguely half-remembered tales of words said and meetings held. The evidence meant very little, but it gave the State the opportunity to stray far and wide, far beyond the scope of the indictment, to acts of sabotage not even charged in the indictment. Evidence was led of acts of assault which, if they were true, could have been the basis for a charge of murder, and yet no such charge had been laid.

At one stage, tiring of this mounting volume of evidence which did not relate directly to the indictment, we objected. Mr Justice de Wet, in what was one of his most remarkable judgments, slapped our objection down without ceremony. This, he said, was not a trial before a jury. He was quite capable of deciding what was relevant and what was not relevant. Any objections we had could stand over until the end of the case when we could argue that irrelevant evidence should be struck out.

If Yutar needed encouragement, this was it. So week after week, material prejudicial to the accused was introduced and bandied about in the press, mountains of evidence irrelevant to the charge and wholly inadmissible according to my understanding of our code of law. After the judge's ruling the prosecution ranged further and further, the witnesses got more and more removed from the case and from reality, till finally we reached a certain Peter Nbomvo.

Nbomvo was a young man. At the time he was called to give evidence he was serving a fifteen-year term of imprisonment on Robben Island, having been convicted of sabotage. His crime had been that he had taken part in the deliberate burning down of a house in Port Elizabeth which belonged to an African supporter of the Government. It was about this very crime that Nbomvo was to testify, since now, it appeared, Umkhonto and our clients were to be held responsible for Nbomvo. Allegedly, on a mission organised and directed by the Port Elizabeth leadership of Umkhonto we Sizwe, Nbomvo threw petrol bombs into two occupied houses. We ourselves knew nothing of the incident, save that it had happened. Why it had happened, who had organised it, if anyone, who had participated in it, we did not know. None of the accused had been in Port Elizabeth at the time or participated in the local command of Umkhonto we Sizwe. Was Nbomvo telling the truth? If so, he would be a most damaging witness, since the defence evidence would be that Umkhonto we Sizwe, in its campaign of sabotage, had at all times instructed its members not to risk human life. In fact, in the earlier stages of the case before the prosecutor's imagination began to run so wild, even State witnesses such as Mtolo had testified that this was the policy of the organisation.

So we investigated the Nbomvo incidents rather carefully. We read the record of the testimony of his own trial. There, the defence claimed that he knew nothing at all about the burning of the two houses, that he had not even been on the scene. The court had rejected this allegation. If we could find this out, the State which had gone to the trouble to bring him from his cell on Robben Island to this case must have known all that, and more. They must have decided, quite cold-bloodedly, to lead his evidence under oath in court, knowing that it totally contradicted everything said in the earlier case and knowing that a judge had already rejected that testimony. Vernon tore Nbomvo's credibility to shreds, and it was left to Dr Yutar to re-examine.

How does one rehabilitate a clearly proven liar? Overnight some preparation was done, and in the morning Dr Yutar asked why he had lied about his part in the arson during his own trial. Nbomvo replied that he had wanted to tell the truth, but his lawyer had told him to deny all knowledge and to lie about his part in the attack on the two houses. Yutar must have been fully aware that he was going to offer this explanation, for otherwise the question of why he had lied would never have been raised. On the one hand he hoped thus to establish that the evidence in this case was true and the lies were all in Nbomvo's previous evidence. On the other hand, he was smearing Nbomvo's lawyer, who happened to be one of the very few Port Elizabeth lawyers who had faced unpopularity to appear in the defence of unpopular causes, such as Africans charged with sabotage. The lawyer, Mr Jankelowitz, had been a thorn in the side of the police in the Eastern Cape.

We had no brief to defend the reputation of Jankelowitz, but we decided that this piece of gratuitous slander would not be allowed to go unchallenged. We reserved further cross-examination of Nbomvo, and went to work to get all the facts about Nbomvo's trial.

By the time Nbomvo returned for further cross-examination, an interesting story had been pieced together. We learned that, while Nbomvo had been under arrest and awaiting trial, he had made not one but three separate sworn statements. Each one contradicted the others. Two of these statements, both lying, if his evidence in our case was to be believed, had been made before ever he had consulted Jankelowitz. The third had been made after the attorney had withdrawn from the case. And so the smear was nailed. But, as is always the case, nailing a slander is not the same thing as undoing the damage which it caused. There had been less publicity of the exposure of Nbomvo than of his original smear.

Some little publicity did, however, surround the Nbomvo incident, for reasons quite unconnected with sabotage or Nbomvo. It so happened that what was normally the jury box stood prominently on the judge's right hand, on an elevated dais in front of counsel. Since it would be empty throughout this case, it had been reserved as a public gallery for VIP's who might attend the trial. On most occasions there had been representatives of the diplomatic corps of several countries. On one occasion a visiting cricket team from one of the minor provinces in South Africa, with a day off in Pretoria, had been brought to sit in this VIP box, as though the Rivonia trial had become one of the tourist sights, like the Kruger Monument or the Botanical Gardens. On this day of Nbomvo exposure, the VIP box was occupied by two well-known American sociologists, Dr Gwendolyn Carter and her colleague professor Tom Karis, on a visit from the United States. They had spent the morning with the Special Branch hearing all about the evil machinations of the agitators, communists and liberalists in the dock, and learning how the Bantu people would be placid and happy if only the agitators would leave them alone. In the afternoon they had been invited by the State PR men to come and listen to the exposure of some of these agitators and communists. Whoever had invited them had apparently not realised that it was Peter Nbomvo who was going to be exposed that afternoon. So there they sat in the VIP box, obviously enjoying every minute of Berrange's scientific and delicate dismembering of Peter Nbomvo.

Dr Carter had met Nelson Mandela and perhaps others of the accused on an earlier visit to South Africa. From the VIP box she greeted them, smiled and generally gave no sign of support for the side which had invited her to attend. The pettiness of Dr Yutar, equalled only by the pettiness of the policemen who surrounded him, was roused to anger. At the end of the day when court adjourned, Yutar strode out in a fury. Orders were immediately issued that from then on the VIP box was no longer to be occupied by anyone at all.

The following evening, the newspapers reported: 'The privilege of seats in the jury box which has hitherto been afforded to foreign observers was withdrawn yesterday. When two officials, one from the Dutch Embassy and one from the American Embassy, took their seats there today, they were told that they must sit in the public gallery. On enquiry they were told by Percy Yutar that it was because of what happened yesterday. He would not comment further. Nothing of which the press was aware happened yester-day, except that during the course of the hearing, Dr Carter caused some amusement by her varying facial expression which mirrored her intense interest in the cross-examination of a State witness by Mr V Berrange for the defence.'

Other forms of retribution seemed also to be connected with Dr Yutar's discomfiture over the exposure of Peter Nbomvo, for the following day police started making arrests amongst the non-white spectators.

Walter Sisulu's 15-year old son, Lungi, who had come to court to get a look at his father, was arrested during the tea interval. Instructions for his arrest were given by a certain Warrant Officer Dirker of the Security Police and one of the senior investigating officers in the Rivonia trial. Lungi was asked to produce his pass. He explained that he was only fifteen, and the law did not require him to have a pass. He was still a schoolboy. The police refused to accept this explanation, marched him off to the police station and kept him there. His mother intervened and was told that he would have to stay in jail; the police officers were too busy to worry about her troubles. I think if I had not intervened and threatened an urgent application to court, Lungi would have stayed in jail for the night. I told the Commanding Officer of the prison that I would sue him personally for unlawful arrest and detention unless Lungi was released quickly. Perhaps it was this that led to a grudging release, without any apologies, after Lungi and his mother had spent the whole day at the police station.

That day all spectators in the non-white gallery were asked by the police to give their names and addresses and two were arrested. After the tea interval Fischer protested to the judge at this obvious intimidation of the public. Mr Justice de Wet was in one of his moods—utterly intolerant.

'I cannot see,' he said, 'how it affects the proceedings of this court. It was not done while this court was in session. The police presumably had good reasons for doing what they did.'

As far as we could see the only good reason was their desire to re-establish their ascendancy, and also to intimidate friends and sup-porters of the accused and perhaps scare them away from the trial.

One of the people arrested was the wife of Elias Motsoaledi, one of the accused. Once again I intervened, and this is how a reporter who was standing in court described the scene for the papers the next day:

'When the police started taking the names of people in the public gallery and detained Mrs Motsoaledi as she was leaving the court, Mr Joffe approached the police and said 'I am the attorney for Mrs Motsoaledi and I want to know why she is being arrested'. One of the policemen replied: 'Keep away from us. If you are looking for trouble you will get it'. Mr Joffe repeated that he was an attorney and wanted to know what the charge against his client was. The other policeman piped up: 'We have had trouble with you before. If you are looking for trouble you will get it'. When Mr Joffe asked the policeman if he was threatening him, the answer was: 'Just keep out of this or you'll find trouble'. Mr Joffe repeated: 'I wanted to know what the charge is'. '90 days' was the reply. When Mr Joffe asked the policemen what their names were one said: 'You know my name'. The other warned: 'Keep away from me . . .'.

Mrs Motsoaledi had seven children ranging from six months to fourteen years. She lived alone with them now that her husband was in jail. They would be waiting for her to come home that night, but there was no way of getting word to them. Mrs Motsoaledi lived in Orlando and her address was well-known to the police. If there had been evidence of an offence, the police could easily have made the arrest at any time, at her home. It required a more easily persuaded person than me to justify it all with the thought that 'they presumably had good reason for doing what they did'.

The taxi driver, 'Mr A' who said he had carried Mhlaba to the scene of a sabotage attack in 1961, also said that some years before, he had fetched Nelson Mandela from a Port Elizabeth hotel, and taken him to a meeting held in one of the suburbs. Thereafter, he had taken him down to the sea for a swim, and then taken him back to his hotel. There was a great deal of evidence to show that at that stage of his career, Nelson Mandela sported a heavy black beard. Here in the court he was clean shaven, as he had been ever since his arrest over a year before.

Mr A was asked to describe Mandela's appearance when he had taken him to the beach. He said he couldn't describe him; there was no particular distinguishing feature. Dr Yutar persisted. Did he recognise Mandela in the dock? Oh, yes, he did. Had he looked then just as he looked now? He had. That was Friday afternoon.

Either Mr A had forgotten his lines, or someone had failed to put him properly in the picture. The court adjourned for the weekend. On Monday morning Mr A was recalled. His memory had somehow miraculously improved. Over the weekend he had been thinking the matter over, it appeared, and he suddenly remembered that when he had seen Nelson Mandela in Port Elizabeth he had had a beard.

This blatant example of the coaching of witnesses was so crude as to be almost laughable. It was not important in itself, but rather as an indication of the extent to which coaching of witnesses was going on. It seemed that it was proving inadequate even to hold a man in a cell for three or six months in solitary confinement, without reading matter, without visits, without conversation of any kind, while constantly interrogating him, planting an idea in his mind, suggesting what his evidence should be. It was not enough that this should go on month after month before the witness was called. Now to all this was added the direct coaching of witnesses in the midst of their evidence and, if necessary, recalling them so that they could change their evidence to what they should have said if their memories had been better.

A worse case of coaching came up shortly afterwards. The other Port Elizabeth taxi driver who told the story of how materials for bombs had been picked up was asked to describe what these materials were. The question was put, not by us, but by Dr Yutar. Again, coincidentally, it was a Friday afternoon. He explained that the powder was like 'mealie meal', that is to say maize meal—off-white. Dr Yutar obviously knew that if this was to be gunpowder, the colour should be black not white. Dr Yutar put question after question in an attempt to get the witness to say that the powder was black. But the powder remained obstinately white. The witness described some plastic tubes which, clearly, were supposed to be transparent so that the contents could be seen. Again and again Dr Yutar asked for a description of these tubes, phrasing the question as carefully as possible to indicate the answer. But again and again they remained opaque.

On Monday morning when the witness returned, he was asked the same questions again. This time, he got the answers right.

We had said time and time again in the course of cross-examination that our clients were going to make substantial admissions which would make them guilty in law, regardless of any further evidence which might be led. Yet Dr Yutar insisted on getting his evidence at any cost, and in leading it all to the bitter end. This was not just a case for him. It was a demonstration, an exposure, an unmasking of people because they opposed the government. It is only thus that I can explain Yutar's determination to lead witnesses who were a disgrace to any court.

One was Suliman Essop, an Indian, and the other Peter Coetzee, a coloured. Suliman Essop was the owner of a fleet of Volkswagen Kombis, which he hired out. Not to put too fine a point on it, he ran a large 'pirate' bus company, not as a licensed bus operator, but taking advantage of the shortage of transport between Johannesburg's city centre and the main African township of Orlando, to run a fleet of unlicensed vans, plying backwards and forwards like a charter taxi service. From time to time he hired out his buses for special charter trips. The State alleged that Umkhonto we Sizwe had repeatedly hired his vans to take young men from Johannesburg to Bechuanaland, the first stage of their trip abroad for military training. Essop came into court and testified to making many such trips. Again the defence did not challenge. But Essop's evidence also purported to explain who had made the arrangements with him for those trips. In this one could almost see the prosecution mind at work.

The case against Kathrada was extremely weak, so Essop testified that on several occasions he had been hired by Kathrada for trips to Bechuanaland. We knew he was lying and so, certainly, did the police. Essop had already testified almost a dozen times before this, in cases where the trainees he carried had been intercepted before reaching the border, and charged with attempting to leave the country illegally, or with attempting to obtain military training. The details of all his trips had been canvassed in these earlier court cases. We obtained all the records; presumably the prosecution had them long before us. In every case, Essop contradicted himself, tailoring his evidence to suit the circumstances of the case. In the Rivonia case, Kathrada had hired him on specific occasions; in a previous case, where Kathrada was not involved, he had said it was Sisulu. Neither Sisulu nor Kathrada, we were told, was concerned with that aspect of the work of the national movement, whatever else they might have been concerned with.

Essop was demolished by reading his own testimony from previous cases to him. In each case he gave different evidence about the same event. We thought by the time we had finished that no prosecutor would ever dare again to call such a witness as Essop. But we underestimated them. Essop become one of the State's star travelling witness, an itinerant liar on request, which these periods of witch-hunting seem to produce in human history. He was still travelling from court to court, giving evidence on the same events in trials up and down the country, long after every shred of credibility had been torn from him in the Rivonia case.

His primary driver, Peter Coetzee, proved to be even less credible. I don't think he was vicious. I think he was either silly or playing silly. I doubt that he was as stupid as he appeared in the box. He said alternatively 'no' or 'yes' to anything he was asked, indiscriminately, and apparently unconcerned which was right. He was asked to identify various people from photographs. Everybody with a beard—Goldreich, Wolpe, Slovo—he identified as Jimmy Kantor. I find it hard to believe that anybody could be as silly as this without trying, except perhaps the prosecution that decided to call this clown as a witness to facts which the accused were not going to deny.

Finally, of all the prosecution witnesses, there was only one other than Mtolo and Davids who I think is worth bothering with. He was Patrick (or Abel) Mthembu. The accused were very bitter about him, because of all the prosecution witnesses in this case—173 of them—he alone had worked with them personally, he alone was know to them all, and he alone had at one time or another been associated with them somewhere in the national liberation movement.

Mthembu was the only person of any standing in the African National Congress who the State could persuade to testify in that case. He had been held in solitary confinement twice. On the first occasion he had been held for some weeks and released. A few weeks later he had been re-arrested, held for some months. Finally he agreed to testify. His testimony from his own point of view was cunning.

He had been an accomplice, involved up to the hilt in the activities of Umkhonto we Sizwe. He knew—because he was intelligent enough to know—that a witness who testifies to crimes to which he is an accomplice will get an indemnity from the court. He was offered such an indemnity by the court before he gave evidence, and knew he would go free. For this, the accused could not forgive him, even though they could understand and even forgive those who broke under solitary confinement.

Mthembu placed responsibility for much of his own part in Umkhonto we Sizwe on the shoulders of a man with whom he had minor political clashes over the years, Elias Motsoaledi. Mthembu made the case against Elias strong, and in doing so ensured a stiff sentence, possibly even death for Elias, while he himself went free.

Another witness was English Mashiloane, an elderly man and a distant relation of Motsoaledi. His evidence was concerned chiefly with the activities of Motsoaledi and Mlangeni. He described how meetings of the African National congress had been held in his house in Orlando. Groups of young men going abroad for military training, he said, had been picked up by Suliman Essop and Pete Coetzee from his house. Mlangeni and Motsoaledi had supervised these operations. Neither he nor Yutar was satisfied, however, to let his story rest there. So he went on to tell stories not only unbelievable in themselves but which were said by the accused to be totally false. He told, for example, how Motsoaledi had brought parcels of dynamite to his house, taken them to the garage and re-packed them into smaller parcels and gone off again, leaving some sticks of dynamite behind the garage door. Motsoaledi, he said, had warned him not to smoke near these sticks. On a certain occasion he said, a letter had come to his post office box. As he could not read he showed the letter to Motsoaledi and asked him to read it. Motsoaledi had said 'Oh, this letter is for me', and had then opened the letter. Inside, to the witness's surprise, there were no letters but only a series of numbers. Motsoaledi had said: 'Let me read this letter to you'. Looking at the numbers he had read: 'You are please to meet the recruits who are coming on the Cape Town train on such and such a date and at such and such a time'. He continued to decipher the code, reading while they walked rapidly down the street.

I suppose Yutar expected the court to believe this. There were many letters as exhibits before the court which were typed in some code, with numbers obviously standing for letters or words. Yet all the combined resources of the South African Security Police failed to decipher a single word. And we were asked to believe that Motsoaledi decoded it as he walked along, without any reference work whatsoever.

Mashiloane had himself been a supporter and member of the African National Congress. What had happened to change this man into one who lied so glibly, not only against his erstwhile colleagues, but also against one of his own relations? Partly, no doubt, it was that he had been kept in jail in solitary confinement. But partly, as we discovered through the prison grape-vine, inducements had been offered. In the jail he enjoyed special treatment once he agreed to testify. He was a herbalist by trade. He had been allowed to practise his trade even in jail, selling herbal remedies to prisoners and others in the jail who might want them, and enjoying special privileges that not even awaiting trial prisoners enjoyed. He also, of course, earned an indemnity for his participation in the affairs of the illegal African National Congress, and in the business of despatching young men for military training abroad. Our cross-examination of Mashiloane brought out one fact very clearly. Even while he stood in the witness box, he was not, he insisted, free or out of police custody. He seemed to feel that he was fighting for his life as fully as the people in the dock, as likely to be punished, convicted and sentenced to long term imprisonment as they.

The man was not a fool. He was a prosperous businessman, despite his illiteracy. Yet the police had persuaded him that his very life depended on what he was saying here in the dock, and that he was not testifying voluntarily to the truth, but was fighting for his life from the witness box. At the end Dr Yutar, it seemed, attempted to deny Mashiloane the indemnity from prosecution to which he was entitled if he gave satisfactory evidence. The legal position ought to have been explained to him clearly by the judge before he testified. This was that, as an accomplice, he did not have to give evidence if he did not wish to do so, but if he did choose to do so and his evidence was satisfactory he would get an indemnity from future prosecution. Dr Yutar, in leading this witness, did not tell the court that he was an accomplice. Either he did not want to draw the court's attention to the fact that, as an accomplice, his evidence must be treated with extreme caution or perhaps he hoped to avoid the indemnity and thus keep Mashiloane in custody as another pliable peripatetic witness for future cases.

Some way through the testimony, however, the judge saw the point, and put the question directly to Dr Yutar: 'You are using a person who is an accomplice. Are you not compelled to warn him, should you not tell him that he should give his evidence satisfactorily or face prosecution?'

Dr Yutar wriggled: 'My Lord,' he stuttered, 'I'm . . . I do not . . . um . . . consider him an accomplice'.

This was so preposterous that the judge did not even bother to comment, but immediately warned Mashiloane of his position and then ordered Yutar to proceed.

This double-dealing on indemnities was even more blatant in the case of Patrick Mthembu. At the end of his evidence the court ruled that he had given his evidence satisfactorily, and was therefore indemnified against further prosecution. Mthembu walked away from court—as he thought—a free man. Three weeks later he was re-arrested under the 90-day detention law and again held in prison. And so, in the way of people who have once started to inform against their colleagues, he became a professional informer despite his indemnity. He too, thereafter, went travelling from trial to trial, giving evidence against more and more of those with whom he had once worked, and probably also against those he had incited to the very deeds with which they were charged. The indemnity covered prosecution. But there was no indemnity from solitary confinement under the 90-day detention act.

Most of the other witnesses for the State were policemen. Generally, their evidence was of a formal nature, of acts of sabotage which they had investigated, what they found at the scene, what explosives had been used. Some of them gave evidence of trials where people named as co-conspirators or agents of the accused had been charged with sabotage in various parts of the country. Some gave evidence of the police raid at Rivonia when the accused were arrested, and of documents which had been found in various places. Explosive experts testified that explosives described in the documents were capable of causing serious damage, and explained the effects and consequence of various formulae, fuses and methods of sabotage which had been described by witnesses such as Mtolo.

The facts generally were not disputed. Some of the slant put on the facts was, but in general the police witnesses were not seriously challenged. There were, however, one or two exceptions.

There was a certain Sergeant Card from Port Elizabeth whom we nicknamed card-index. He appeared to have a photographic memory for people and names. He rattled through a list of some fifty or sixty people from Port Elizabeth district. He knew all their first names. Of each he said: 'This man I know. He was a member of the African National Congress'. 'He was a Group Officer!' 'A Commander', 'A Sergeant!' 'An Intelligence Agent!'—whatever title he wished to give—in such and such a branch of Umkhonto we Sizwe. 'This man I know. He was a Sergeant.' 'This one I know. He was an Officer . . .' and so he went on, down the line. It was a very impressive performance, complete with all their nicknames, police records and whereabouts.

The point of Sergeant Card's evidence was that everybody who had been convicted of any charge of sabotage in the whole of the Eastern Cape was known by him to be a member of Umkhonto we Sizwe and the African National Congress. When we asked the sixty-four dollar question how he knew, the answer was 'Sometimes they told me'.

One finds it hard to understand how anyone would tell a policeman which branch of a sabotage organisation he held what office in. On other occasions, the answer was 'Through police records!'—that is to say, by hearsay or by the word of informers recorded in the dossiers. Sergeant Card as an experienced policeman must have known that this evidence was not admissible in a South African court. The prosecution led by 'the most qualified prosecutor in South Africa' certainly knew it was inadmissible. Yet they led it, with a reckless disregard for the law made possible by Mr Justice de Wet's ruling that this sort of evidence was admissible unless we proved that it should be struck out.

Sergeant Card, however, made one admission worth noting. He was asked how he obtained information from persons who were detained for interrogation. The answer came out straight: 'We tell them what we know, and wait until he confirms it!'. It is no doubt not unimportant that the two lying taxi-drivers were both from Port Elizabeth, both victims of Sergeant Card's methods of interrogation. 'We tell the witness what we know, and hold him in solitary until he confirms it!'

The other police witness who should be mentioned is Detective-Sergeant Dirker. I have referred to him before, as the one who gave orders for the arrest of Sisulu's son in court. Sergeant Dirker must have been nearing retirement age in the police force. He had been in the Security Branch longer, I should think, than any other Security Police officer involved in this case. Most of the accused had known him for years, as he had known them. Yet he remained Sergeant while other men many years his junior in experience had been promoted to Lieutenant, to Captain, and even to Colonel. He stands about 6 ft tall, heavily built, with a paunch. He affects a lock of black hair that hangs down from a balding pate over one eye in the Hitler fashion. Perhaps the likeness is not his fault, but to go with it he affects a little black Hitler-moustache. Coupled with the same beady black eyes, these features make him into a gross, inflated version of the fanatical Adolf Hitler.

In the witness box he spoke in the sanctimonious butter-wouldn't-melt-in-my-mouth tones of a lay preacher. We were prepared for Sergeant Dirker. Our clients had had experience of him in the past. We did not expect to hear the plain unvarnished truth, and we didn't. Sergeant Dirker told the court of the raid on Rivonia and what he had found there. That was straight enough. But from this he went on to tell how the document 'Operation Mayibuye' came to be found. The accused had told us categorically that this document had been left in the soot box of a little heating stove which stood in the corner of the thatched cottage. Sergeant Dirker, giving evidence under oath, said the document was found open on the table in the centre of the room. It could, of course, have been an error. There were so many documents. But the error, strangely, was of considerable importance to the whole State case. If the document had been open on the centre table, it would appear to have been the centre piece of the discussion taking place in that room at the time the police closed in. And that was precisely what the prosecution alleged. It was on this basis, chiefly that all those in the room that day were alleged to be members of the National High Command of Umkhonto. This document, dealing as it did with the launching of guerrilla warfare and armed insurrection, the State argued, was only revealed to the members of the High Command, and so the position where this document was found was, in a way, central to the case against those of the accused who did not admit membership of the Command.

Dirker was lying about where the document was found. We knew he was lying, and he knew that we knew. He lied in a sickeningly sanctimonious tone. He went on to another fiction. He said he had walked into Sisulu's office sometime in December 1962. There he had found Kathrada with one arm across the shoulders of Mr Duma Nokwe, the only African barrister in the Transvaal, who had been sent abroad by the ANC early in 1963 to work in the foreign mission of the African National Congress. Nokwe was cited as a co-conspirator in this case. There was little significance in this evidence. As far as we could see, it was made merely to bolster the statement by another lying State witness, Suliman Essop, that it was in Sisulu's office that Kathrada had hired his vans to carry military recruits to the border. Dirker went too far in this petty lie. He had to be lying, because at the time both Sisulu and Kathrada were subject to ministerial orders which prohibited either of them from communicating with the other, or with any other banned or listed person. Kathrada, found with his hand on Nokwe's neck in Sisulu's office, would unquestionably have been arrested by Dirker on the spot, and charged with a breach of the order. So would Sisulu and Nokwe.

Dirker is not a subtle man, and had apparently not realised the glaring improbability inherent in his evidence. His final lie in the witness box was to strengthen the case against Bernstein. He said that after he had entered the thatched cottage at Rivonia and found the people gathered there, he went outside and found Bernstein's car. He had opened the bonnet and put his hand on the engine. The engine was cold. This lie, no doubt, was to tie up with the prosecution's story that the document 'Operation Mayibuye' was found on the table, that the accused were in the course of an important discussion on it. The fact that the engine was cold showed that Bernstein had obviously been present for hours. Here again, Sergeant Dirker's limited subtlety trapped him. Bernstein at the time was under a house arrest order. He was allowed to leave home during daylight hours only, but had to report to the police daily between the hours of 12 and 2 p.m. The raid at Rivonia had taken place, according to police evidence, at 3 p.m. Bernstein had reported at Marshall Square, Johannesburg Police Headquarters, at 2 p.m. He had signed the duty book in the office, his signature witnessed by the policeman on duty. His presence there could not be challenged. The fastest possible journey from Marshall Square to Rivonia would have taken half an hour. Bernstein could not possibly have been at Rivonia more than thirty minutes and his engine could not possibly have been cold. In fact, accordingly to all the accused, Bernstein had arrived at Rivonia less than ten minutes before the police.

But there was even further evidence that Dirker was lying, quite coldly and deliberately. Bernstein's car had a burglar alarm, for which the switch was buried under the front carpet. Unless that switch was first depressed, the hooter would blow until it was closed. No one had told Dirker about it. It was too easy to trap Dirker in lies. He was shown his own lies, and asked if he would now tell the truth. He preferred to stick to his lies. So we had to show the judge the character of Dirker.

We had a judgment from a previous case, in which the judge had found that Dirker was a witness whose evidence could not be believed. That was a case in which Walter Sisulu and another co-conspirator, Michael Harmel, had been stopped in a street by Sergeant Dirker. Dirker alleged that they had passed documents from one to the other. The judge disbelieved his evidence. We put the judge's comments to Dirker. He defended himself, obstinately. In that case, he said, the real facts did not come out fully. The judge, he implied, had been misled. Dirker then was as completely and utterly truthful as he was now.

Dirker's evidence posed only one real problem for us: how to handle the testimony that 'Operation Mayibuye' had been open on the table. Dirker was not alone in this evidence. Similar evidence was given by Detective Sergeant Kennedy. Whether Kennedy was manufacturing his tale or whether at the time the document was drawn to his attention it had already been taken from the stove and put on the table by somebody else, I do not know. If we challenged both Kennedy and Dirker on this point they might well call further police witnesses to show that the document was on the table. We would then ourselves have to testify on the point, and thus open up the possibility that the judge would disbelieve us. Whatever else happened, it was essential that our witnesses should be believed. A direct dispute on this point therefore—even though it was of importance—could well be disastrous for our whole defence. We wanted no possible grounds for the judge to find that any of the accused should not be believed. And so we decided to leave the document where the police put it, on the table in the middle of the room, and take our chances on the consequences.

That then was the State case, except for the evidence against Jimmy Kantor. Kantor had had a remarkable in-prison, out-of-prison existence during the course of the State case. For the first few months of the State case he had remained in prison, bail refused. Shortly before Christmas 1963, by which time Makda had punctured the case against him, the judge had himself raised the question of Kantor's bail for review. After argument, he had overridden Yutar's objection to bail, since it had become clear that

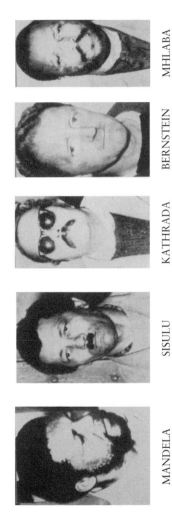

MANDELA   SISULU   KATHRADA   BERNSTEIN   MHLABA

GOLDBERG   MBEKI   KANTOR   MOTSOALEDI   MLANGENI

Plate 1 The accused at The State vs. Nelson Mandela

Plate 10 Denis Goldberg rejoices at the 40th anniversary celebration of the founding of Mkonto we Sizwe at the great stadium in Soweto. All the founding members were awarded medals in 2001

Plate 11 From left to right: Walter Sisulu, Arthur Goldreich, Denis Goldberg

Plate 12   Nelson Mandela, 2001. 40th anniversary celebration of the
founding of Mkonto we Sizwe

Plate 13 Nelson Mandela visits Thatched Cottage at Rivonia 2001

the case against Kantor was threadbare. With bail fixed at £5,000, Kantor had left Pretoria Jail just in time to celebrate Christmas at home. It seemed to us that Jimmy was half-way to his freedom. And then suddenly, one Saturday afternoon several weeks later, he was re-arrested and taken to a special hearing before Mr Justice Cillie, where the police applied for a cancellation of his bail and his return to custody. It could have been fortuitous that this was Saturday and, Mr Justice Cillie, the duty judge for special hearings. I think it was more likely calculated. On the last occasion when the police had talked about Kantor's escape plans to prevent his getting bail, Mr Justice de Wet had been clearly sceptical. Mr Justice Cillie was apparently convinced.

Piet Cillie had been elevated to the bench at a time when he had very limited legal experience, having by-passed the normal routine of long experience as an advocate and senior counsel. At the emergency hearing, Lieutenant Swanepoel testified that he had confidential information that Kantor was planning to leave the country. State security, he said, made it impossible to tell the Judge where his information came from. Mr Justice Cillie ruled that Swanepoel need not then disclose the source of his information or details of the escape plans. This effectively hamstrung cross-examination by Kantor. Kantor then volunteered to go into the witness box and submit himself to cross-examination, and did so. Neither the police nor the judge, afterwards, suggested that anything that was in his evidence, on which he was cross-examined, substantiated the police allegation. Nevertheless, Mr Justice Cillie ruled that bail be forthwith cancelled, and Kantor was returned to custody. So, for the last part of the State case, Kantor was back in Pretoria Jail with the other accused. I suspect that all this was really just stage-setting for what the State intended to be its most damaging evidence, the testimony of a certain Mr Cox, called in as an expert. He was a senior member of a respected firm of Johannesburg accountants. He was to give evidence on what he had found in the books and financial records at Kantor's office. Cox came with all the appearance of being a scrupulously fair and impartial witness. His evidence was that certain matters handled by Kantor's office, particularly the purchase of the Rivonia Farm and the disposition of certain monies for the bail and defence fund operated by Walter Sisulu—were not handled 'according to the norm'.

Dr Yutar led him though this evidence about 'the norm' and departures from 'the norm' at great length. The court was being asked to infer that, because these transactions had not been handled according to 'the norm', they were necessarily sinister and illegal. It was left to the defence to establish how this all-important 'norm' was arrived at. Mr John Croaker did a very thorough job on Kantor's behalf, until it emerged that Mr Cox's much-quoted 'norm' was based on a study of files and accounts forming a small sample of Kantor's voluminous records, which had been selected for his study by the police. Immediately Mr Cox had been released from the witness box, not quite so spruce as he had started out, Mr Croaker applied for Kantor's discharge, on the basis that there was no case for him to answer. There was a short and telling argument, and Kantor was discharged from the case—free at last.

7 The Defence

We had five weeks in which to prepare our defence. It was at once simple insofar as so much was admitted by us, and yet extremely complicated. Because of the sheer volume of evidence, especially documentary, the defence virtually divided into two separate sections. On the one hand, consideration had to be given to the individual position of each accused, the extent of the evidence against him. On the other hand, there was the overall consideration—which to the accused seemed to be the most important—that of establishing the true facts of the movements in which they had been engaged and their true aims as distinct from the gross distortions presented by the prosecution.

For both aspects, a monumental job of analysis of the verbal, and more particularly the documentary, evidence was required. The documents numbered several hundred, many of them lengthy, involved, political treatises of many pages. They all had to be considered in detail, analysed, interpreted and fitted into the right place in the overall story in a way which the prosecution had scarcely ever attempted to do, and when it had, had done wrongly. The documents were tackled by one part of our legal team, the individual positions of the accused by another. It was evident from the beginning that the case against the individuals was not of equal strength. For at least three—Bernstein, Mhlaba and Kathrada—in that order, there was virtually no evidence of complicity in the alleged conspiracy. For the others, the evidence was either over-whelming, or complicity had already been conceded by counsel in the course of cross-examination of witnesses.

So far as Bernstein, Mhlaba and Kathrada were concerned, a detailed explanation of every piece of evidence would have to be given, and their pleas of 'not guilty' argued fully. So far as the others were concerned, what was of importance was chiefly that the record should be set straight, and distortions in the prosecution case rectified. This at least was how they saw it. We lawyers saw it somewhat differently, our bias being not politics, but law.

The lives of the accused were at stake. The State case alleged that they had already embarked on the organisation of armed insurrection and guerrilla warfare, and that in pursuit of this plan they had already arranged for the intervention of military forces of foreign powers against the Republic of South Africa. By way of aggravation of sentence, the State had led much evidence of cases of murder, and of sabotage where murder could be said to have been attempted. With this case accepted by the court, the peril to the lives of the accused was real and grave.

The accused denied absolutely that they had decided to launch guerrilla warfare, though they admitted that all their planning was based on a realisation that if all else failed, the time would come when they would turn to guerrilla warfare. They were quite pre-pared for it and ready to admit it. But that time had not, in their view, been reached at the time of their arrest. They had not con-templated direct intervention by foreign military forces at all, and most of them in fact thought that even to visualise such a prospect was a political error. It was then vital for us to clarify the signifi-cance of the document 'Operation Mayibuye' on which the State relied to establish its allegations, and which the prosecution described as 'the corner-stone of the State case'.

It seemed almost certain that the three I have named, Bernstein, Mhlaba and Kathrada, would all have to go into the witness box and give evidence. So far as the others were concerned, there was a very serious question in our minds over whether they should give evidence.

At the commencement of our preparations, our legal team was inclined to the view that they should not. We argued that they could say little that would prove that guerrilla warfare had not been decided upon or initiated—nothing that could not be as well or better deduced by counsel, from documents. Under cross-examination they might make statements or admissions which could damage the chances of argument on their behalf being believed. Our hesitation to put them in the witness stand was based on the assumption that Dr Yutar would not cross-examine the accused on matters of politics; he would stick closely to the law, and the facts. On matters of politics he had shown himself throughout this case to be a complete amateur. He had approached politics precisely as so many people do, as though it is unlike all other branches of human knowledge and activity, in that on this subject every man is by nature an expert, and knows it all. This belief had led him time and again into making political utterances so fatuous and far removed from reality that we knew that he had no understanding of the politics of the accused, of their organisations, or for that matter, of South Africa itself.

The very nature of the case, we thought, had driven him to attempt to present his case in the light of his limited understanding of the politics involved. But surely, he would change when he came face to face in debate with the accused who had spent their entire adult lives in politics? Insofar as there are experts in politics, almost all of the accused would be classed as expert and professional. We were sure Yutar would fight shy of the political issues and stick closely to the facts.

Whenever opportunity permitted during the State case, the accused had been discussing amongst themselves their versions of the facts. They had laid down for themselves a very clear basic principle: they would state the facts as fully as possible, but they would not under any circumstances reveal any information whatsoever about their organisations, or about people involved in the movement, where such information could in any way endanger their liberty. They would reveal what was necessary to explain and justify their political stand, provided only that it implicated no one other than themselves, and that it did not in any way undermine the safety and continued existence of their organisations which were still operating illegally.

We explained to them that once in the witness box, they were obliged to answer all questions put. They insisted, quite simply, that they would refuse to answer any questions which they thought might implicate their colleagues or their organisations. We told them that in doing so they might well antagonise the judge and make their case worse, not better. They were unimpressed. They felt from the outset that because of their standing in their movement and in the country, it was not only their right but also their obligation to go into the witness box and explain precisely what they had been aiming to do and why. Thus, the record would be put straight and the falsifications and distortions of the State against them would be answered in public.

George Bizos proved, however, to have a deeper psychological insight into the workings of the mind of Dr Yutar. He said—and perhaps he was only half-serious when he said it—that in his view Yutar would attempt to debate politics with the accused. We all felt that not a single prosecutor anywhere under these circumstances would dare tackle the accused on basic political questions, but George began to offer us bets that Yutar would tackle the accused on their home ground—politics. We were all fairly certain that he was wrong. But we began to feel that there was something in Yutar's personality which could drive him to such a mistaken course. Whether the accused agreed with George or not, they insisted that they go into the witness box to nail what they regarded as slanders and distortions made against them by the prosecution. We had no option but to accept their decision, though we did it at the time unwillingly.

The next problem was how to present the case they wanted. At first working on the assumption that the accused would go into the witness box in numerical order—either all of them or only some— we assumed that Mandela would be first and would take the first hammering from the prosecution. We started preparing the evidence we would lead, but the more preparation we did, the more unhappy he and his colleagues became. They had begun to realise that the case which they wished to put to the world—their side of the case—would not emerge forcibly through Mandela in the witness box. It would come out in a jumble of bits and pieces, led in the spasmodic fashion which question and answer necessarily provides. There would be no cohesive statement which they and their supporters in the country and abroad would be able to build upon, or even to understand. Second, they began to feel that Mandela's voluntary entry into the witness box for cross-examination would appear to be a retraction from the position he had taken during his own trial on the charge of incitement in which he had been sentenced to the five-year term he was currently serving. At that trial he had refused to enter the witness box. He had made a strong statement from the dock attacking the institutions of white supremacy, including particularly white supremacist justice, in terms of which, he had said, he was being tried by an all-white court, white magistrate, white prosecutor and white police investigating officers. Under such circumstances he had said, equal justice, real justice could not be done. And accordingly, he had told the court, he refused to plead before such a court. Let the court decide his case as it chose!

Would it be possible on this occasion to give evidence without apparently contradicting that stand on principle, which had had an exhilarating effect on his followers at the time. It would appear, he said, as though he was like Sam Goldwyn, saying firmly 'those are my principles, gentlemen. But if you don't like them, I've got others'. It was these two factors that finally led all the accused to the decision, Mandela himself being the most insistent supporter of this point of view, that he should not go into the witness box for cross-examination. We decided that instead he would make a carefully prepared, lucid and exhaustive statement of the political aims of the accused, their attitudes and their work, which would stand as the frame into which we would set the defence of all the others. Thereafter, the others would go into the witness box for cross-examination.

Having decided this we set to work on the individual cases, and gradually came to a further decision that neither Mlangeni nor Motsoaledi should go into the witness box at all. The evidence against each of them showed that they had participated in the recruitment and transportation of young men for military training abroad. The evidence showed that, in so doing, they were not leaders in the conspiracy. We did not feel that they could improve either their own case or the general case of the accused by entering the witness box.

Put like this, it sounds as though the making of these vital decisions was a simple process. In fact, it was hedged about with difficulties. We discovered, for example, when we came to the prison for our first consultations after the adjournment, that a new consultation room had been set aside for our benefit. The building staff at the jail had apparently been busy preparing it specially for us. It was long and narrow with a partition down the middle of it, composed of perforated hardboard. With great difficulty and much sweating and swearing of warders, these perspex windows could be removed, leaving a heavy metal grating in their place, over a wooden counter. There were loose bar stools on either side. We were told that counsel were confined to one side of this bar counter, the men across the grating on the other. When we were first ushered into this 'consultation room' the accused were already seated on the other side of the counter, in a long row, like customers in a milk bar. Nelson smiled politely, stood up and said 'What will it be today, gentlemen? Chocolate or ice-cream soda?'.

Colonel Aukamp, commanding the jail, was present, symbolically cutting the tape on this newest acquisition of his empire. He didn't like Nelson's remark. There were many things about us and the accused that he didn't like, and the feeling was fairly mutual. He asked us how we liked the new arrangement, and we told him bluntly that we didn't. It was not only the indignity of asking senior counsel to sit perched on bar stools, holding consultation across a counter like teenagers in an ice cream parlour. More important was the fact that it was now virtually impossible for us to hold an adequate consultation at all. There were, after all, nine accused spread out in a single line along the counter. There were four counsel and myself on the other side. It was impossible for any one of us to be heard by all the accused simultaneously without shouting, and debate became virtually impossible stretched out as we were in single file. Even if the accused sat shoulder to shoulder, one end of the line was some twenty feet away from the other. Exhibits and notes had to be slid through a tiny space under the bars. Nobody could lean over another's shoulder to read or to see what was going on. The procedure was impossible and we protested. We had no doubt that when this new consultation room was specially planned for our benefit, thought had been given to the installation of listening devices. Subsequent events at the jail, so some prisoners later told us, confirmed that things said in that room were being picked up outside and repeated.

We protested at the arrangements, but Colonel Aukamp insisted. This was where he had put us in accordance with instructions, and this was where we had to stay. We decided that while we carried on a fight about it, we would have to get on with our preparations despite the difficulties. Immediately another impediment was put in our way. Our hours for consultation were severely restricted. We were permitted to enter the jail at 9 a.m.—which meant getting up at 6.30 a.m in order to make the 30-mile drive from Johannesburg. But at mid-day we had to leave, and were not permitted in again until 2 p.m. This, we were told, was to enable the accused to have their lunch. More important, what we weren't told, but gleaned from the accused themselves, was that this arrangement was to allow the warders to go off duty and have their lunch. It left all of us with two hours to kill in Pretoria and nothing to do. We had nowhere to work. We suggested that it would suit us better if we could work right through uninterrupted by lunch. If necessary we would provide sandwiches so that the accused would not have to return to their cells for lunch. The Colonel seemed stunned by this suggestion. It would set a dangerous precedent, it seemed. Mandela was a convicted prisoner. So was Walter Sisulu, who had been convicted on a charge of incitement shortly before his arrest and who, since he was in jail anyway, had now elected to start serving his sentence even while his appeal was still pending. Convicted prisoners, we were told, were not allowed to eat 'outside' food. It was 'regulations'—that formidable prison word we heard so often in those months. If we fed the other accused, there was a definite danger that Mandela and Sisulu might eat 'outside food', including—the Colonel's imagination boggled—possibly even such luxuries as bread! The hours could NOT be changed for any reason at all. And so we worked like that, preparing our case—three hours in the morning, a two-hour break fiddling around in restaurants in Pretoria, two hours in the afternoon—and then, for the lawyers, back to Johannesburg to work through into the early hours of the morning, usually at Bram Fischer's house.

We divided the responsibility for various aspects of the case. Vernon Berrange took the case of the three 'possibles'—Bernstein, Mhlaba and Kathrada, and prepared to lead their own evidence. Arthur Chaskalson undertook the incredibly tortuous job of analysing all the documentary evidence. George Bizos and Bram prepared the remainder of the accused for their testimony, and assisted Mandela to compile his statement to be made from the dock. My own job was to co-ordinate all their work, and to start gathering material to be led in mitigation of sentence.

Since the issues in this case were largely political, much of the material which we brought to the jail for the accused to use in preparing their defence was political, always subject to censorship by the prison authorities. All books and documents we brought had to be handed in at the office and censored before they could be passed on. An element of gamesmanship developed in our conduct here, as soon as we realised that the jail was keeping the prosecution posted. If we wanted Dr Yutar to think we were concentrating on a particular branch of evidence, we learnt that it was useful to hand in to the prison authorities documents relating to that aspect. The word got back. At one time, partly for real preparation, partly to distract Yutar, we started handing in volumes of the 100-volume record of the mammoth Treason Trial of 1956–61. It seemed that the prison authorities might as well educate themselves while censoring. And we rather liked the idea of Yutar engaged in the futile task of reading the 100-volume record for himself. Our gamesmanship paid off. There were piles of the thick black Treason Trial record on his desk when we next called on him.

It was during this period that I, and I think all the counsel, began really to know the men for whose lives we were fighting. Their personalities began to emerge clearly before us, and their differing characters, qualities and capabilities showed themselves. Nelson Mandela emerged quite naturally as the leader. He has, in my view, all the attributes of a leader—the engaging personality, the ability, the stature, the calm, the diplomacy, the tact and the conviction. When I first met him, I found him attractive and interesting. By the time the case finished I regarded him as a really great man. I began to notice how his personality and stature impressed itself not just on the group of the accused, but on the prison and the prison staff themselves. Somehow Nelson was treated in a particular way—not quite with deference, for that is not the word—rather with respect. Everyone in the jail from the Colonel down to the most unenlightened, uneducated and unfeeling warder, treated him in a special way. I think they realised that, with Nelson, they were dealing with a bigger man than themselves, though this did not mitigate their hatred for all that he stood for. In some ways, coupled with their fear and their contempt, there was a strange inverted awe for one whom they regarded as a 'Kaffir' better educated, more able than they could ever hope to be. It was perhaps part of Nelson's greatness that he never dictated, nor made himself a law unto himself. He would always consult, discuss, argue, and finally be guided by the opinions of his colleagues around him. Yet he was never a follower; he was one who worked and moved with the group and at its head.

And so sitting daily huddled round a table, with little notes passing backwards and forwards, and obscure conversations with coded key words which we hoped only we understood, we prepared the case for the defence. While the others worked at their own evidence, Mandela worked steadily at his statement to be made from the dock. But at no time did we disclose to the prison authorities or to the prosecution that he would not go into the witness box.

I have said before that I don't think Dr Yutar ever came to understand the accused or their attitude to the charges against them. Certainly in this preparation for the defence innings it seems to me he went wildly astray. On the day that court reassembled, it appeared to us that he had prepared himself as though the only man to be cross-examined was Nelson Mandela. In a normal case

Mandela was the one accused who would certainly have taken the stand to exonerate himself on the basis that his culpability was minimal because he had been in jail throughout the period of the main offence. And Yutar, I think, imagined this case would run like any other. In his failure to understand the accused, he must have imagined that Mandela would behave as the run-of-the-mill criminal does in court, lying, distorting, concocting alibis and explanations, and relying on every possible legalism. I believe that it was on this basis that Yutar prepared himself to tackle Mandela, and what he fully expected would be Mandela's lies about himself, his activities, his organisation, his leaders, his own part in the conspiracy and the plans and tactics of Umkhonto we Sizwe. In this, perhaps more than anything else in the case, Yutar revealed how deeply he was out of his depth.

On Monday, 23 April, the courthouse was packed with spectators. Dozens of uniformed police were inside and outside the building, mingling with the plain clothes detectives, friends and relations of the accused, and interested outsiders, mainly African. There was a large contingent of students from the Pretoria University, hostile to the accused. As the crowd milled about in Church Square outside the Palace of the Justice, a special branch photographer rested his telephoto lens on the shoulder of a sergeant and took snapshots of spectators to be tagged and filed amongst the anti-government dossiers at Security Police headquarters.

We went down to the cells below the court to have a last discussion with the accused before the session began. By this time the colour bar even in the Supreme Court was breaking down. At the start of the case Bernstein, Goldberg and Kantor had been regularly locked up in a 'Europeans Only' cell, while all the non-whites were locked up in a 'Non-European' cell. The two groups were only brought together at our special request for consultation or immediately before time for them to be ushered into the court. By now, however, the arrangement had broken down, partly because the accused themselves markedly ignored the colour demarcation unless instructed on each occasion to abide by it, and partly because it was part of the atmosphere of the case that colour lines did not operate either between the accused or between the accused and counsel. Nelson was calm and completely unperturbed by the task before him.

In court, as planned, Bram Fischer led off for the defence. He summarised what the defence would state, what it would try to prove, which parts of the State case it conceded and which it would deny.

'Amongst the matters which will be placed in issue by the defence are the following: First, that Accused Nos. 1 to 7 (that is, all except Kantor, Mlangeni and Motsoaledi) were members of the National High Command of Umkhonto we Sizwe. The defence evidence will show that the accused Goldberg, Kathrada and Bernstein were not members of the High Command of Umkhonto or members of Umkhonto at all. The defence evidence will also explain what the relationship was between Mandela, Sisulu and Mbeki, and with Umkhonto and the High Command of Umkhonto. It will also show what the relationship was between Goldberg and Umkhonto, and between Mlangeni and Umkhonto, and Motsoaledi and the African National Congress.

'Second, my Lord, in issue will be the allegation by the State that Umkhonto was a section of the African National Congress, to use the phrase so frequently used by the State, "the military wing" of the African National Congress. The defence will seek to show that the leaders both of Umkhonto and of the African National Congress, for sound and valid reasons which will be explained to your Lordship, endeavoured to keep these two organisations entirely distinct. They did not always succeed in this for reasons which will also be explained, but we will suggest that the object of keeping the two organisations separate was always kept in mind and every effort was made to achieve that object.

'Thirdly, my Lord, it will be put in issue that the African National Congress was a "tool" of the Communist Party, and that the aims and objects of the African National Congress were the aims and objects of the Communist Party. Your Lordship will remember that great point was made of this in the State's opening. The defence will deny this emphatically, my Lord. It will show that the ANC is a broad national movement, embracing all classes of Africans within its ranks, and having the aim of achieving equal political rights for all South Africans. The evidence will show further that it welcomes not only the support which it received from the Communist Party but also the support which it receives from any other quarter. Now on this point, the evidence will show how Umkhonto we Sizwe was formed, and that it was formed in order to undertake sabotage only when it was considered that no other method remained for the achievement of political rights. Finally, on this point, my Lord, the defence will deny the allegations made in the state's case that Umkhonto or the African National Congress relied, in order to obtain support, on what was referred to as being 'the alleged hardships' suffered by people.

'All this will be relevant particularly to the fourth point, and that is this—the fourth issue—that Umkhonto had adopted a military plan called Operation Mayibuye and intended to embark upon guerrilla warfare during 1963 or had decided to embark upon guerrilla warfare.'

Mr Justice de Wet: Will that be denied?.

Mr Fischer: That will be denied. Here the evidence will show that while preparations for guerrilla warfare were being made from as early as 1962, no plan was ever adopted, and the evidence will show why it was hoped throughout that such a step could be avoided. In regard to the last issue, the court will be asked to have regard to the motives, the character and political background of the men in charge of Umkhonto we Sizwe and its operations. In other words, to have regard amongst other things to the tradition of non-violence of the African National Congress; to have regard to the reasons which led these men to resort to sabotage in an attempt to achieve their political objectives; and why, in the light of these facts, they are to be believed when they say that Operation Mayibuye had not been adopted, and that they would not have adopted it while there was some chance, however remote, of having their objectives achieved by the combination of mass political struggle and sabotage.

Bram paused at this point, while the judge finished making notes. He then said: 'the defence case, my Lord, will commence with a statement from the dock by Nelson Mandela who personally took part in the establishment of Umkhonto, and who will be able to inform the court of the beginnings of that organisation and of its history up to August 1962 when he was arrested.'

This statement seemed to cause consternation. Dr Yutar was behaving as though he could not believe his ears. As Nelson rose slowly, adjusting the spectacles which he wore only for reading, Yutar jumped to his feet. His voice rose to that falsetto which we came to know as the crisis call of the prosecution. 'My Lord!' he squeaked, 'My Lord. I think you should warn the accused that what he says from the dock has far less weight than if he submitted himself to cross-examination!'.

The judge looked at him rather sourly, 'I think Mr Yutar, that counsel for the defence have sufficient experience to be able to advise their clients without your assistance'.

Yutar seemed unable to get his breath back. Bram, somewhat less biting than De Wet, replied in the gentlemanly manner which he could never abandon, even when he was very annoyed. He appreciated, he said, his learned friend's advice. But 'neither we, nor our clients are unaware of the provisions of the Criminal Code'. Mandela, let it be remembered, was himself a qualified attorney with several years of practical experience in the courts before his conviction and sentence in 1962.

Standing in the dock he began very slowly, very quietly, reading the statement which he had prepared, in a flat even voice. At no stage did he raise his voice very much, or change from the slow, measured speech with which he had started. His voice carried clearly across the court. Gradually as he spoke the silence became more and more profound, till it seemed that no one in the court dared move or breathe.

He started from the days of his youth, explaining how he had come into the national movement, what had led him first of all to the African National Congress and later, from the African National Congress to the founding of Umkhonto we Sizwe in which he himself had played a leading part. He explained why Umkhonto we Sizwe had chosen sabotage of a particular type, that is to say, attacks against government buildings and installations where no loss of life could be involved. Throughout its existence, he said, Umkhonto had recognised that the time might well come when it would have to turn to more militant struggle and guerrilla warfare. That time had never been reached. His explanation was at once legal and political. He set out the political reasoning which had guided himself and the African National Congress in all that had been done and the reasoning which led him now to believe that what had been done was not only right, but the only possible course of action for them. He described how he had travelled abroad on a mission for the African National Congress and how, while abroad, he had himself received military training. He had solicited and been promised that men from the liberation movement in South Africa would be trained by friendly African States in the arts of guerrilla warfare and military arts generally. He had returned from this mission to South Africa, and taken up the struggle again, living an underground life until his arrest. In this clandestine life as a politician and organiser, he had lived and worked in hiding at Rivonia. He dealt with the character of the Rivonia house and of the fact that, to his knowledge, this house had been used also by members of the Communist Party for their own political affairs.

Once he had been anti-communist. But he had learnt from his experience that his duty to his people made it necessary that he cooperate with the Communist Party, as the African National Congress had cooperated with it. The Communist Party alone, he said, had shown a willingness to throw in its lot with the national liberation struggle of the African people. He explained his attitude to communism, and the Communist Party, denying that he himself was a member of the Communist Party, though he found much to admire in their programme and behaviour. He had been influenced, he said, by Marxist thought, and so in fact had almost all the significant leaders of the national movement in every country in Africa. In a short, detailed and documented statement of the way in which Africans live in South Africa, he threw back in the teeth of the prosecution the allegation that the African National Congress had been motivated by imaginary or bogus allegations of grievance. He showed that in fact the grievances of the African people were very real indeed, and very genuine. He finished, with his voice slightly roused, in a peroration on the aims of the African National Congress.

'Africans want to be paid a living wage. Africans want to perform work which they are capable of doing, and not work which the government declares them to be capable of. Africans want to be allowed to live where they obtain work, and not be endorsed out of an area because they were not born there. Africans want to be allowed to own land in places where they work, and not be obliged to live in rented houses which they can never call their own. Africans want to be part of the general population, and not confined to living in their own ghettos. African men want to have their wives and children to live with them where they work, and not be forced into an unnatural existence in men's hostels. African women want to be with their menfolk and not left permanently widowed in the reserves. Africans want to be allowed out after 11 o'clock at night and not to be confined in their rooms like little children. Africans want to be allowed to travel in their own country and to seek work where they want to and not where the Labour Bureau tells them. Africans want a just share in the whole of South Africa; they want security and a stake in society.

'Above all, we want equal political rights, because without them our disabilities will be permanent. I know this sounds revolutionary to the whites in this country, because the majority of voters will be Africans. This makes the white man fear democracy.

'But this fear cannot be allowed to stand in the way of the only solution which will guarantee racial harmony and freedom for all. It is not true that the enfranchisement of all will result in racial domination. Political division, based on colour, is entirely artificial and, when it disappears, so will the domination of one colour group by another. The ANC has spent half a century fighting against racialism. When it triumphs it will not change that policy.

'This then is what the ANC is fighting for. Their struggle is a truly national one. It is a struggle of the African people, inspired by their own suffering and their own experience. It is a struggle for the right to live.

'During my lifetime I have dedicated myself to the struggle of the African people. I have fought against white domination, and I have fought against black domination. I have cherished the ideal of a democratic and free society in which all persons live together in harmony and with equal opportunities.'

At this moment he paused, a long pause, in which one could hear a pin drop in the court, and then looking squarely at the judge he finished: 'It is an ideal which I hope to live for and to achieve'. Then dropping his voice, very low, he added: 'But if needs be it is an ideal for which I am prepared to die'.

He sat down in a moment of profound silence, the kind of silence that I remember only in climactic moments in the theatre before the applause thunders out. Here in court there was no applause. He had spoken for five hours and for perhaps thirty seconds there was silence. From the public benches one could hear people release their breath with a deep sigh as the moment of tension passed. Some women in the gallery burst into tears. We sat like that for perhaps a minute before the tension ebbed.

Mr Justice de Wet turned to Bram and said, almost gently: 'You may call your next witness'.

Bram called on Walter Sisulu.

From our point of view Walter was the key defence witness. If his evidence was believed, the court must find in our favour that Umkhonto and the African National congress were separate organisations with individual identities and that Operation Mayibuye had not been adopted by Umkhonto as a policy, although Umkhonto had always envisaged that it would have to prepare for guerrilla warfare at some date in the future. It was a difficult decision to place such tremendous responsibility for the defence case on Walter. It was not that we doubted his staunchness, but some of us at least doubted his ability to cope with the formidable cross-examination which would be unleashed against him since Mandela had not been in the witness box.

Walter is not a man of much formal education. He had left school at Standard Six. He had worked underground in the mines, and he had been a clerical worker, a salesman, and for a long time an administrative official of the African National Congress, for some years its Secretary General. To pit this man against Dr Yutar, B.A., LL.D., seemed in some ways to be taking on a battle of unequal intellect. If Dr Yutar confined his cross-examination to the legal niceties, and the splitting of fine hairs, we were worried how Walter would come through. We put these doubts to the accused. They knew Walter better than we did. They had little doubt that, on this issue, he was perhaps the most expert of them all. He was the one who knew more than any of them of the inner workings of the African National Congress and of Umkhonto we Sizwe. On these issues they had no doubt whatsoever that he would more than prove a match for Dr Yutar.

In the evenings after we left Pretoria Jail, we lawyers used to argue about this on our long drive home. Quite early on, George Bizos, backing his hunch, laid odds that Yutar would choose to avoid the straight matters of fact which would prove the guilt or innocence of the accused and would tackle Sisulu on matters of politics. He would attempt not only to prove the guilt of the accused, but also to prove particularly the innocence of the Government, its good intentions, and its ascendance over the African majority in the country. George found lots of takers. We did not credit that any prosecutor anywhere would choose to tackle a witness like Sisulu on the one subject in which he is expert, and the prosecutor is not. We believed that the prosecutor would steer clear of all political debate, would attempt to confine the cross-examination to matters in which the prosecutor was the expert—the detailed wording and meaning of documents, the precise places where they had been found, the significance of the documents to the overall conspiracy, and the implications which the prosecution was going to draw from the documentary evidence. He would keep as far away as possible from politics and any political implications. George said that, in normal circumstances, he would agree. But Yutar was not a normal prosecutor. And so Yutar, he was convinced, would wade out into the deep waters of politics and quite likely drown. We took his bets, and lost.

Bram led Walter's evidence. He took him first through his own personal history and the story of how he came to be interested in politics and how he rose gradually to be a leader of the African National Congress. From this he passed on to political questions, the aims of the African National Congress and the disability suffered by the African people.

Question: And have you suffered from these hardships personally?.

Answer: I have suffered. I have personal experience of various disabilities, as for instance the pass laws, and the question of being underpaid, and the question of persecution. I have been banned under the Suppression of Communism Act. I have been confined. I have been ordered to resign from political organisations to which I have belonged. I have been house-arrested. I have been detained. I have been separated from my family.

He then dealt with the growth of the African National Congress up to 1960, when the Government had proclaimed a state of emergency, during which his organisation had been declared illegal while he and most of the other leaders of it had been in jail, held without trial or without charge.

Question: What was your attitude then to the banning of the Congress?.

Answer: We could not accept the ban on the African National Congress because it was the mouthpiece of the African people. It was the only hope that the African people had which could liberate them from oppression.

He went on to describe how it had been decided to maintain the African National Congress organisation, illegal though that decision was, and how they had carried on with their policy of mass organisation and agitation on a non-violent basis. He covered the same ground as Mandela in explaining how some of the leaders of the African National congress and other people of other races had come to the conclusion, finally, that violent struggle in South Africa was inevitable. And if it was inevitable, better that it should be led by leaders of experience and reliability, than be left leaderless and to the whim of inexperienced men. He went on to explain how he himself, as representative of the African National Congress, had arranged with Umkhonto we Sizwe that he attend meetings of the High Command from time to time, and how he had been present when Operation Mayibuye had first been presented to the High Command as a plan for consideration. It had been decided to seek the views of other bodies including the African National Congress. On the High Command itself opinions for and against Operation Mayibuye were very much divided. He said that at the time of his arrest at Rivonia, no decision had yet been taken. Many leaders of the African National Congress and of Umkhonto itself had expressed doubts about various aspects of the so-called plan. Bram then led him to explain his position to the court.

'Mr Sisulu, you have chosen to give evidence under oath so that your story can be tested by cross-examination in the ordinary way. Is that so?'

'That is correct, my Lord. Except that I must explain to the court that I would like to make my position very clear. I am prepared to testify in this case in regard to the part I have played and in regard to the part which my organisation has played and some of the people connected with it. But my Lord, I would certainly find it difficult to testify or to answer any questions relating to my organisation which might lead to the prosecution of my people. I would not do anything which would lead to revealing the workings of my organisation and confidential matters. I would not be able to testify insofar as that aspect is concerned. I am aware that by so doing I might worsen my position. But I find that I cannot do otherwise.'

He thus made it clear to the court before his evidence in chief was finished that questions outside his own activities and the activities of the other accused in the box would not find him a willing informer. Finally, having finished with his evidence in chief, Mr Fischer said to him: 'Looking back on it, Mr Sisulu, do you consider that you could or should have acted otherwise than you did?'.

This was the point for Walter, if he wished to do so, to recant, apologise for, or retract any of the things he had done in the African National congress or Umkhonto we Sizwe. Instead he answered straight:

'I can't see how I could have done otherwise, other than what I have done. Because even if I myself did not play the role I did, others would have done what I have done instead.'

And so Bram sat down, leaving Walter to face Dr Yutar in a cross-examination, which was going to last for several days. Thus we came to the test of the representative of the African National Congress against the representative of the white South African State. This is how it appeared to all in court; this was how in fact it unfolded.

Dr Yutar started off on a tack which he had shown over and over again during the prosecution case, on the attitude of the African National Congress and Umkhonto we Sizwe to the taking of human life. In my view it should never have been permitted to be voiced in court at all, for no such charge or suggestion of culpability for any killing had been made in the indictment before the court. Yutar asked whether it was correct, as Sisulu had said in evidence, that in acts of sabotage committed by Umkhonto there was to be no injury to life and no killing of persons.

Sisulu: That is absolutely correct.

Yutar: Did the African National Congress or Umkhonto ever take precautions to see that, as a result of the commission of various acts of sabotage, nobody was injured, that nobody was killed?

Sisulu: The manifesto of Umkhonto makes it perfectly clear; the choice of targets makes the position perfectly clear—that the intention was not to injure anybody at all.

At that moment Mr Justice de Wet intervened. 'There was a trial during the last war that I remember in which a bomb was placed next to the Benoni post office. Some unfortunate passer-by came to post a letter; the bomb exploded and he was killed.

If you are going to start bombing buildings is it possible to avoid that type of accident? Can you ever be sure that you have avoided killing or injuring people?'.

Sisulu answered quite calmly: 'My Lord,' he said, 'an accident is an accident. But the precaution in fact is in the intention, and the method used—for instance at night, when people are not there. These are some of the things we take into consideration, that it should not be done at any time in any manner, in order to avoid the loss of life.'

Mr Justice de Wet: Your argument is that as long as you have not got the intention to kill people, it does not matter if you kill people. Is that your argument?.

Sisulu: No sir. I am saying that precautions are taken in order to avoid such a thing. I am not saying that it can't happen. But I am saying that precautions are taken that it should not happen.

This intervention by the judge seemed to us to be rather sinister. We did not expect that he would not intervene at all to cross-examine a witness, for clearly he is entitled to clarify any point which does not emerge clearly from the evidence, if he thinks it is germane to the issue before him. We were dismayed, however, by the way he put these questions and the fact that he put such questions at all, when killing, injuring or maiming people was not charged in the indictment. In fact several State witnesses, including Mtolo himself, the star of the prosecution team, had testified that the intention and clear instructions of Umkhonto at all times had been to avoid loss of life. In this question Mr Justice de Wet seemed to be revealing a very sinister bias against the accused. Sisulu answered him well enough, but the judge's intervention made us feel very uneasy.

Dr Yutar took advantage of it, as he did of every opening made for him by the judge. For a long period he dealt with the likelihood of people being injured or killed during sabotage attacks, playing up quite outrageously to the judge's prejudice, and facing Sisulu with allegations so far removed from the indictment that a better judge would have brought him to a halt. Only when he had exhausted this topic did Yutar turn to the real questions of the case, and firstly to the ANC's links with the Communist Party. Sisulu dealt with this topic confidently, in precisely the same way as had Mandela. Yutar then brought his questions round to a direction which we would find reappearing more and more often—questioning not designed to reveal facts about the offence charged, but to extract information from the accused about their colleagues, assistants and co-workers, for the benefit of the Security Branch of the police. Often in the course of this case, the questioning of defence witnesses began to resemble interrogation sessions by the Security Police, which the accused themselves called 'fishing expeditions'. Repeatedly the accused were forced to face up to the fact that they could not maintain their personal integrity and yet answer the questions. As we had foreseen, they would have no option but to refuse to answer.

Yutar came round to one of the documents in evidence, and started questioning Sisulu about how this document had come to be issued by the African National Congress.

Question: Now where did this discussion take place?

Sisulu: In Johannesburg.

Yutar: Where in Johannesburg?

In the townships.

Whereabouts in the townships?

Sisulu: Are you trying to get the house?

Yutar: I am not trying to get the house! I am trying to get the truth. Where was this discussed?

Sisulu: I am saying the townships, in the North-Western areas.

Yutar: I want the truth. I want to know where in the townships.

Sisulu: That means what house it was.

Yutar: Really!

I am not prepared to answer that.

You are not prepared to answer that?

No.

Why not?

I have explained the position. I am not going to implicate people here. What difference does it make in whose house?

Yutar: Don't ask me questions please. I want to know in whose house this discussion took place.

Sisulu: I am afraid, my Lord, I would implicate people if I answer that question.

Yutar: You are not going to answer that question?

No, sir.

In what way will you be implicating this person?

Because it's a question of so-and-so's house, and the next thing is that policemen go and detain that person under the 90-days law to find out who the people were.

Yutar, holding up one of the exhibits: Who was the member of Umkhonto who drafted this pamphlet?

Sisulu: I can't mention the name.

Why not?

Because I am not mentioning names.

Yutar's voice was rising in anger. Walter refused to be driven into a corner. His low-toned, unmoved and unflurried responses seemed to feed Yutar's fury. The very fact that Walter was clearly protecting someone who was still inside the country seemed to fire Yutar's anxiety to elicit the information.

Yutar: Well, unless his Lordship stops me, I'm going to insist on a name. I want to know who, on behalf of Umkhonto, drafted this pamphlet.

Sisulu: It doesn't help you to insist on the name. I have explained that insofar as people who are in the country are concerned, I will certainly not answer.

Yutar: Not answer?

Sisulu: No. But I will answer to people who are outside.

Yutar: Oh. They're safe!

Sisulu: Of course!

I want to know who drafted this pamphlet.

Well, my Lord, I am not prepared to answer that question.

Mr Justice de Wet: You are not prepared to answer?

Sisulu: I am not prepared to answer.

De Wet: Yes, very well.

This was something new in the South African courts, and certainly new as far as recent political trials were concerned. Prior to this case, there had been a series of trials of people said to be members of the Pan-African Congress, or the organisation sponsored by it called Poqo. One of the things which we had been told by Sisulu and his colleagues during our preparations was that in these PAC/Poqo cases, many of the accused had attempted to exonerate themselves by naming and implicating dozens of others who had participated in their activities, and so spreading the persecution ever wider. By refusing to answer such questions, the Rivonia accused broke new ground. They hoped thus to set a new standard which would be followed by others in subsequent political trials. In fact, the example they set became a precedent, and in many political trials the accused followed it. Many unwilling witnesses also refused to testify and faced the prospect of twelve months imprisonment for this refusal.

Sisulu's refusal to answer Yutar's prying seemed to leave Mr Justice de Wet unmoved. It was part of the contradictory nature of this man that, at one moment, he could make interjections which seemed so biased and sinister, and at the next could tolerantly accept Sisulu's determination to say just as much as he pleased, and to hold back whatever he thought necessary to protect his own movement and its supporters from prosecution.

Only a few moments later Mr Justice de Wet intervened again. Sisulu had said of the African National Congress: 'We educate people in this country and the people abroad that the only solution in South Africa is living together as black and white—that there is no other solution'.

Mr Justice de Wet: Living together? But doesn't that involve—according to your ideas—control by the non-white element because they have more in numbers?

Sisulu: My Lord, we have always maintained that because of historical conditions in this country the mere fact that the Africans are in the majority would not mean black domination.

Mr Justice de Wet: No, but black control! Won't it mean black control?

Only in the sense that the majority of rulers will be black.

That necessarily involves control, not so?

Well it might be that control can be exercised by both races together. We have in the history of this country, an example in the Cape Province where the Africans themselves elected a European.

De Wet: You would never agree to that, would you?

Sisulu: Why not?

De Wet: You being represented by a white person?

Sisulu: No, not to be represented, my Lord. We don't want to be represented. But we say if the people of South Africa elected Dr Verwoerd, by all means let him come to Parliament—he is elected by the whole lot. We are not fighting the issue on the basis of colour.

The cross-examination went on, Yutar fishing continuously for information, Sisulu refusing continually to give it, the judge intervening every so often to reveal crass prejudice and bias, not I think, as a conscious thing, but as a built-in part of the unconscious outlook of a white South African. Possibly the judge thought he was asking in an unbiased, interested way. But it didn't come out like that, nor could it. The man, even though he was probably trying to be judicial and impartial, had all the prejudices of an average white South African.

Yutar was not only 'fishing', he was also smearing the anti-government movements, and particularly Chief Albert Luthuli, President General of the African National Congress, who had been awarded the Nobel Prize for Peace in 1961. Time and again he attempted to bring Chief Luthuli's name into the evidence, and to convict him in absentia of complicity in sabotage.

Despite his position in the African National Congress, Luthuli had *not* been named as a co-conspirator. His exclusion, I feel sure, was designed to drive a wedge between him—a proponent of non-violent action—and the accused. Evidence about Chief Luthuli was clearly inadmissible. Since he was not a co-conspirator, nothing he said or did was relevant to this case. But by his earlier ruling that evidence could stand unchallenged until the end of the trial, Mr Justice de Wet had opened the door to this too, and Yutar meant to keep his foot in that door. He asked a question about 'President Luthuli—the Nobel Prize winner for peace', with a sneer on his face for the benefit of the public gallery and the press. Sisulu answered shortly: 'I will not answer anything about Chief Luthuli'.

Question from Yutar: Did Slovo tell Mthembu that President Luthuli had agreed? (to the policy of Umkhonto).

Slovo only can answer that!

You are not prepared to answer?

No, I am not prepared to.

You are not prepared to?

No.

And you were present?

I was present, yes.

What I am interested in is whether the new operations had been put before the President, Chief Luthuli, and that he agreed?

You won't get that from me. You won't get anything from me about Chief Luthuli!

The smearing passed from Chief Luthuli to Canon Collins. The prosecution attempted to show that since Canon Collins and

Christian Aid had sent money from London for the defence of the people charged with sabotage, they were actually giving money to aid sabotage. Sisulu would have none of this reasoning. Eventually Yutar came to the question of what brought Goldberg to Johannesburg. Sisulu said that Goldberg told him that he had left Cape Town because he was afraid the police wanted to arrest him.

Yutar: What for?

Sisulu: 90 days (solitary confinement).

Yutar: What for? The police don't arrest people indiscriminately, unless . . .

Sisulu: They arrest many people indiscriminately. For no offence people have been arrested.

Yutar: Would you like to make a political speech?

Sisulu: I am not making a political speech. I am answering your question.

How do you know they arrest people innocently?

I know. They arrested my wife. They arrested my son. That was indiscriminate.

Without any evidence whatsoever?

Sisulu: What evidence?

Yutar: I don't know. I am asking?

At this point, for the first and only time Sisulu momentarily lost his composure. 'I have been persecuted by the police', he said bitterly, with anger in his voice. 'If there is a man who has been persecuted, it is myself. In 1962 I was arrested six times. I know the position in this country.'

Yutar: You do?

Sisulu: I wish you were in the position of an African! I wish you were an African and knew the position . . .

Yutar dropped the subject sharply, and turned to questions dealing with the illegal broadcasts by Radio Liberation. Sisulu said that, though the trials of the apparatus had taken place at Rivonia, the broadcast had been done elsewhere, so that if the broadcast was traced by the government location devices, it would not lead to Rivonia. Mr Justice de Wet expressed scepticism that a broadcast not previously advertised could be traced down quickly. Sisulu said he was only repeating what the technicians advised.

De Wet: I think some of your clever colleagues like Dennis Goldberg would be able to tell you that if they don't know beforehand that a broadcast is taking place, they wouldn't be able to trace the place.

Sisulu: Well, that's what they suggest, my Lord.

De Wet: If the technicians are so clever that they can trace the origin of a broadcast within a few minutes, then it doesn't matter where you hold the broadcast, they will catch you red-handed.

Sisulu: We would still take the risk. There was no doubt that those who were there were taking a big risk. But the point is that we were in hiding, and that is the reason it was not done at Rivonia. We were staying there, and we would have been exposing it to the police.

De Wet: So you don't mind the people who were working the broadcast and putting your recording over the air—you wouldn't mind their being caught so long as you are not caught? Is that the position?

Sisulu: No, that's not what I'm trying to say. One does take the risk. But you would not put all your eggs in one basket. Those who were to do it were there. That's why we were not there—not that we don't care about any particular person who might be arrested.

De Wet: Isn't that rather typical of patriots? That they are always prepared to let the rank and file take the risk, and see that they don't put themselves in danger. Isn't that the position?

Sisulu: I don't think that that interpretation is correct. Take the case of war . . . the generals are sometimes not very exposed, not because they want to expose others.

De Wet: But exactly the same thing happens with people who are plotting a rebellion or revolution. They look forward to being the government in due course. And they see to it that they preserve their own skins, not so?

Sisulu: My understanding, my Lord, is that we, to the best of our ability, want to preserve everyone.

Looking back on it, I think this passage most clearly reveals the inner attitudes of Mr Justice de Wet to politicians. It seems to me that, over and above his dislike for the politics of the accused and his instinctive belief in white supremacy, his inborn prejudice against blacks and particularly what he would regard as 'cheeky' or 'clever' 'up-start' blacks, he also had a prejudice against politicians—all politicians. He seemed to regard politics as a dirty business, and politicians as rather slimy, scheming characters, untrustworthy and generally moved by despicable motives. It was in this sense that I began to understand the speech which Mandela had made so forcibly at his previous trial, in which he had declared quite positively that, despite the fairness of the individual judge, so long as the courts remained exclusively white, with white prosecutors, white judges and white magistrates, an African could not get a fair and equal trial. The scales were loaded against him by the prejudices of which even the best judge is unconscious, but which nevertheless influence his attitude.

Sisulu stood up magnificently against this double-barrelled attack from the prosecutor on the one hand and the judge on the other. He was in the witness box under cross-examination for five days. In the main his evidence covered much of the ground of Mandela's statement—the story of how Umkhonto came to be formed, of the relations between it and the African National Congress, and of the part he himself had played.

Five days under cross-examination without any hesitation or lapses, and without any notes, was a feat of considerable merit, and under extremely difficult circumstances. From the moment he started giving evidence Sisulu was segregated from all contact with lawyers and accused. This was something quite new in our experience. It is usual practice in our courts that an accused person who has started evidence should not discuss the case with his lawyers until that evidence is completed. But this was something different. Sisulu was isolated at all times. He was carried from jail to court in a separate vehicle, and not allowed to mix with the other accused during lunch adjournments or recesses, or during exercise periods in the jail.

In a way this seriously hampered the preparation of other accused, because their preparations required consultation with Sisulu. We considered a protest at this segregation, but decided not to protest unless Sisulu himself felt so inclined. We had no doubt that if we protested and Sisulu returned to the company of his co-accused, Dr Yutar would claim that he was being 'coached' between sessions, and seek thus to account for his coherent and unshakeable story. We therefore made no move. For over a week Sisulu was kept in complete isolation with no human contact at all, day after day in the witness box being hammered by judge and prosecutor. The way he came through revealed his real qualities of stability, calmness and certainty in himself which had made him a leader in his organisation, and which had ultimately made him Secretary General of the African National Congress.

Operation Mayibuye was in many ways the crux of the entire case for most of the accused. Guilt on the charge of attempting to overthrow the State by armed force had been admitted by most of the accused themselves. The question which had been the focus of our preparations throughout was not this question, but rather what sentence the court would impose. And the crux of that question was Operation Mayibuye. If the court found, as Dr Yutar was asking it to find, that Operation Mayibuye had in fact been adopted, then the picture was very black indeed. For Operation Mayibuye was a draft plan for the deployment of a guerrilla army, and the launching of widespread military struggle with assistance from friendly countries abroad. The accused, in their brief to us, told us that Operation Mayibuye was not adopted but was under discussion. Mandela's statement in court had not touched on this issue because the document had not seen the light of day until Mandela was already in jail.

The question was whether Sisulu's evidence would serve to prove the defence case on this document, for if it did so, it would fatally weaken the case for capital punishment which the State was pressing. In his evidence in chief, Sisulu explained that when Umkhonto was formed, the leading officials of the African National Congress in South Africa had continued exclusively in that organisation, maintaining their duties there. They had not, generally speaking, joined Umkhonto. Liaison between the African National Congress and Umkhonto had been carried out by Nelson Mandela who served in both committees. After Nelson's arrest it was felt necessary by the ANC that a leading official of their organisation should be appointed to maintain contact with Umkhonto, so that any decision with political implications taken by Umkhonto could be discussed and advised on in good time by the African National Congress. Thus, from time to time, Sisulu had attended meetings of the High Command, although he had not formally been a member of it. He had participated in discussions on the broad general policy of the armed struggle, but had not been in any way responsible for the daily workings of the organisation. His evidence had been that Operation Mayibuye had been placed before the National High Command as a draft for discussion. It had been prepared by a group of its members, amongst whom was Arthur Goldreich, who had lived in the main house at Rivonia, and who had made a dramatic escape from Marshall Square after his arrest. When the draft was presented, Sisulu said, there had been those who favoured it very strongly, there had been some who had opposed it very strongly, and there were many who were undecided and wanted further discussion.

Any decision to launch guerrilla warfare would be so far-reaching that the National High Command felt it should not decide this issue alone, unilaterally. Such a decision would require at least the agreement and fore-knowledge of the African National Congress. Sisulu himself had participated in the discussions on the National High Command, and in preliminary discussions at the Working Committee of the African National Congress on the question of guerrilla warfare as raised by Operation Mayibuye. His evidence was that, at the time of arrest, no decision had been taken. There was still much opposition, although there was also considerable support for Operation Mayibuye. He himself, he said, did not feel that Operation Mayibuye correctly outlined the tasks before the national movement.

On this evidence he would surely face a gruelling cross-examination; or so we thought. But Dr Yutar, for all his reputation as a devastating cross-examiner, became the victim of his own psychological weaknesses. He proved incapable of sticking doggedly to the points at issue, one by one. Instead he was carried away by his own emotions into fields where chinks that might have been opened up in Sisulu's story were lost from sight, the main burden of the State's allegations on Operation Mayibuye became forgotten, and the defence case remained unassailed to the end. A typical passage between these two runs like this:

Yutar: Were the conditions right for Operation Mayibuye?

Sisulu: No. My view was that conditions did not exist at that time for Operation Mayibuye.

On the basis of this reply Dr Yutar read the document paragraph by paragraph, and questioned Sisulu whether the paragraph in his view, was correct. Sisulu disagreed with some of the formulations in the document, accepted others. Yutar suddenly drifted away on to a sideline, carried by something Sisulu said, on to an irrelevant, incidental thought.

Incidentally, what is the membership of the African National Congress?

Sisulu: When it was banned (1960), it was 120,000.

And what is the total Bantu population in South Africa?

It was twelve million.

So, despite your fifty years of trying to persuade the Bantu in this country that they were being oppressed you only had in 1960 a total enrolment of about 120,000 out of 12 million?

Yes. The reason is obvious. There is no country which conducts greater intimidation against political movements than South Africa. And yet that does not mean that because we have 120,000 we do not represent the aspirations of the African people. The point you are making is this: that we are not representative of the African people, that we don't have a following. Political organisations don't get everybody. The organisations themselves are smaller in numbers, yet they represent the aspirations of the people.

Yutar did not attempt to argue against this short lecture in politics. But instead he allowed his cross-examination to be led off the track he had been following, to an errant trail—the statement in the document which said 'we are confident that the masses will respond in overwhelming numbers to a lead which holds out a real possibility of successful armed struggle'.

Seizing on the remarkable similarity between this statement and Sisulu's words in the witness box, he asked, 'Do you agree with this statement?'

Sisulu: If the masses knew that we were leading them and there was a real possibility of success they would respond in overwhelming numbers. The reason for this is that the people do want to have a vote in this country.

At this point Mr Justice de Wet got into the argument; confusing the trail yet further. 'Would they really? Is that correct, Mr Sisulu? You think they should have the vote, but how do you know that the ordinary Bantu about town wants the vote? You think that he ought to have it, and you are telling him that he ought to have it. But how do you know that he really wants it? You only know that you think he ought to have it, but how do you know that he wants it?'

This was really reaching far outside the bounds of this case, but Sisulu was not ruffled: 'Well', he said, 'Well, I have not come across meetings where I have heard people saying, 'No, we don't want the vote!'. People always support the idea of the vote'.

Mr Justice de Wet subsided. Yutar, his place in this attack lost, turned to a phrase about planning 'for insurrection by the guerrilla units, armed invasion, whether by sea or air, leading eventually to open rebellion'.

Sisulu: We were not planning any armed invasion.

Was it not discussed?

Yes. I am saying that a plan like that could not possibly be adopted. Certainly the National Executive of the African National Congress would not take a matter like this lightly. It is a serious matter, a serious matter of war.

Yutar: Of course it is. It is High Treason.

Sisulu: I know. But I am not talking about the legal liability. I am talking about the seriousness, even to embark on a thing like this. It requires serious consideration. It will involve the life of people.

Mr Justice de Wet: But I can't understand, Sisulu, this being put unless some arrangement had been made with outside countries. Has there not been an arrangement that they would help if they were asked?

Sisulu: No, my Lord, definitely not. We had not reached the stage of asking anybody for armed intervention. Certainly not.

De Wet: How could the man who drew up this plan put this had there not been some preliminary arrangements for that?

Sisulu: I don't know. I don't know why it was done because there was certainly no such arrangement.

I did not feel very happy about these interventions from Mr Justice de Wet. They appeared to indicate that he had made up his mind about one of the crucial points—that armed intervention from outside had been agreed upon by the leaders of the ANC, that arrangements for it had been made before this trial started. Yutar presumably sensed something of the same sort. So he continued to press and press, attempting to elicit some response from Sisulu which would strengthen this finding. Document after document was perused paragraph by paragraph; question after question was put to Sisulu. And again, gradually, Yutar began to lose track of the main point of the case, and to follow this issue with a neurotic tenacity. From the point of view of the State, he was pursuing a red herring, of importance only to a man of Yutar's psychology, bent not on justice but on vengeance. Sisulu came through the ordeal well.

At the end of the fifth day of cross-examination, shortly before the court was due to adjourn at 4 o'clock, Mr Justice de Wet said: 'I think the witness looks tired. Is there much more you wish to question him on, Dr Yutar?' That was Friday. I thought that perhaps Mr Justice de Wet wanted to start his weekend early.

Dr Yutar replied: 'I couldn't possibly finish today my Lord. I will try and finish on Monday'.

This surprised us. In our view the crux of the case against those of the accused who were going to deny participating in the affairs of Umkhonto and the sabotage campaign had not even been reached. For them the crux must be the meeting at Rivonia on 11 July at which they had all been arrested. What purpose had that meeting served? Had the meeting not in fact been a meeting of the National High Command? And convened in fact to implement Operation Mayibuye? This seemed to us the crux of the State case. But up to that moment, Dr Yutar had scarcely touched on the meeting of 11 July. We doubted, therefore, whether we could place any trust in his promise to finish cross-examining Sisulu on Monday.

The court adjourned. Walter spent a solitary weekend while we finished preparations for our next witness, just in case Yutar did finish early on Monday.

Normally if we followed the numerical order in which the accused had been cited, our next witness should have been Dennis Goldberg, to be followed by Govan Mbeki. But by now, Dr Yutar and Mr Justice de Wet had opened up some broad political questions of which we had not originally seen as relevant to the case, and which we had not prepared ourselves to tackle in defence. There was, for instance, the question whether the African National Congress represented the African majority, and whether an organisation of 120,000 members can claim to be the voice of a 12 million strong population, and whether the Africans were in fact oppressed, or whether it was the propaganda and agitation of the African National Congress which sought to convince them that they were oppressed when they were not. We decided that the best man to handle this would be Govan Mbeki. Govan would therefore have to stand down to a later date when we had fully prepared on these issues.

Goldberg's case was in the main outside the general case against the accused, centred either on his Cape Town activities, or on his specialised investigation into the manufacture of arms and weapons. We did not want this special aspect to interrupt the general thread of our defence. And so accused No.5, Ahmed Kathrada was our next witness.

Yutar's conduct proved even more mysterious to us on Monday morning than it had on Friday. As soon as court commenced, he said: 'My Lord, on reflection over the weekend and in the light of admissions made by this witness, I have decided to curtail my cross-examination considerably and I hope to conclude it by the tea adjournment'.

And so it was. A few minor questions of no particular significance, and Yutar's attempt to shake Sisulu was over and done with.

Bram Fischer re-examined in his quiet, undramatic manner. We wanted to rebut the judge's suggestion that Sisulu and other leaders stayed safe in the background, in the security and hiding of

Rivonia, while their followers had been sent out on dangerous missions of sabotage and illegal radio transmissions. To rebut this, he took Sisulu through the last few years of his political activity. The record is perhaps a piece of South African history that needs to be recorded.

Fischer: You were first convicted in 1952 in the Defiance of Unjust Laws Campaign?

That is correct.

In consequence of taking a lead there you were convicted a second time under the Suppression of Communism Act, for organising the Defiance Campaign and taking a part in it?

That is correct.

That could have given you ten years in jail, couldn't it?

That is correct.

Then again you were arrested in 1954 and convicted for attending a gathering. At that time you had been banned from gatherings?

Yes.

You were convicted, but acquitted on appeal?

That is correct.

In 1960 you were detained during the State of Emergency?

That is correct.

In 1961 you were convicted twice, and in 1962 you were first arrested for attending a gathering and then the charges were withdrawn?

That is correct.

In April you were arrested again in Johannesburg under the Suppression of Communism Act, and there you were acquitted on the charge of attending a gathering?

Yes.

Then in 1962 I think you were arrested on several occasions?

Six times in 1962.

One of these occasions was when your mother died and people came from your neighbourhood to your house to sympathise?

They came as you say. And I explained the position to the police, but despite my explanation they arrested me. Eventually the charge was withdrawn.

When the ANC became illegal, you have told the court you continued to participate in its activity. And that of course exposed you I think to a sentence of ten years?

That is correct.

And when you were detained for 90 days (that is to say, from day of the arrest at Rivonia) were you approached and interrogated in any way?

Yes, I was interrogated by members of the Special Branch several times. They said they believed I was in possession of vital information which would help the State, and that I was facing a very grave charge, the penalty for which is death. They told me I could escape if I was prepared to give evidence, or rather to give them information confidentially. They said it would not be known by anybody. And they told me that some of the Europeans had already spoken and given information about me. They repeated examples of the rebellion of 1914 when Jopie Fourie was hanged. I, however, said that I would never give information about my colleagues and they could do what they wished.

So you did not accept any offer, though it may have saved you from the death penalty?

Yes.

By the time Bram sat down, we felt that Walter in the witness box had been a triumph. His colleagues who had persuaded us beforehand that he would be more than a match for Yutar had understood him well. He had been. The whole court, I think, had been impressed by this small man of meagre education but of tremendous sincerity, calm, conviction and certainty. It was difficult to say what the judge felt. His comments had been, in the main, snide if not sinister. He had betrayed a bitter prejudice against Sisulu and probably against the defence as a whole. But at least we felt that during the days in which he had been in the witness box, the judge had come to understand that in Sisulu he was dealing with no run-of-the-mill criminal of the type he was accustomed to in his court. To sentence such a man to death would not be easy for any judge.

Our next witness, Ahmed 'Kathy' Kathrada, was quite a different character. Only 34 years of age, he had been active in the South African Indian Congress since he was a schoolboy. For many years he had been a full-time official and employee of the Indian Congress. He was essentially one of the doers, the organisers, the men who get things done. He did not claim to be a policy maker or a theoretician. In discussions he seldom expounded an opinion at any length. But what he did with remarkable effect was to heckle pointedly, with biting and pertinent interjections, and often with a great deal of sarcasm and humour. The evidence thus far did not implicate him deeply in the offences charged. The main thing against him seemed to be that he had been arrested at Rivonia and had been shown by the servants on the farm to have lived there for several weeks before that date. It was shown by evidence that during his time there he had disguised himself as a ginger-haired, swarthy Portuguese. At Rivonia, it was said, he went by the name of Pedro. So successful was his disguise that detectives who had known him intimately for many years failed to recognise him when the Rivonia raid took place.

There was Mtolo's evidence that he had been in the room while Mtolo discussed Umkhonto matters with Govan Mbeki. There was evidence that he had used typewriters and duplicating machines at Rivonia, with the inference that some of the duplicate material belonging to Umkhonto, the African National Congress and the Communist Party found at Rivonia must have been his handiwork. There was also the evidence of Essop Suliman, a taxi owner, who said that Kathy had paid him money for the carrying of military recruits to the Bechuanaland border.

Vernon Berrange led Kathrada's evidence. He was as much concerned to let the judge see the man as to get him to see the case. Berrange led Kathrada through the story of his life—how he had come to dedicate himself to the national liberation struggle of the non-white people. He described his reaction when the African National Congress had been declared illegal in 1960. 'I was greatly disturbed', he said. 'For many years the African and Indian Congresses had co-operated on numerous issues which affected both races. I believed that the disappearance of the ANC from the political scene in South Africa would deprive the African people, or should I say all the oppressed people in the whole of South Africa, of a most responsible leadership.'

Question: And as a member of a minority group where do you think your future lies?

Answer: I have long come to the conclusion, and so have the Indian people, that our future lies with the policies of the African National Congress.

He described how he had been placed under a house arrest order in 1962. This prohibited him from entering factories, though his work at that time required his daily entry into printing works for whom he was a canvasser. It prohibited him from communicating with any other banned or listed people, from attending social gatherings, or from being out of doors during the hours of darkness or over weekends. He made applications to be allowed to continue his work as a printer's representative, and this was refused. He said that when the law was introduced in 1963 permitting the police to hold any person for up to 90 days at a time for interrogation under conditions of solitary confinement, incommunicado, he had little doubt that he would be one of the first victims.

'I think that at the time', he said, 'I had been arrested something like seventeen times since 1946—or rather not arrested, but I had been charged on seventeen occasions. I was arrested many more times and I am not including charges for just putting up posters or distributing leaflets or that sort of thing. In fact I was acquitted on nearly every charge except five'.

Berrange: What were the charges on which you were convicted?

Answer: Apart from my participation in the Defiance Campaign of 1952, I was charged and convicted on a charge of being in the Cape Province without a permit. (All Indian citizens of South Africa who wished to travel from one province to another had to obtain permits.) In 1955 I was convicted in Bloemfontein for entering a location (that is, a segregated African residential area). And in 1961 I was convicted for contravening a banning order by going from Johannesburg to visit my mother who at the time was ill.

He had then decided that he would go 'underground' rather than be detained indefinitely for interrogation by the police and would carry on his political work in secret. He knew Arthur Goldreich and Goldreich had offered to prepare a disguise for him, and to give him accommodation at the cottage in Rivonia, while he was having his hair and facial appearance changed. This is what had brought him to Rivonia. He told the court that, after staying at Rivonia for some time to complete his disguise, he had moved out to another place about the beginning of July. He had returned to Rivonia on the night of 10 July in order to make a tape-recording of a speech which was to be broadcast over the illegal ANC radio, in reply to a claim by the Minister of the Interior, that all races in South Africa were happy and thought in the same way about the beauties of apartheid. Kathrada had decided to reply to this speech on behalf of the Indian population. He had come to Rivonia on 10 July, and he had been there on the afternoon of the 11th when the police raided. Hepple had arranged to drive him back to his normal place of residence after the afternoon meeting at which Hepple was to be present. Kathrada had not been invited to the meeting but would probably have sat in on the discussion if the police had not intervened.

Dr Yutar cross-examined in an aggressive fashion and this acted as the spur to the aggressive sarcasm so characteristic of Kathrada in discussion.

Yutar: Do you agree that this proposed broadcast of yours in response to the speech by the Minister of Finance was a very vicious document?

Kathrada: I don't agree. I agree that it was in immoderate language, but I don't agree that it was vicious. I think that what the Minister was saying was vicious.

Question: You have called them (that is the Nationalist Cabinet) amongst other things, criminal?

Kathrada: That's what they are.

Yutar found it hard to keep his temper with Kathrada, especially when Kathrada refused to answer questions about other people and *their* activities.

Yutar: Your oath is to tell the truth, the whole truth and nothing but the truth.

Kathrada: I am aware of that.

So that when it comes to giving evidence which might implicate somebody either in this court or outside this court were you not prepared to give that evidence?

I am honour bound not to.

Honour bound to whom?

To my conscience, my political colleagues, to my political organisation, to all of whom I owe loyalty.

What about being honour bound to the Almighty?

I am not telling any lies.

You are not honour bound to that, are you?

Well I don't know if the police are doing the Almighty's work! But I am not prepared to give the police anything that might implicate other people.

Sisulu adopted that attitude in the box and you are doing the same.

Is there anything wrong with that?

Don't ask me. I'll tell his Lordship what I think about it in due course. And I am telling you now that you are adopting the same attitude as Sisulu.

That's obvious.

And this political organisation to which you owe this loyalty; does it also include the African National Congress?

Yes.

It also includes the Umkhonto?

If I knew anything about the Umkhonto I would not tell you. If the fact of it was to implicate anybody, I would not tell you.

Then how am I to test your story and what you are telling us?

I am afraid I have no suggestions.

In his irritation Yutar was again drawn from his own ground of law and on to Kathrada's territory, politics. 'Did you incite people not to move from Sophiatown to Meadowlands?' This was in reference to a vast operation carried through by the Nationalist Government, in which the entire freehold township occupied by Africans and coloureds and known as Sophiatown was declared a white area. The whole African population was forcibly removed to a municipal African township where they had no freehold rights, living surrounded by a fence, in municipally-owned housing, controlled by a multitude of regulations, without any of the freedoms they had known in Sophiatown. The operation, known as the Western Areas Removal Scheme, had been bitterly fought by the African National Congress and its allies, the Indian Congress, the Congress of Democrats and many others, including a very redoubtable Anglican parson, Father Trevor Huddleston, who later became a Bishop in Southern Tanzania.

Kathrada: I called upon the people not to move.

Yutar: Which do you prefer, Sophiatown or Meadowlands?

I prefer to live where I like to live. Not where somebody in Parliament tells me to live.

But of the two places, Sophiatown with all its slums and she-beens or these beautiful garden houses in Meadowlands, which do you think is the better place of the two?

Sophiatown, with its comparative freedom, rather than Meadowlands which has got a hundred and one restrictions, permits and where your own mother can't come and visit you without a permit.

It's all very well to complain about conditions in South Africa but what about the Indians in India? By the way, have you been to India?

I have not been.

Do you know about the suffering of the people in India?

In India? I know about the suffering of my people in this country where I was born. I don't know anything about India.

You have never been there and you have never done any research?

I have read about India.

And so it went. The clash was much to the amusement of the accused and the public, who enjoyed nothing quite so well as seeing Kathrada strike out to the discomfiture of Dr Yutar. At the end of the day when court adjourned, the segregation procedure which had been followed with Sisulu was applied to Kathrada. We decided on this occasion to challenge it, and the following morning Berrange made a protest in court. 'The defence', he said, 'feels strongly about this because it is a matter of principle. Ever since Mr Kathrada completed his evidence in chief the jail authorities, on the instructions of Dr Yutar, have isolated Mr Kathrada and kept him away from his fellow prisoners. That means, of course, my Lord, that during the day when he is here he is not entitled to mix with his fellow prisoners during intervals, he is not entitled to have tea with them, to have lunch with them or to have any form of intercourse or contact with them. I don't think that we counsel are unaware of our obligations and we are very conscious of our duties. We certainly would take no steps to interview or have consultation with any of the accused prisoners once they have finished their evidence in chief. But this is an interference with the rights of the prisoners themselves, and I accordingly seek your ruling on this matter.'

Yutar in his reply was as smarmy as even he could get. 'My Lord', he said, 'I share the feeling with my learned friends and feel equally as strongly about this matter. For reasons, my Lord, which would not be in the interest of the accused himself to disclose in this court, I felt obliged to take that precaution in order to avoid, my Lord, the possibility of consultation between the accused under cross-examination and their fellow accused. My Lord, I must just mention one thing. My learned friend, Mr Berrange, spoke to Mr Sisulu in the midst of cross-examination and amongst other things he concluded his conversation with the words 'Your colleagues in the dock want you to know that they are proud of you, and also the legal team are proud of the way in which you have been giving your evidence'. My Lord, I don't know whether that pride stems from the reluctance of the witness under cross-examination to disclose certain people, or from the plan of sabotage which had been embarked upon. But I do feel very strongly that it is irregular for counsel to speak to an accused person under cross-examination, and my Lord, the danger of the co-accused speaking to an accused under cross-examination is a very real one.'

This was the most outrageous smear. Vernon, in his capacity as counsel, had asked to see Sisulu at the jail during one of the recesses. He had done so specifically to ask him whether he was capable of standing up to his isolation, since his long ordeal in the witness box was dragging into its second week. The prison authorities must have 'bugged' the interview room, and reported Vernon's conversation to Yutar. Mr Justice de Wet blandly ignored all this. He merely told Yutar that he had never heard of such a procedure before, and as far as he was concerned there was no necessity for it whatsoever. Yutar rather reluctantly agreed to recall his instructions to the jail authorities. Kathrada's cross-examination was resumed again on the subject of India.

Yutar: Kathrada, do you know that India has a three-year detention no trial law?

Kathrada: It is quite likely.

Did you ever voice any protest against that?

I did not.

You did not?

I live in South Africa. I suffer from the laws in South Africa. My objection is to what goes on to me and my people.

Do you know that Ghana has a five-year detention no-trial law?

That is correct.

Have you ever spurned assistance from Ghana?

Never.

Never?

No. I'd get assistance from the devil, provided it was for my people in this country, and for the freedom of my people.

But you choose to attack the country of your birth?

I choose to attack it, and I'll go on attacking it until things are put right.

Dr Yutar picked up one of the Mandela diaries in which there had been some entries referring to a certain 'K'. He was rather anxious to prove that the K referred to was Kathrada.

Question: Are you sometimes referred to as K?

Kathrada: I am not referred to as K. I don't know of anybody who refers to me as K.

Do you know anybody else who goes under the initial of K?

Yes.

Who?

Mr Kruschev.

There was laughter in court. Yutar is incapable of laughing at a joke at his own expense. 'So you are trying to be funny at my expense?' he said.

Kathrada: I wasn't. You asked me if I knew of any Mr K, and I told you.

Yutar was getting rattled, and Kathrada was getting increasingly aggressive.

Yutar turned to what he described as 'the irresponsible leadership' of the African National Congress who had planned a campaign of sabotage, and asked: 'Did you have confidence in those irresponsible leaders of the ANC?'.

Kathrada: I have said that I regard the leadership of the ANC as responsible. I have said that those who have been in Umkhonto have been forced to resort to these methods. I have the fullest admiration for their courage, and when you talk of responsibility, I also know that members of the Ossewa Brandwag (a Nationalist supported, extreme right-wing Afrikaner movement which existed during the second world war) committed acts of sabotage when they had the vote and they had every other means of expressing themselves in this country. They resorted to sabotage and some of them are in the government today.

Yutar attempted to prove that Kathrada had not been truthful when he had stated his own views of sabotage in his evidence in chief. Kathrada had said that he had had reservations about sabotage. He had thought it would not be effective unless it was directly related to some mass campaign, for instance a mass anti-pass campaign when people were going to jail for burning their passes. If, in the course of such a campaign, someone committed an act of sabotage as, for instance, blowing up a pass office, he could see the effectiveness of sabotage. But except in such circumstances, he did not think that sabotage would be politically effective. He had not supported the sabotage campaign, but he recognised the right of the organisations to conduct such a campaign, and he would respect their decision if they saw fit to decide upon such an action. On this basis, Kathrada could not be shaken. Finally, Yutar brought his cross-examination to what he thought was going to be the dramatic end. 'You are a member of the Communist Party?'

Kathrada: I am.

You are a follower of the Communist Party?

I am.

Whose aim and object is to secure freedom for what you call the oppressed people of this country?

For what are the oppressed people in this country.

To which doctrine you subscribe?

I do, fully and unequivocally.

Are you determined to see the fulfilment of the policy, the aims and objects of the Communist Party?

I still am.

Which involves the overthrow of the government of South Africa?

That is so.

By force and violence if necessary?

When and if necessary.

Yutar sat down. If he thought he had scored a point he was, in my view, mistaken. His cross-examination, I believed, had shown the court Kathrada's bona fides. He had made a forthright statement of his political principles without any equivocation at a time when those principles were fiercely unpopular and illegal, and where a shifty character would certainly have tried to prevaricate. And in his irritation with Kathrada, Yutar—characteristically—had missed the vital question which we felt must decide Kathrada's guilt or innocence. This question was: had he or had he not been at a meeting on 11 July at Rivonia when the police raided, and when they alleged the document 'Operation Mayibuye' was before the meeting, on the table? But not a word of cross-examination was directed to this. Nor was there any investigation of the other crucial matter—had the broadcast which he had prepared or the typing and duplicating which he had done at Rivonia been connected with Umkhonto we Sizwe or not? As matters now stood, there was no evidence to show that they had. Nor, on the face of it, was there anything to suggest that the typing or the broadcast was part and parcel of a scheme of sabotage and violence to overthrow the government. It was a political attack on the government certainly. But this was not the charge.

These two vital questions in the case of Kathrada remained completely untraversed, and the State inference thus completely unproved. If the case was judged on the evidence and the evidence alone, Kathrada should be found 'not guilty'. He had admitted to knowledge of the conspiracy to commit sabotage which was conducted from Rivonia, but that was all. Would he be judged on the facts and the facts alone? Or would the judgement be swayed by the prejudices and hysteria running riot in the country? Kathrada's admission that he was a Communist by belief and also a member of the illegal Communist Party might have impressed the judge with his honesty. But it might also have persuaded a prejudiced man that anyone capable of such an aberration was also capable of the deeds charged in the indictment and indeed likely to have taken part in them.

Kathrada stood down, and his place was taken by our next witness, Raymond Mhlaba. He hailed from Port Elizabeth. To some extent, like Goldberg, he had been out of the close circle of co-workers in the Transvaal around the national head offices of the organisations comprising the Congress Movement, of which Mandela, Sisulu, Mbeki, Bernstein and Kathrada had all been part. Mhlaba was a very large man, rather stolid, giving the impression of great strength and solidity. He had a sudden crashing laugh which burst out unexpectedly on very small provocation. He had been a member of the African National Congress for many years, and was probably the best-known member of the African National Congress in the Port Elizabeth region where it had its greatest strength. He rarely spoke of his family. His wife had been killed in a motor accident some years before and his eight children lived with his sister. We had found him to be a man of tremendous sincerity and a single-minded simplicity which expressed itself in a laconic turn of phrase.

One day, for instance, we had heard him discussing the question of hanging with Govan Mbeki. Ray had remarked off-handedly, somewhat to Govan's consternation, 'What does it matter. You go there. They put a rope around your neck, pull a lever, and it's all over. What is there to be frightened or bothered about?'.

For some strange reason his sincerity, his honesty and his simplicity did not come across from the witness box. Though we had not foreseen this, of all the defence witnesses he alone made a rather unfortunate impression in the box. I have been unable to decide why it should have been so, or what there was in his attitude, except perhaps that being a rather slow-moving man, he was also somewhat slow to answer. This might have given the impression that he had heard the question but was busy manufacturing or tailoring the answer in his mind before speaking it. This impression was to prove fatal, for the evidence against him was not very strong. The strongest part of it was that he was shown to have lived at Rivonia for some short while before his arrest. There was one witness who had given evidence that Mhlaba had taken part in certain acts of sabotage in Port Elizabeth on 16 December 1961. His evidence had gone into impressive circumstantial detail of the way in which the bombs for this episode had been collected from various places, of the people who had been in the car, of the route they had travelled, of the times at which they got off at various places and of conversations that had taken place there. It was impressive enough to persuade us that much of his account was true. Perhaps the only lying part of it was that Mhlaba was there. We had it from the accused that Mhlaba was not only not in Port Elizabeth, but that he had not even been in the country at all when Umkhonto we Sizwe staged these first acts of sabotage. Had it not been for this impressive yet false evidence, we would not have felt it necessary for Raymond to go into the witness box at all, so weak was the rest of the case against him. But if he did not go into the box to contradict *this* evidence, he would inevitably be found guilty.

Raymond's evidence was brief. Led by Vernon Berrange, he explained briefly that he had been a member of the African National Congress for many years. He said that in 1961 he had been called from Port Elizabeth to ANC Headquarters in the Transvaal. There he had been asked to undertake an African National Congress mission. He had gone on that mission and as a result had not been in Port Elizabeth from that time, October 1961 until June 1962. On his return he had reported to ANC Headquarters and had again been sent on a mission. This second mission had ended shortly before his arrest. He had returned from his mission and was taken to rest up for a short while at Rivonia, living in hiding until it was decided where or what his next activities would be. He thus acknowledged that he had been an active member of the African National Congress throughout the period of its illegality. He denied that he had been involved in Umkhonto we Sizwe or been a member of the National High Command.

Yutar started his cross-examination on his usual 'fishing expedition' basis: 'who were the members of the ANC in Port Elizabeth?'.

Mhlaba: I'm afraid I can't assist you there.

Yutar: You are taking up the same attitude as Sisulu and Kathrada? In fact I have just heard an aside that you are all going to take up this same attitude!

According to what I understand, yes.

Who gave you instructions not to divulge their names?

Nobody gave us instructions.

But you are all acting alike?

We are acting alike because we feel that it is not in the interests of the organisations and not in the interests of the oppressed people in this country.

But you have taken an oath. Does that mean anything to you? What does it mean to you?

It means that I must assist this court insofar as I can, in giving evidence.

Having drawn another blank in this direction, Yutar turned to the crux of the case against Mhlaba—where had he been on 16 December, 1961, when acts of sabotage took place in Port Elizabeth. His first question was not a question, but a statement: 'I want to put it to you that in December 1961 you were either in Port Elizabeth or in Leipzig'. This confirmed for us what we had been fairly sure was the position. The Security Policy knew that at the time of the sabotage in Port Elizabeth in December 1961, Mhlaba had been outside the country! They thus knew that their chief witness against Mhlaba must be lying. We had been prepared for exactly such a question as this.

Vernon suggested to the judge that 'the witness should be warned by your Lordship in regard to the latter part of the question as to whether he was in Leipzig. That is a question which might tend to incriminate him on another charge, and under those circumstances he need not answer it'. The further charge if Mhlaba admitted to being in Leipzig would be one of leaving the country without a passport. The judge agreed. He told Mhlaba 'You need not necessarily answer the question which may be an admission that you left the country without getting the necessary permit. It doesn't follow that if you left for Leipzig you didn't have a permit. But if you feel that the question incriminates you, you can refuse to answer it on those grounds.'

Mhlaba had been briefed by us about this beforehand. He knew that he was living dangerously and in refusing to state where his mission had taken him, he would be indicating to the court quite clearly that he had in fact been outside the country. It would be impossible, later, to deny it. At this moment Dr Yutar intervened.

'I want to tell you Mhlaba, on behalf of the Attorney General, that here and now in the presence of his Lordship, I grant you full indemnity for any prosecutions so you needn't worry about incriminating yourself.'

Mhlaba thought for a little while. 'My Lord, I am not taking your assurance.'

Dr Yutar: 'Even though I state it in open court, in the presence of the presiding judge? I give you the solemn assurance in open court, and every word I am speaking is being taken down, that I grant you here and now full indemnity, and that no prosecution will be instituted again you no matter what offences you might have committed as a result of your leaving the country without a permit, so you need not worry about it.'

Mhlaba again refused to answer. The wording of Dr Yutar's statement is interesting. It confirms that he knew that in the vital period, Mhlaba might have been outside this country. Nevertheless, he had led the evidence which implicated Mhlaba in the sabotage of 16 December and he was persisting in it, contradictory though it might be.

The judge summed the situation up. 'The position is, Mhlaba, that you say you were not in Port Elizabeth on 16 December, but you refuse to tell the court where you were on that date. Is that the position?'

Mhlaba agreed that it was. The rest of the cross-examination was extremely short. It was directed entirely towards getting information about where Mhlaba had been or what his mission had been, or else about other people who might have been participating in the affairs of the African National Congress. On all these matters Mhlaba refused to talk. And so the evidence that he had taken part in sabotage on 16 December stood, though it was clearly false and everyone on both sides knew it was false.

Had Mhlaba made a better impression in the witness box, had his manner been more convincing or won greater sympathy from the judge, Mhlaba could only have been acquitted at the end of this case. In fact, on the law, my impression is that even as matters stood, he could still well be acquitted. We had done a great deal to undermine the credibility of the taxi-driver's evidence against him. For the rest, he was shown by his own evidence to have taken part in the affairs of the African National Congress at the time when that was illegal. However, the evidence which in my view was necessary if the State was to prove its case against Mhlaba, was never given in open court—neither then nor later.

Our next witness was to be Lionel Bernstein. As he had been incriminated by a witness who had been kept in solitary confinement for several months, we thought this a convenient stage to introduce medical evidence on the effects of solitary confinement.

The two leading authorities on this topic were both psychologists, Professor Danziger of Cape Town University and Dr Albino of Natal University. After careful studies they had concluded that in certain prisoners solitary confinement produced brain damage leading to marked abnormalities of mind. Prisoners became disorientated, their judgement was destroyed, and they became easily prone to confuse fact with suggestion. After solitary confinement, these authorities claimed, witnesses were not normal. Any evidence they gave was accordingly highly suspect. Whereas to all outward appearances the witness might seem perfectly normal, he might in fact be suffering from brain damage as a result of solitary confinement which would not be apparent to the judge. This brain damage could well result in the witness believing that the evidence he had given was true, when in fact it was not, but had been suggested to him by the police.

Many people when they had been detained in solitary confinement had told us that after a time they were unable to distinguish truth from fantasy, and began to believe even suggestions by the police that they had committed acts which they had not. We considered it then imperative that such evidence should be led, so that the judge could assess the value of evidence by the State witnesses correctly.

Percy Yutar scarcely objected, save to claim the tendering of such evidence was an attempt 'to make political capital out of the provisions of the 90-day detention clause'. But Quartus de Wet would not have this evidence. His views were typically arrogant and intolerant. No doctor, he said, was needed to tell him what weight should be attached to the evidence of witnesses. He and only he could decide that. He said nothing to explain how he could assess the value of the evidence without expert knowledge of possible hidden effects of solitary confinement. He merely refused to allow us to call expert testimony. And so Lionel Bernstein took the stand.

There was less evidence against him than against anybody else in the case. The evidence boiled down to this—that on the day the police raided Rivonia he had been present in the room where a meeting was alleged to be taking place. From evidence given by employees at Rivonia, and by builders and others who had done work on the premises at the time that Goldreich took occupation, it appeared that Bernstein had been architect for the alterations. These alterations included the conversion of an outside storeroom into what had come to be known as the 'thatched cottage', where most of the accused had lived while at Rivonia, and where the alleged meeting of 11 July was held. Bernstein had been a regular visitor at Rivonia for purposes not clearly defined throughout the three yeas that Goldreich had been in occupation. One of the farm labourers testified that, on a day when radio aerial masts were being erected at the farm, Bernstein had been on the roof of the cottage connecting the wires. Detective Sergeant Dirker, as I have recorded, had said that when the police raided Rivonia, he had felt the engine of Bernstein's car and found it to be cold, implying thereby that he had been there several hours. There was also a piece of hearsay evidence by Bruno Mtolo, who had said that he had been told by someone else that a certain 'Rusty Bernsteam or

Bunstead' had been in Durban to start the Umkhonto we Sizwe branch and initiate sabotage. This last piece of evidence was clearly inadmissible and scarcely worth worrying about from a legal point of view. It was however interesting, because it seemed completely out of character with the clear, almost photographic memory which Mtolo had about everything else. His hesitancy over the exact name, at this stage when Bernstein's name had been in the press for weeks, appeared almost theatrical, as though rehearsed rather than a genuine lapse of memory. What precise dramatic effect Mtolo or the prosecution sought to produce by this act we never discovered, but somehow it struck a wholly false note in Mtolo's evidence. Bernstein, as I think I have said before, denied that he had been either a member of Umkhonto we Sizwe or of the National High Command.

Vernon Berrange led him through the formal part of his evidence. He recounted his political experience which dated back to 1937 when he joined the Labour League of Youth, and later the South African Labour Party. He had joined the South African Communist Party at the time it was legal, early in 1939, and had remained a member until it was formally dissolved by the Central Committee of the Party after the passing of the Suppression of Communism Act in 1950. During that time, he said, he had been a member of the Johannesburg District Committee, and at one time its Secretary. His political activity had been mainly in the fields of propaganda and publicity. He had written consistently, both before and after the banning of the Communist Party, on a large number of political topics. He had been a regular contributor to left-wing periodicals and had written several pamphlets. He had been an executive member of the ex-serviceman's organisation, the Springbok Legion, and also of the South African Congress of Democrats until banned from it. After that, he had carried on writing for various organisations and periodicals.

The crucial part of his evidence was that of his association with the Rivonia property, and with things that went on there. His evidence was that at the time that Rivonia was being purchased, he was asked to inspect the place and to act as architect for alterations to an out-building to provide a self-contained flat in the grounds of the house. He had done so. While carrying out this work he had found Mandela living there, and he had visited Mandela from time to time and lent him books. He had learnt, he said, that the property had actually been bought by the Communist Party. After Mandela left, he continued to visit the place from time to time. He had attended meetings both in the thatched cottage and in the main house. On 11 July 1963, he had been invited there to discuss the conditions of people detained under the 90-day detention law, with a view to mounting a campaign of protest and agitation for their release, and for an improvement in prison conditions, as well as to raise funds for the maintenance and relief of their dependants.

He denied that he had been on the roof when the radio masts were being erected, or taken any part in this operation.

In many ways he proved to be an ideal witness, one of the best I have come across in the course of my legal career. His answers were clear, concise and to the point. He was at all times extremely polite and unruffled, and yet he would not concede anything which he did not want to concede, no matter how he was bludgeoned by Dr Yutar.

Yutar's cross-examination took a strange turn. We expected that he would stick closely to a couple of main topics; to the evidence which had been led about his share in the erection of radio masts, to his alleged visit to Durban to found Umkhonto we Sizwe, to his presence at the meeting on 13 July, and to questions concerning the meetings he had attended at Rivonia and the documents found there relating to the Communist Party and its activities.

Our expectations once again proved to be wrong. Dr Yutar opened his attack on the Communist Party and on Bernstein personally. He got so carried away by this vendetta that he failed at any stage during his peculiar cross examination to refer to any of the evidence against Bernstein whatsoever. As Yutar's cross-examination developed we could see the judge visibly warming towards Bernstein. I suspect that it was the first time in his life that he had come face to face with that rather rare South African creature, an avowed white communist. In this experience, he had found one who defended his beliefs clearly, concisely and without rancour or jargon. The judge seemed favourably impressed.

Dr Yutar, as we had anticipated, questioned Bernstein about a large number of documents, the majority of which were said to be produced by the Communist Party in its period of illegality. Bernstein was being questioned about the contents of the documents and their meaning as though he were an expert on communism. It was not suggested by Dr Yutar that he had written the documents, or that he even knew of their existence before they became exhibits in this case. Nevertheless, Bernstein was asked to interpret them, comment on them and discuss their politics, which he did. Where he agreed with what was written he said so, and where he disagreed he also said so. We could not see the relevance of the questions, but made no objection to this line of cross-examination. Dr Yutar was clearly getting nowhere.

In one small, certainly unwitting manner, he began to reveal how typical a white South African he was. He called Bernstein 'Mister' throughout his cross-examination, though none of the other accused received any such courtesy. Partly this was a reaction to Bernstein's own demeanour in the box, but even more, I think, Yutar was reacting unconsciously to the fact that he was, after all, a white man despite his off-beat politics and his criminal tendencies.

Dr Yutar again probed for information; names of people who had been present at meetings, people who had taken part in various activities. Bernstein also refused to name anyone who was still in the country. Finally he came to the key questions: 'Were you,' he asked 'a member of the Communist Party?' Bernstein replied that up to the time of its dissolution in 1950, he was. 'Did you remain a member of the illegal Communist Party?' Bernstein declined to answer, on the grounds that to do so might incriminate him in an offence which was not charged before the court.

We had discussed this matter with him before his evidence. We had advised him that, if he took this line, he would be well within his legal rights. But it would certainly leave no doubt at all in the mind of the judge that he had, in fact, continued to be a member of the illegal Communist Party. He was well aware of this. In fact, this might be said to be his very purpose. Again Yutar pressed and

Bernstein resisted. Yutar then asked the judge to instruct the witness to answer. Mr Justice de Wet informed Bernstein that he was required to answer the question put to him, and if he failed to do so he could be sentenced to imprisonment for contempt of court. He would then he held for eight days in prison, and could be brought up and asked the same question again, and again returned to prison if he refused to answer. At that moment the thought must have crossed Justice de Wet's mind that Bernstein had already been in prison for over nine months. A smile crossed his face, as he added: 'I don't support that will make much difference to you under present circumstances'.

Bernstien replied: 'No, sir. I am afraid not.' And that was where the matter ended.

Dr Yutar gave up, and turned to perhaps his most despicable smear. He produced a document which could only have come from the police archives. It had not been put in evidence, and was not an exhibit. It was a copy of a magazine called *Fighting Talk*, published in 1954, in which there appeared an article about Bram Fischer. It was signed only with the initials 'LB'. It had been written on the occasion of Fischer's banning from all organisations by edict of the Minister of Justice. The article dealt with Bram's career, making the point that whenever the writer despaired for the future of South Africans, he remembered Bram Fischer and his career, and this restored in him the belief that white South Africans were human beings, not all indistinguishably reactionary and racialistic. The article described Fischer as a leader of the Congress of Democrats, an organisation which had been declared unlawful in 1962. It catalogued his activities in the South African Peace Council and in the Communist Party, of which he had been a member of the Central Committee. Yutar put this article to Bernstein, and asked him who had written it. Bernstein identified it as his.

Dr Yutar: 'Who was the Secretary General of the Communist Party?'.

Bernstein declined to answer the question.

Dr Yutar: 'Well, since you are unable to answer that question, perhaps we may conclude that it was the gentlemen referred to in the exhibit before you. Will you please hand it to the judge'.

The document was handed to the judge, evidence of nothing at all, not even an exhibit, not found anywhere relevant to this conspiracy, or in possession of anyone. It had one purpose only—to allow Yutar to suggest that Bram was a senior member of the Communist Party, and so smear him in the eyes of the judge.

Yutar returned to the question of Bernstein's membership of the illegal Communist Party. Once again he offered a blank indemnity for all offences which Bernstein might admit to, other than those charged in this court, if he answered the question whether he was a member of the Communist Party. He repeated this offer again—an indemnity against all further prosecution. Bernstein asked the judge for an adjournment so that he might consult counsel. Court adjourned briefly, and we turned up the law books to check the validity of this offer. We discovered that Dr Yutar did indeed have power to offer an indemnity, but his superior, the Minister of Justice, was not bound by this offer regardless of whether it was accepted by the accused or not. Dr Yutar could indemnify and his chief could, nevertheless, prosecute. Whether Dr Yutar was aware of this or not we were not sure. He should have been. He was the Deputy Attorney General.

We returned to court with our knowledge. Bernstein refused the indemnity and again refused to answer the question. Dr Yutar turned from this fruitless enquiry to one of the most remarkable of the whole case.

Question: Have you ever accused the State of coaching its witnesses?

Answer: I possibly have said that, sir.

In this case?

Yes, possibly.

Have you accused the police in this case of acting improperly?

I can't recall if I have, sir. But I think it is possible.

What grounds have you for saying that the police in this case have acted improperly?

Well, my Lord, I can only testify to the testimony of one police witness, who himself said here under oath that when you have a 90-day detainee and you want to get a statement out of him, you tell him what you know of the facts, and then he confirms them.

Question: And he confirms it?

Answer: Well, he says this is the only way you can get a statement out of a detainee—when you tell him what you know, and then you put it to him like that.

And if the detainee denies it are you suggesting then that the police force him to agree?

No, they just keep badgering him.

Until he agrees?

Possibly until he agrees. Or possibly they give up at some stage.

You say that you might have said that the State coaches witnesses?

I might have.

That is a reflection on the State Prosecutor?

I am afraid so, sir.

Have you any evidence to support that wicked suggestion?

'My Lord, we did have an incident here in court.' And then turning to the judge, 'I don't know if I am forced to deal with this question, sir'.

Yutar: It affects your credibility.

Bernstein: Well, I would like his Lordship to tell me if this is all strictly relevant to the case.

Mr Justice de Wet: It is a relevant question, Mr Bernstein. You can answer it.

Bernstein: Well, my Lord, we did have one case of a witness who testified here on Friday afternoon and who went away for the weekend, and who came back on Monday morning, was asked precisely the same question he had been asked on Friday afternoon, and he gave different answers. From which I deduce that some coaching had taken place over the weekend.

Yutar: That was the witness we were having a certain measure of difficulty with the interpreter?

Bernstein: That is so.

But you don't ascribe it then to the difficulty of interpretation. You say directly that the witness was coached?

Well that is my deduction.

Did you ever say—'Apart from police evidence and documents, all the substantial witnesses other than people who gave purely technical evidence about, for example, who bought a particular car—all the substantial witnesses have been detainees who made statements under pressure and while subject to detention and solitary confinement, and subject certainly to threats of either indefinite detention or prosecution, or both.' Did you make that statement?

Yes, I did, sir.

Is it true or false?

I think it is probably true, sir.

These statements were being read by Dr Yutar from a letter which Bernstein had written from the Pretoria Jail to his sister in Britain. The letter, handed in to the prison authorities in the normal way for censorship, had been forwarded to the addressee, but a photostat copy had been handed by the prison authorities to the Security Police, and by the Security Police to Dr Yutar. The letter contained Bernstein's observations on how evidence was being obtained.

The purpose of the cross-examination was to force Bernstein to state whether or not the court in which he was being tried was fully fair, and whether he was getting a fair trial. Anything more unfair it is difficult to imagine. If he thought he was getting an unfair trial, would he say so in the presence of the judge, when his life might be at stake? The only purpose of such a cross-examination was to prejudice the judge against him, and Yutar made a great deal of it. He took Bernstein's allegations that all the substantial witnesses had been detainees, who had testified under the pressure of solitary confinement and threats. He began to cite each of the twenty-nine witnesses the State had called who, he said, had been under 90-days detention, apparently trying to prove that the defence had conceded that the evidence of these witnesses was true. It was an unbalanced action, and a stupid one, contradicted by the facts.

The fact was that we had attacked witness after witness and attempted to prove that much of the testimony had been obtained only by threats while the witness was under detention. Dr Yutar must have forgotten all this. Perhaps he thought Bernstein and everyone else-had forgotten it too. For example:

Yutar: We have Cyril Davids. He was cross-examined. But it was never suggested to him that he was forced to give the evidence he gave.

In fact, almost the entire cross-examination of Davids had been spent on suggesting just that.

Yutar: Now we come to Essop Suliman, and he in effect spoke about the conveyance of over 300 recruits across the border. That has been accepted by the defence.

Bernstein: I don't think a word of what Essop Suliman said has been accepted by anybody, sir.

In fact has it not been admitted by your co-accused that recruits were conveyed across the border?

Yes, sir. But I don't think the dates, the arrangements, the payment or anything else testified to by Essop were accepted.

You remember Harry Bmbani, that is, a recruit who is serving a two-year sentence. It was never suggested to him that he was either coached by the State Prosecutor or forced by the police to give false evidence.

That may be so. I can't be sure.

Mr Berrange: My Lord, my learned friend is completely wrong. I don't know where he gets this evidence from. In fact, it was suggested that he changed his evidence three times.

Yutar: Do you remember the witness Peter Mbomvu who testified to the commission of two acts of sabotage? Do you think he was forced to say that he committed two acts of sabotage and not one?

Bernstein: My Lord, he was either forced, or induced, or he was persuaded by some fantasy. But it was shown in court that he had made three different statements about the same subject, all under oath, at different times.

Yutar: So the police must have been awfully inefficient in forcing him to make one statement—they got three different statements out of him.

Bernstein: Yes. And they led all three in evidence here.

After a little more of this Yutar read a passage of the letter which said 'The whole thing disgusts me, the unprincipled timidity of people, and even more the unprincipled willingness, eagerness of the authority to use them'.

Yutar: You adhere to that?

Bernstein: I adhere to that.

That is the condemnation of course, not only of the investigating officer, but also of the State Prosecutor in this case.

A condemnation of the State, sir, which has provided facilities for witnesses' statements to be taken from them under duress.

Yutar seemed to lose control more and more as this went on, straying even further from the charge, the evidence or the case. He began to get Bernstein to comment, paragraph by paragraph, on a large number of documents found at Rivonia, which were alleged to have been issued by the Communist Party. Bernstein was commenting freely on the political line and tactics outlined in the documents. One of my colleagues, a counsel from the Johannesburg Bar, happened to be in Pretoria that morning. He was sitting in the VIP Gallery, listening to this cross-examination while Bernstein commented freely on passages from documents dealing with armed uprising, rebellion and sabotage, stating his opinion on their appropriateness or truthfulness. When we adjourned for tea, he told me that it appeared to him that Bernstein had completely cooked his own goose. We had to explain to him that all this was really irrelevant. The documents were neither found in Bernstein's possession, nor written by him, and they were not alleged by the State to have been distributed by him or even by an organisation of which he was a member. Put this way, my colleague was as completely mystified as we were about the purpose of this whole cross-examination.

Yutar completed this section by quoting again from the letter: '. . . so this is now patently the basis of the operations. You arrest the man, hold him in solitary confinement, tell him that he will be held indefinitely unless he answers satisfactorily, that is the key word, and tell him what he knows are the right facts, and just keep at it until he answers satisfactorily . . .'. Is that a correct description of what occurred in this case?'

Bernstein: I think it is a correct description of what occurs to a 90-day detainee.

I am talking about witnesses in this case.

Those who are 90-day detainees, I think it is very likely what happened.

And then you go on to say—you pay me this compliment— 'Here too Vernon did a great job exposing this very patent, or blatant coaching of witnesses'. How dare you say that if you have nothing to support it?

My Lord, I have explained the case on which I think it is an adequate statement.

We were waiting naturally for Yutar to get down to the substance of the case against Bernstein, the three questions: Had he been on the roof the day the radio aerials were being erected? Had his presence at Rivonia on the day of the arrest been connected with the discussion of the National High Command on Operation Mayibuye? Had he gone to Durban to start a branch of Umkhonto we Sizwe? These were the only substantial allegations against him. And though the third was clearly hearsay and inadmissible, it had been allowed to get into the record by virtue of Mr Justice de Wet's ruling, and cross-examination on it might well have extracted something from the witness which would make it admissible.

Finally, of course, we expected Dr Yutar to try to rehabilitate one of the chief investigating officers, his witness Detective Sergeant Dirker, who had been shown in evidence to be a blatant liar when he said that the engines of Bernstein's and Hepple's cars had been cold. Surely these points had to be reached. But Dr Yutar, as I have said before, got carried away, and lost sight of his case. It was blatantly so in Bernstein's case. Having exhausted his mysterious examination on Bernstein's letter to his sister, he sat down abruptly as though satisfied that his job was well done. None of the evidence against Bernstein had been so much as mentioned.

Bram Fischer's re-examination was brief. The evidence we had wished to lead about the medical, psychological and mental effect of 90-day detention had been excluded by the judge's ruling. But Yutar had opened this whole question for us by his cross-examination of Bernstein. We decided to re-examine on it. Bernstein told briefly of the effects which solitary confinement had had upon him. He spoke of irrational fears which he had developed over many minor matters; of an extremely severe, nervous tremor of the hands which he had developed, and which had stayed for a long time after the end of his solitary confinement; he found himself completely unable to concentrate, and when first released from solitary confinement and entitled to write letters or read, he had found it impossible to write more than two paragraphs at a time without taking a ten minute pause, walking around his cell to recover his concentration.

At the end of Bernstein's evidence we had no doubt whatsoever that the case against him had disappeared. If this case was to be judged on its merits, his acquittal was a virtual certainty. But he, and we, retained some reservations about the actual outcome, not because of the legal situation which was clear, but because we could not know what would be the effect of the political hysteria which surrounded this case.

At this point we re-introduced Govan Mbeki whose evidence we had deliberately held over, so that we could prepare him to deal with the derogatory political remarks which had been made throughout Sisulu's cross-examination, both by Dr Yutar and by the judge. Whether Yutar knew it or not, his evidence would go most completely and clearly to the heart of the case. For Mbeki, more than any of the accused, had been at the centre of Umkhonto we Sizwe and the National High Command during much of the period covered by the indictment. He had also been a key figure in the African National Congress during the whole period, and had more information about and could—if he chose—throw greater light on the inner workings of both organisations, their policies, their purposes and their decisions than any of the earlier witnesses. In a way he was ideally equipped to do so. He had a quiet, calm manner covering an iron-hard determination. He had the best education of all of them. He had won a bursary after completing his schooling, which had taken him on to University, where he obtained his Bachelor of Arts Degree, and subsequently also a Bachelor of Economics Degree, majoring in Education and Social Sciences.

At this time he was at 53 the oldest of the accused, grey haired and with a tremendous experience of politics and of social work behind him, mainly in the Eastern Cape and the Port Elizabeth district, but also in Natal and in the Transvaal, stretching right back to the early depression years of the 1930s, when some of the co-accused were new born babies.

We decided that Mbeki would deal with all the political allegations which had been made by judge and prosecutor in the earlier stages of the case. He would give as exhaustive an account of the state and condition of the African majority in South Africa as the judge would permit.

Bram Fischer led his evidence, starting as he did with all the witnesses—by getting him to recount his own life and experience, and how he had come to take part in politics.

Mbeki told how, as a child who lived with his family in Johannesburg during school holidays, he had seen mass police raids for passes or for illegal liquor, practically every weekend. 'Some police closed the entrances to the alleys behind the houses, while others combed the back yards, beating up almost indiscriminately the men who were found in the back yards, and arresting those who were unable to produce passes. Living in a state of fear like this resulted in one never having any rest at weekends, more particularly after a long week of hard work. It was during this time that I realised, as others had realised amongst the Africans, that if the African is to restore his respect at all and enjoy any measure at all of freedom, then he would have to struggle hard to see that the pass laws were repealed.'

He then dealt with his political history, which had led him to membership of the African National Congress and, through many years of active work, to positions on the national executive of the African National Congress, and finally to the office known as 'National Speaker' of the annual conference. This was before the ANC was banned. Dealing with the banning, he explained that the whole organisation had felt unable to accept a ban, and had decided to carry on illegally.

Fischer: Had you good reason for this?

Mbeki: Yes. The ANC after a number of years, a number of decades, has been the vanguard of the struggle of the African people for national liberation. And it was something that I just couldn't accept. At the time thousands of people looked up to the ANC to lead them in the struggle against the laws which were threatening practically every right that the African had enjoyed before. As I say, I just could not accept the fact that the government should destroy the ANC. I therefore continued to be a member of the ANC under conditions of illegality.

Bram led him to describe his views of the attitude of white South Africans to their African compatriots. Mbeki quoted the statement of the Prime Minister, General Hertzog, in Parliament in 1936, which said in justification of white supremacy 'self preservation is the first law of nature'. He then described the varying forms which this 'first law of nature' has taken in South Africa—how with different governments in differing international and national climates, the consistently white supremacist policy has been known as 'segregation', 'trusteeship', 'baasskaap', 'apartheid'—and now 'separate development'.

Fischer: Has the policy itself changed, apart from the name?

Mbeki: No. Apart from that, the leopard has not changed its colours at all. The position was very clearly expressed by the late Prime Minister, Mr JG Strydom, when he said 'die wit man moet altyd baas wees' (the white man must always remain the boss).

Has any one of the last three Prime Ministers including the present Prime Minister ever met any leading member of the African National Congress?

Not one of them.

Talking about methods of protest. Since this government has been in power what has happened to the right of Africans to hold meetings or demonstrations or processions?

In the reserves (i.e. African occupied rural areas), since the early 50s meetings have been banned except those that have the approval of the Native Commissioners. In an area like the Transkei, Proclamation 400[2], which was passed about four years ago to meet the specific situation, has become a permanent feature of the administration.

In the urban areas it is virtually impossible to find a place to hold political meetings of Africans chiefs or headmen who do not approve of government policies have either been deposed or banished. I think that since the Nationalist Party came into power in 1948, no less than 133 chiefs have been banished to different areas where their language is not spoken, or where they couldn't make a living.

And so his evidence moved from political oppression to social and economic conditions, to health and poverty, particularly in the

Transkei area which Mbeki knows best, to taxation and wages and standards of living. Then Mbeki came to deal with the pass laws.

Fischer: I think you worked for eight years in Port Elizabeth?

Mbeki: Yes, I worked for eight years in Port Elizabeth and during that time I was never able to live with my family.

Why was that?

I was not allowed to rent a house because I had not qualified to be permanently resident in Port Elizabeth because I had not worked for one employer continuously for a period of ten years.

So you were never able to bring your family to live with you?

For the eight years I was there I was never able to do so.

Your case is not unique?

No, it is not unique. Not at all, because lots of other men who live in single men's barracks lived there without their families.

This critique of white supremacy was delivered by Mbeki in a quiet, soft voice, slowly, with a slight smile on his face. His manner seemed to irritate Dr Yutar, and that irritation showed itself very clearly when he rose to cross-examine. Pointing a finger at Mbeki he said: 'I want to remind you that this court is trying issues of sabotage and other offences, and it is not a court of enquiry into grievances of the Bantu. So I hope you will forgive me if I don't even attempt to challenge the correctness of some of your complaints'.

For a moment we thought that Dr Yutar had finally decided wisely to steer away from the arena of politics and social conditions into which he had led this case, and to return to the facts. We were misled. It turned out to be only a piece of irritation, with no significance, because he began immediately to question Mbeki on politics. He used all the standard questions which are used by all the apologists of the South African way of life. Why, he asked, was it, if conditions in South Africa were as Mbeki described them, that a million foreign Africans flock to South Africa from territories outside in order to work here? How, he asked, could Mbeki have complained about hospital facilities for Africans, which were almost free. In one case—and Dr Yutar cited this with a tremendous dramatic effect—in the case of the St John's Ambulance Eye

Hospital in Johannesburg, there were facilities for optical treatment for Africans which were not even available for whites. This tub-thumping, inevitably, came round to the last stronghold of white South African racialism—ritual murder, a form of witchcraft practically unknown in South Africa, though cases do occur in neighbouring territories across the border.

Yutar: I think you will also agree that, despite the evil influences of the South African government, we have not got ritual murders in this country.

Mbeki: What would that explain in any case?

Do you know that the South African Medical Research officials, apart from helping the Bantu in this country, have sent some of their serums to help the non-Europeans in other countries? Do you know about that?

I have heard about that.

Do you know that if you present a balance sheet, you should present a true and fair account? Have you, when you fulminated against the South African government and its people, represented the other side—the benefits which the Bantu have in this country?

What benefits? What benefits have they been given? I am not aware of any benefits the Africans are getting from the South African government.

Not aware at all? And yet millions try to remain here in this country?

That does not explain it.

You have given your evidence here in a calm quiet voice. To make certain I was listening to the same person, I had your tape played back (the tape of a speech by Mbeki broadcast over the illegal Radio Liberation). You don't always speak that way do you? You can raise your voice?

If I must raise it, yes.

And you speak a little faster than you have spoken here?

If I must speak a little faster, I do.

And not so sanctimoniously as you have tried to speak here?

That is your opinion.

Dr Yutar read from an issue of the newspaper *Spark*— Mbeki had been the Port Elizabeth reporter. 'Beneath his quiet charm and gentle smile, a ruthless determination to reach his goal—the emancipation of his people.' Is that a fair description of you?

I think so.

A ruthless determination. And in some of your speeches you could be ruthless, not so? And in fact you were in speeches which you addressed when you attended meetings throughout the country. Do you deny that?

I spoke the truth and exposed what was the hardship of the Africans. If you call that ruthless—speaking the truth—then I was ruthless.

No. I am just trying to convey, not the subject matter, but the way in which you put it across. You were not the gentle, quiet, sanctimonious human being that you are now showing in the witness box.

Well, that would have to be the opinion of whoever was listening to me. Mbeki's testimony on the facts was that at all times he had been a member of the National Executive of the African National Congress, including the period after it was banned. He had remained one of its executive members on the day of his arrest. In that capacity he had been drawn into the activity of Umkhonto we Sizwe and on to its National High Command. For some years he had been a member of the Communist Party, in a group in Port Elizabeth.

Yutar: Which group?

Mbeki: The Communist Party group.

I know. Which group? I am asking you which group?

The Communist Party group, I say.

But how many groups were there in Port Elizabeth?

I don't know. I was only concerned with my group.

That is the group I want. What was its name?

The Communist Party group has no name. It is not like a football club.

And who were the members of your group?

That I am not prepared to say.

You are not prepared to tell us? Why not?

Why should I do so? I am not prepared to incriminate anybody.

Dr Yutar then put to Mbeki each of the four charges in the form of questions, asking at the end of each—'Did you do this?' and Mbeki answered 'Yes'.

'Well, Mbeki, I will put it to you in very brief form. Four charges against you, and you have replied to all of them. You have replied 'yes' to all of them. Can you tell his Lordship why you have pleaded not guilty to the four counts?'

Yes. I did not plead guilty to the four counts for the simple reason, firstly, that I should come and explain from here under oath some of the reasons that led me to join Umkhonto we Sizwe. And secondly, for the simple reason that to plead guilty would to my mind indicate a sense of moral guilt to it. I do not accept that there is any moral guilt attached to my actions.

Alright, let us forget about moral guilt. Having now admitted, after making some political speeches, that you were on the National High Command, have committed sabotage, that further acts of sabotage had been conspired to be committed, and you furthered the aim of communism, that you and your colleagues solicited money both here and abroad in order to advance these campaigns, do you now plead guilty?

I am not pleading guilty!

No, you don't. You don't even admit you are legally guilty?

I have explained my position.

A better prosecutor, or perhaps a bigger man would at that stage have left Mbeki. His 'guilt' was established beyond doubt. He could perhaps have concentrated on aspects of the State case which had been disputed by earlier defence witnesses. But not Dr Yutar. Just as he could not suffer defeat without visible indignation, so he could not take victory without bragging.

He turned to each of the thirteen documents which directly implicated Mbeki, and to the twenty four witnesses who testified against them. Citing each one in turn, he asked 'Are you suggesting that these documents are lying?' 'Are you suggesting that these witnesses are lying?'—for two and a half days, document after document, point after point. It could not affect the case. He did it partly because in the course of it, he and the Security Branch hoped to elicit information which they had not already got, and partly because this was Dr Yutar's way of celebrating his triumph over another accused clearly and unmistakably proven guilty. Mbeki consistently refused to answer anything that implicated anybody else or gave away any information about his organisation which was not already in evidence.

We had left Dennis Goldberg to the end, not because he was the least important of the accused, or because his evidence was unimportant, but because to some extent the case against him was separated from that of the rest of the accused.

Unlike the others he was from Cape Town. He had come to Johannesburg shortly before his arrest at Rivonia. When the arrest took place, he had not been together with the other accused, but was sitting by himself in the main house, while all the others were together in the thatched cottage in the grounds outside. It was alleged that he was a member of the National High Command of Umkhonto we Sizwe. But it was clear from the evidence that the case against most of the accused was that they had led and directed the organisation, while against Goldberg, the evidence indicated that he had not been involved at the same level, and not in the leadership. The evidence against him had been led thoroughly and at great length, and had occupied a large part of the time spent in court. It was essentially evidence against Goldberg; it was never shown by the State that the rest of the accused knew of, approved of, or directed what Goldberg was doing, although the State sought to hold them equally responsible for it.

The evidence showed that he had come to Johannesburg in a rather mysterious fashion, after disappearing without warning from his home in Cape Town. In Johannesburg he had assumed a false name, or rather a series of false names. It was hard at times for us to sort out which name Goldberg was using for what purpose, and he called himself sometimes Williams and at other times Barnard. In fact, by the time the case came to trial, he himself couldn't always recall which name had served in which transaction. The evidence showed that Williams had purchased a house in the district of Travellyn near Johannesburg. Some weeks after the Rivonia arrest, the owner of the house had come to find out why the rent had not been paid. He found a window broken and called the police. The police entered, and documents belonging to the African National Congress and Umkhonto we Sizwe had been found. It was shown that in the name of Barnard, Goldberg had lived for a short time in the cottage at Mountainview where Kathrada had also stayed, and which had been used later by Goldreich and Wolpe after their escape when Goldberg was already in prison. It was shown that he had purchased a Kombi van which was found at Rivonia and which was said to belong to Umkhonto. But the most damning part of the evidence against him was given by about twenty witnesses, factory owners, wholesale distributors and machinery merchants. They testified that Goldberg, using one or another of his pseudonyms, had made enquiries at foundries about the manufacture of castings, had obtained quotations for iron castings which were shown to match designs for a hand grenade which had been found amongst Arthur Goldreich's papers. Goldberg had also obtained quotations for wooden boxes which matched in shape and size a design for the making of land mines, also found in Goldreich's notes. There was a typewritten report found at Travellyn and allegedly written by Goldberg to the National High Command. It surveyed the problems to be met and methods to be adopted in setting up explosive devices—grenades, bombs, land mines. The report specified the equipment that would be required, and the type of place needed if such work was to be carried out secretly, under cover of some legitimate business, such as poultry farming. There were manufacturers to testify that the fans, the furnace, tools and other equipment required for such a factory had all been the subject of enquiries by Goldberg. Copies of many written quotations addressed to Mr Barnard or Mr Williams at addresses used by Goldberg had been produced in court. If Goldberg's stay in Johannesburg had been short it had certainly been extremely busy. He had assembled all the information but the evidence was that no orders at all had been placed for any of this equipment.

To handle this busy business operation, Goldberg had also hired post office boxes in different names and arranged certain cover addresses for himself at which to collect correspondence. The State alleged that the enquiries were made by him on behalf of

Umkhonto because the National High Command had already decided to go over to guerrilla warfare, and these were its first actions. The house at Travellyn which lay secluded, in large grounds, in a rural area close to the city, tallied exactly with the specification Goldberg had described in his report for a manufacturing centre. The State thus alleged that Goldberg had bought this property for the purpose of manufacturing grenades, land mines and other devices, as part of its guerrilla war preparations. This was one side of the case against Goldberg.

The other side related to some of his activities in Cape Town. The previous December a camp was organised outside Cape Town at a place called Mamre, at which, the State alleged, Goldberg had trained young men in the arts of guerrilla warfare. In addition, there was evidence that he had been found in suspicious circumstances together with people who were alleged to have committed sabotage or been convicted for it. On this basis the State made Goldberg a member of the National High Command and the Umkhonto we Sizwe. They also put him on the list as Accused No.3 in order of precedence, immediately behind Nelson Mandela and Walter Sisulu.

Most of the evidence was completely factual and most of it had gone unchallenged by us. It was clear to us that Goldberg had no chance of getting off, but was bound to be found guilty on all charges. However, when it came to interpreting his actions, Dennis and the other accused put forward a very different explanation from the one the State had given the court.

Dennis said he had come to Johannesburg with the intention of leaving the country. He had been so repeatedly persecuted by the police in Cape Town that he had reached the stage where he could take no more of it. He had come secretly to Johannesburg both to avoid a police trail and in the hope of finding someone there who would know the route by which he could cross the border illegally. While in Johannesburg, he had been persuaded to do a short job of investigation for Umkhonto for which he was peculiarly equipped, but which Umkhonto itself was finding itself unable to do. He was a qualified engineer, and the job of investigating and reporting in detail on the possibilities of manufacturing armaments on a large scale was essentially a job for someone with technical knowledge. Goldreich had been asked to investigate the feasibility of guerrilla warfare, and Goldreich had enrolled Goldberg as a technician to get all the technical information together. With this information, they would be able to give the High Command a true picture of what they would be up against if they decided to go ahead with guerrilla operations.

Had this been a legitimate enterprise, I would say that Goldberg approached his job with great professionalism, skill and energy. He seemed to have found out everything that needed to be found out; he considered all the angles of costs, of manpower, of materials, of transport, labour, promises, storage and everything else, in a way which I think did credit to his ability as an engineer. On the other hand, as it was not a legitimate enterprise, he left behind him a trail so wide, so fully documented, so completely covered in every detail by both his own and other peoples written records, including his own pocket book found on him at the time of his arrest that I must say that in my view his skill as an engineer was not matched by his ability as a conspirator. The evidence was overwhelming, and we had a great deal of difficulty in deciding whether Dennis should give evidence or not. If he was to give evidence it could only be in order to show that he was not a prime mover in Umkhonto or a member of the High Command, but rather a technician at one of the lower levels under the instructions of the High Command. He could possibly also show that the result of his manufacturing enquiries had convinced him, and would ultimately probably also have convinced the National High Command that they were nowhere near ready to dream of guerrilla operations on the scale visualised in Operation Mayibuye, which was far beyond their technical resources. The advantages seemed slight for the case as a whole, though it could well be very important to Dennis personally. Though it could not affect the verdict, it could well materially alter the gravity of his sentence.

Despite all this we were not sure that it was wise to put Dennis in the box. Both Yutar and his police aids seemed to have a particular hatred for Dennis. So far as the prosecutor was concerned his special antipathy had two roots. Yutar was Jewish and one of the few Jews in a senior position in the service of a somewhat anti-Semitically inclined bureaucracy. He lived surrounded by anti-Semitic policemen. And as a Jew, he seemed to regard it as a duty to prove to the government that there were 'good Jews', through his own enthusiastic persecution of these subversive Jews like Goldberg. But in part, his feelings were the direct consequence of Goldberg's manner. He has an irrepressible sense of humour, and a tendency to wise-cracking and smiling in the grimmest situations. This flippancy and irreverence irritated Yutar beyond words. So far as the police were concerned there were other reasons. Dennis had been the only one of the accused who had made any sort of statement when interrogated during his period of solitary confinement. I have little doubt that, when he did so, he had ulterior reasons. However, he agreed to make a statement, and he began the statement. The police were highly pleased with him; they decided to separate him from any other 'politicals' so that no possible counter-influence could be brought to bear on him by any means whatsoever. So they removed him from the Pretoria prison, where the rest of the Rivonia people were held, and took him to Vereeniging. It was a smaller prison, without 'politicals', and less restrictive. Goldberg himself was somewhat freer.

Having got this far, he strung the police along, making a long statement about matters of which they were aware and carefully avoiding giving them any new information whatsoever. Between sessions he was getting to know the ropes of the Vereeniging Jail, and planning an escape. One afternoon by ingenious means he unlocked the door of his cell, climbed over a roof, through a window, dropped to the ground and ran. He had something like a mile to cover before he reached the protection of a plantation. But in dropping off the roof he made the mistake of dropping past the window of another prisoner who gave the alarm, presumably hoping for some reward from the authorities. Before Goldberg reached the trees he was recaptured, badly kicked about by the warders who objected to racing about in the sun at a time when they normally had their afternoon siesta, and was then returned to Pretoria Jail. At this time, Goldberg stopped co-operating with the police and refused to make any further statements. This brought on him an undue measure of their enmity, for I think they sensed that they had been the victims of a confidence trick by Goldberg, which had led them to provide him with the opportunity for a nearly successful escape bid.

Goldberg's ability to joke and laugh while sitting in court listening to the evidence had been very noticeable. And this had done nothing to improve feelings between him and the police who found it infuriating that what they thought was shattering evidence would be met with a broad grin from Goldberg. Goldberg, we felt sure, would get a rough and fierce cross-examination, with little sympathy from Mr Justice de Wet, who had also betrayed signs of some antipathy to Dennis.

During Sisulu's evidence, for instance, de Wet had asked him with something of a sneer in his voice 'surely your *clever* colleagues like Goldberg would have told you that'. The sneering reference to Goldberg's 'cleverness' was not just anti-intellectualism. It was also, I think, a symptom of de Wet's arrogant belief that without white agitators to 'mislead' them, Nelson, Walter and the others would have remained the simple, happy, smiling golliwogs he believed 'good natives' to be. Dennis smiling and joking with the other accused in the dock must have given the judge the impression he was something of a 'smart alec', just the type of fellow a judge feels it is his duty to take down a peg or two.

From what we knew of Dennis, and his tendency to wise-crack, we thought that in the witness box he could well annoy the judge bring down some heavy retribution on his own head. Govan and Walter, we felt, had by this stage persuaded the judge as fully as anyone could that guerrilla warfare had not been decided upon, and that there had been agreement only to investigate the problems of guerrilla warfare fully and carefully. By his testimony, Dennis might well upset this position. There was, of course, also the special danger that came from being white in a country where the white population are extremely hostile to the accused, and almost unanimously supported the government. It was possible that Dennis might be found to be the 'mastermind' behind the guerrilla warfare business, in which case the judge might well sentence him to death without fear of creating a martyr or causing any such public upheaval as would be the case if this were to happen to any of the African accused.

We put all these fears to Dennis, but he was quite adamant. If he was going to be hanged he wanted to have his say first. He made only one proviso—that there should be no danger that his testimony might affect the others adversely. We felt, after thinking about it carefully, that in fact there was no such danger, and on 12 May we called him to the witness stand.

Vernon had read him the riot act beforehand, threatening fire and brimstone if he departed from the rules—no wise cracks and no clever answers. Just be quiet, respectful and to the point. Dennis followed this advice to better effect than we had imagined he could. He turned out to be an outstanding witness, articulate and clear.

After dealing briefly with his history and background, he gave evidence on the camp at Mamre. His evidence was that this multiracial camp of young people was organised by various political movements in Cape Town. He was asked to take charge. The camp had been quite patently political in its purposes, the intention being to train up-and-coming young people in politics as well as in such technical matters as operating a duplicating machine or a loud-speaker system—knowledge that would be useful in the course of their political work. As far as training in guerrilla warfare was concerned, Goldberg gave complete denial. He would never, he said, attempt to do any such thing in an open camp which he knew would be subject to police surveillance, and where there was a large group of young people, none of whom were known to him, and whose reliability or ability to keep secrets he could not trust. To do any guerrilla training or propaganda in such circumstances, he said, would have been suicidal. Everything about the camp had happened more or less as testified to by Cyril Davids except that Davids had added that at each lecture Goldberg had given the campers the gratuitous advice that this lecture was for the purpose of training in guerrilla warfare.

Goldberg recounted the persecution he had been subjected to in Cape Town. He said the Special Branch of the police had followed him wherever he went, driving up and down past his house, hooting and shouting late at night. They had arranged with a neighbour of his to keep a list of all people who visited him, and would afterwards interrogate these people. In December 1962 a bomb had exploded in his garden one evening, and he was fairly certain it had been put there by the Security Police. When he said this to them, they did not deny it, but only argued they could not have been responsible as they did not know how to make such a bomb! About that time he began to receive anonymous telephone calls and an obscene slogan was painted on his car one night. In May 1963 he had left Cape Town for Johannesburg intending to get assistance to leave the country secretly. As I have explained before, he had been asked to undertake the investigation of armaments production which featured so strongly in the case.

To our surprise, cross-examination of Goldberg was undertaken not by Dr Yutar, but by his assistant Mr AB Krog. I should explain that the prosecution team in the case consisted of four people—Dr Yutar, Mr Krog, Mr Theron and another. Yutar had in fact monopolised the entire public side of the case. The others had not been given any public part at all, but had operated throughout almost as stenographers, taking notes and passing up books and documents to Yutar. But Yutar, the senior, was not going to give them any chance to share the limelight of what was probably the most publicised case in South African legal history. At this stage, however, Krog got his chance to shine. He had the reputation of being an extremely good cross-examiner, and this more than worried us. We had expected Yutar to be characteristically led astray by his almost pathological dislike of Goldberg, but were afraid that Mr Krog might do a cold job of destruction. We need not have feared. He had sat for several months watching Yutar in action, and I suppose had decided that Yutar's acclamation from the police and government officials proved that the Yutar method was a good one. Krog abandoned his usual sound and straightforward cross-examination and resorted to Yutar's.

What in Yutar was dramatic if irritating, in Krog was merely pathetic. He lacked that righteous indignation which enabled Yutar to sneer so effectively and rant so convincingly, and his whole act was quite out of character. He asked a few questions in an attempt to smear Goldberg with communism. Then he asked theatrically: 'You have heard defence counsel in this case speak of evidence being *tailored* to suit requirements. Do you not feel a little overdressed at the moment?'.

This sneer was the best that Krog could do on this level. He embarked on a strange cross-examination, designed to show that Dennis could not possibly be believed, and that he was naturally deceptive and untruthful. To establish this, he harped over and over again on the admitted fact that Dennis had used a false name when making enquiries about grenades and parts for land mines. He seemed to think that a truthful witness would go to a foundry manager, ask for 240,000 castings, and say in the interests of truth: 'My name is X. These castings are required for a revolution, and will be parts of a hand grenade'. Since Dennis had not done this, Krog argued that he was patently untruthful, and nothing he said could be believed.

It was a tedious cross-examination, and in my view utterly pointless. Dennis remained unruffled to the end. Only once did he come back with a wise-crack, and then Vemon looked up so fiercely, with that cold terrifying stare which Vernon can manage when he is angry, that Dennis almost blanched in the witness box. After that he never put a foot wrong. By the time Krog sat down, Dennis had succeeded in putting a completely hopeless case into as reasonable a light as was possible. And that was all. He could not possibly hope to avoid conviction on the story he had told.

I suppose special considerations apply in cases of this sort. The accused had dedicated his life to a cause, and now, his behaviour and conduct at what was a climax in that life cannot be viewed as it would be in a normal court case. To some extent the way the accused behaves, the things he says and does in the witness box, are the summation and partly the vindication of his life. Strictly speaking, they are not part of the orthodox legal process of a normal criminal court. So it was with Dennis, perhaps even more markedly than with the others, because the case against him was so heavily weighted and his evidence of so little effect in contradicting any part of it, or presenting it in any new light.

By the time his testimony was over, the defence case was almost complete. There remained only Elias Motsoaledi and Andrew Mhlangeni. We had decided that neither of them should enter the witness box, but they should make short statements from the dock. There were several reasons for this. They had not been at the level of leadership in Umkhonto we Sizwe, and had they gone into the witness box, they might well have distorted the picture of Umkhonto, its aims and its relations with the ANC which had been so well stated by Mbeki and Sisulu. Nor did we feel that their testimony could improve things for either of them. The evidence showed that they had been at very much a rank and file level, with far less responsibility than the members of the National High Command. The indictment in fact did not even allege that they were members of the National High Command. In the witness box, they might well be trapped into admissions which could remove them from this lower level of responsibility and in the view of the judge put them fairly and squarely in the same category as the members of the National High Command.

In their statements they were both going to admit to guilt, as minor participants in the overall activities of Umkhonto.

I think Elias Motsoaledi's statement moved me more than anything said by any of the other accused. We had all grown to like and respect him. He was always cheerful, always smiling. The only exception to this was when his wife Caroline had been arrested in court while listening to the case where her husband was on trial for his life, and taken off to solitary confinement for interrogation. For a short while he was angry and bitter, but it wasn't long before he recovered to announce proudly that his Caroline would never agree to be a State witness against anybody—even if she knew anything. How right he was. His statement was short and to the point.

'My Lord, I am 39 years old. I was a clerk and canvasser. I am a married man and have seven small children. I joined the African National Congress in 1948 and remained a member until 1954 when I was banned from membership of this organisation. Although I am a listed communist I did not join the Communist Party after it had been banned, but I do admit that I was on the technical committee of the Johannesburg Region and was recruited to Umkhonto we Sizwe during the end of 1962.'

He went on to tell the court how he had grown up in the Sekukuniland Reserve, one of a family who lived on four acres of ground. Across the border thousands of acres of land belonging to white farmers lay unused. He came to Johannesburg to earn a living, started work in a boot factory at twenty-four shillings a week, took part in a strike for better wages and was sacked. From this he had come to the trade union movement, and from the trade union movement to a realisation of the need for political change. He joined the ANC and took part in its activities for many years. Then he was banned from membership by order of the Minister of the Interior. Later the ANC itself was outlawed; meetings were stopped and newspapers were closed down.

'There was nothing left for us to do except suffer. Then Umkhonto we Sizwe was formed. When I was asked to join it I did so. There was nothing else I could do. Any African who thought the way I did about my own life and the lives of my people would have done the same. There was nothing else.'

He dealt with the evidence against him, describing much of it as untrue, particularly that given by Abel Mthembu. He admitted participating in the transportation of recruits out of the country for military training, and that he had taken reports to the technical committee of Umkhonto on the practical carrying out of acts of sabotage by Umkhonto units. While admitting so much, Elias denied almost all the evidence which was given by people who had been 90-day detainees. Their evidence, he believed, was manufactured to suit the requirements of the police. He finished up by saying: 'I did what I did because I wanted to help my people in their struggle for equal rights. When I was asked to join Umkhonto we Sizwe it was at the time when it was clear to me that all our years of peaceful struggle had been of no use. The government would not let us fight peacefully anymore and blocked all our legal acts by making them illegal. I thought a great deal about the matter. I could see no other way open to me. What I did brought me no personal gain. What I did, I did for my people and because I thought it was the only way left for me to help my people. That is all I have to say.'

He put down the notes from which he was reading and looking at the judge he said: 'In addition, my Lord, I want to say that I was assaulted by the Security Branch in an attempt to make me make a statement'. He said that he was prepared to give evidence under oath about this if there was any enquiry into it. The assault had not taken place at the Pretoria Jail but at Witsdrag Police Station where he had been kept in solitary confinement. And even then, he said, the police were not satisfied. 'More than three months ago they arrested my wife and detained her under 90-days. And when she finished her 90-days, she was re-arrested again. As it is she is still in jail. I consider this disgraceful on the part of the police, my Lord, that a woman with seven children should be punished because of offences committed by me. That is all I have to say.'

He sat down. The effect in the court was considerable. Andrew Mlangeni followed. He too gave a short account of his own life and activity and how he joined the African National Congress in 1954. He said that in October 1961 he had left Johannesburg for family reasons, and had not returned until February 1963. Thus the evidence given by several State witnesses about his activities in Johannesburg in 1962 was completely false, and he denied it entirely. He said that in February 1963, when he returned to Johannesburg, he had heard of Umkhonto we Sizwe and had been asked to join it. He had agreed and had become a messenger for one of the Umkhonto leaders, Mr Joe Modise, who was then living in hiding underground. Joe Modise was, by that time, a representative of the African National Congress abroad. Mlangeni said that as part of this work he had taken some messages from Johannesburg to the Durban Regional Command. He contacted the Durban Regional Command through Bruno Mtolo whom he had previously known as a trade unionist, and delivered his message of instruction for certain young men to be sent to Johannesburg as the first leg of a trip for training abroad. He told the Natal Regional Command how the men were to travel to Johannesburg, and how they would be met in Johannesburg. He returned from this trip bringing with him a car which the Natal Region felt was 'too hot' for them—a car found at Rivonia on the day of the raid. The police had become suspicious of Mlangeni and visited and searched his house several times.

Mlangeni decided to protect himself against possible arrest, especially since he had to undertake a further trip to Durban for Umkhonto. A friend of his in one of the lesser separatist churches had issued him a certificate showing him as a Minister of the Church. Thereafter he had worn a priest's collar and gone around disguised as a Minister of the Church. 'The court can now see that some of the evidence given against me is true and some false. I have chosen not to give evidence, my Lord, because first of all I do not want to be cross-examined about people I have worked with and places I have visited in case I might give these people away. Also, my Lord, I have frankly admitted that I have assisted Umkhonto we Sizwe. I want to say that I joined the ANC in 1954. I did it because I want to work for my people. I did this because of the treatment my people have received from the rulers of this country. In the ANC I found a political home where I was free to talk against the government.

'South Africa, my Lord, is a very rich country, the resources could be exploited for the benefit of all the people who live in it. This government and the previous governments have exploited not the earth but the people of various racial groups whose colour is not white. But the government daily makes suppressive laws in its white Parliament, which laws are aimed at suppressing the political aspirations of the majority of the people who have no say. I know that you, my Lord, have to administer the law, but when you do so, I ask you to remember what we, the Africans and non-white people, have had to suffer. That is all I have to say except to add that what I did was not for myself but for my people.'

Mlangeni too, having finished his prepared statement, then went on to describe an assault which had taken place on him at the Central Barracks, Pretoria, which he said he believed to be the headquarters of the Security Police. He described being tortured with machines which gave severe electric shocks. He recalled that the Minister of Justice had recently told Parliament that such electric machines were not used by the police. 'But I don't blame the Minister, my Lord. He probably does not know that this is happening in some of the police stations. This is my personal experience that this has happened to me. It is absolutely not hearsay.' On that note he sat down.

This ended the evidence of the accused. We called only two other witnesses whose testimony was of little significance. They were to testify to the fact that Mlangeni had been out of the country from October 1961 to February 1963—the period during which several of the State witnesses claimed to have seen him involved in aspects of recruiting and transporting military trainees. These witnesses were fabricating, but in the light of Mlangeni's own admissions, their lies didn't really alter the case against him, so we had almost decided to let the matter rest. But Andrew was very aggrieved about this false evidence and he asked us to call two of his neighbours to testify that he had not been in Johannesburg during the whole of that time. He gave us the names of four people to interview.

We ran into real trouble. They were frightened to talk to us. Such was the atmosphere in South Africa at that time that they feared that if they gave evidence for the defence they would be victimised by the police, perhaps detained without charge in solitary confinement, and we could do nothing about it. But Andrew still wanted these witnesses called and, finally, on his suggestion, we asked Winnie Mandela—Nelson's wife—to try to persuade them. Eventually three agreed to give evidence. But on the vital day, the courage of one failed, and only two arrived. They were both obviously unhappy. We decided to see Yutar and try to get an undertaking that the police would not persecute these witnesses. After all, they had committed no crime. Their evidence was completely unconnected with politics, being merely that at a certain time their neighbour, Andrew Mlangeni, was not in Johannesburg. At this time Yutar was ill and Mr Abe Krog, deputising for him, immediately gave us such an undertaking. But the police investigating officer, Warrant Officer Dirker, would not go along with it. We said that, in that event, we would explain to the court that our witnesses were afraid to come because they had no guarantee against police reprisals. It was only under this pressure that Dirker reluctantly promised to leave our witnesses alone and, with equal reluctance, our witnesses who would have preferred to have the undertaking in writing, gave their evidence. That closed the defence case. There was nothing left now but our closing address, counsel's argument and judgement.

8 Final Speeches and Verdict

I have throughout written of this case as though the courtroom was sealed off from the world, a vacuum into which nothing happening in the world or the country outside penetrated. This is the only way I have been able to describe coherently what happened in court. But, in fact, the heart and kernel of this case was not in this courtroom, but in the world outside. When the case opened in a dreadful atmosphere of hostility towards the accused, in a country whipped up into hysteria against the accused, their prospects were ominous and heavy with danger. Gradually as the case went on the atmosphere changed. Partly, no doubt, this was due to the bearing and behaviour of the accused themselves. But partly it was due to factors outside the courtroom. The United Nations had taken a unanimous vote with only South Africa's vote cast against, calling for the immediate release of the Rivonia accused. This had been followed up by a succession of resolutions of protest, of demonstrations against the trial and in favour of the accused, of acts of solidarity with the accused. These many actions not only heartened the Rivonia trialists throughout the case and sustained their morale. They also had a considerable effect in conditioning the atmosphere in court.

Here were ten men accused of plotting civil war and military overthrow. And yet, though the offence was generally admitted by them, we had such strange happenings as the award to them by the

World Peace Council of a medal for meritorious service to the cause of peace. Midway in the trial, Nelson Mandela was elected President of the Students Union of London University, an institution he had never attended, by people he did not know. And so, day by day, the volume of pressure in the outside world accumulated to influence the turn in favour of the accused. They were all deeply conscious of it, their morale sustained perhaps more by what was happening outside the court than what was happening inside it. And we likewise felt that while a judgement of guilty in most cases was a foregone conclusion—there was only doubt in the case of Bernstein, Kathrada and Mhlaba—the sentence would be decided as much by outside events as by those inside.

The case for the defence might appear superficially thin, unsustained as it was by any outside witnesses. But we were beginning to feel as we certainly had not at the beginning—that there was considerable hope that no death sentences would be imposed. By the time the court adjourned, we felt that the longer the case had gone on the better the chances of our clients became, and the greater the hope of their coming through alive to see another round in South Africa's history of change and development.

We had only one more thing to do, and that was to prepare evidence in mitigation of sentence. There was doubt whether such evidence should be led at all. But finally, somewhat reluctantly, the accused agreed that it should be and the question was who would give it. We cast many ideas around and finally we decided to ask Alan Paton. He had never at any time been a supporter of violence as a means of political struggle. A devout Christian, and an equally devout believer in non-violence, Paton had in fact at times crossed swords with some of the accused on this very question of violence. His views were well known and basically, I suppose, very much at cross purposes with the accused in their attitude to violence, to Umkhonto, and almost to everything they were doing. Nevertheless, we decided to ask him because his integrity and honesty could not be doubted. His reputation as a reformer and liberal thinker was high both inside and outside the country; he could not be accused of being a communist, concealed or otherwise. He was a devout Christian of high principles and conviction, and a leader of the Liberal Party. We approached him. It was not an easy thing to ask anybody to do in that atmosphere in South Africa. But he put only one simple question to us—'Are their lives in danger?'.

We said 'yes'.

'In that case' he said, 'there is no question at all. I will give evidence if I am called'.

He was one of a breed that was in danger of becoming extinct in South Africa—the liberal of principle and courage, who is not afraid to raise his voice against the stream. How few there were we had discovered from all our contacts with the public during the case, when we found so many terrified, so many backing away from their former stands and ideas, swaying before the winds of reaction which tore through South Africa at the time of the Rivonia trial.

Before we would need Paton there was only argument and judgement. On the 20th May, Yutar began his final speech, the purpose of which is supposed to be to assist the court in summing up and assessing the evidence. Counsel delivering the speech normally evaluates all the evidence, relates each piece of evidence to the charges specified in the indictment, and attempts to present the entire case to the court coherently, clearly and without verbal frills. In general it is unheard of in South African courts that comment, wit, or sarcasm at the expense of the accused should form any part of this speech. At its best, the closing address to a judge sitting by himself should be a sound legal analysis of the evidence, and laws bearing on the charge.

But from Yutar we were to learn a new method of presenting argument. He and his team arrived in court, staggering under a load of thick blue volumes, which were carefully arrayed on the State tables. There were four volumes to a set, all newly bound, crisp and with neat gold lettering on the covers to indicate the contents. About five of these sets were handed to the press. We sat waiting for our turn to come. When it did, Yutar in an almost predictable piece of pettiness, handed us one copy, unbound, without covers, to do duty for our whole team, consisting of four counsel and myself. To the bitter end, it seemed, he was playing this great drama in the career of Percy Yutar, as though the press benches ranked more importantly than judge or defence. In the few minutes before the judge appeared, we skimmed through the document. It was a quicker task than might have been guessed from the size of the volumes, for in fact the volumes did not contain any argument as we understood it but rather a summary of the evidence in some sort of sequence. No effort had been made to analyse the evidence, to point out discrepancies, to suggest why one witness should be believed and another disbelieved when they contradicted each other, or to show where witnesses corroborated each other and where there were discrepancies.

I said what I thought about it in a loud voice, loud enough for Yutar to hear—'This is not a closing address. It's just a garbled summary'.

Yutar had long since stopped speaking to me, so he didn't reply. But when the judge was seated, he handed up four volumes, with the explanation—'My Lord, to assist the court I have had my address typed out and bound up and I beg leave to hand it in, and crave (Dr Yutar was always craving) that it may be of some assistance to your Lordship'.

He proceeded to read three of the volumes from cover to cover. One volume for some obscure reason he ignored completely, possibly because it had been prepared by his assistant, Mr Vorster, in Afrikaans, which Yutar spoke rather poorly.

As he read Yutar interspersed little comments and asides. Bram, summing up Yutar's handling of the case said 'His evidence in chief consisted largely of reading of documents, either solo or to witnesses. His cross-examination consisted of reading the document to the judge'.

Introducing the four volumes, Dr Yutar said; 'Although the State has charged the accused of sabotage, this is nevertheless a case of High Treason par excellence. It is a classic case of the intended overthrow of the government by force and violence with military and other assistance of foreign countries. The acts have been corroborated by the accused themselves. Nevertheless, for reasons which I need not here detail, the State has preferred to charge the accused with sabotage'.

The reasons which he did not choose to detail were very apparent. In a charge of treason, the law requires a preparatory examination which would have apprised the accused of the evidence against them and enabled them to prepare their defence properly. It also requires that every overt act is attested to by two witnesses. It would also have placed an onus on the State to prove the case beyond a reasonable doubt, whereas a sabotage charge leaves much of the onus on the defence.

'The deceit of the accused is amazing', he said. 'Although they represented scarcely more than 1% of the African population (a reference to the evidence that the ANC had 100,000 members), they took it upon themselves to tell the world that the Africans in South Africa are suppressed, oppressed and depressed. It is tragic to think that the accused, who between themselves did not have the courage to commit a single act of sabotage should nevertheless have incited their followers to acts of sabotage and guerrilla warfare, armed insurrection and open rebellion and ultimately civil war.'

In this flourish Dr Yutar apparently got so carried away that he forgot the evidence which he himself had led to show that Raymond and Govan had both personally participated in acts of sabotage.

'Having done that, they would then from the safety and comfort of their hideouts at Rivonia, Travellyn and Mountainview, have surveyed the savage scene of slaughter on both sides of the opposing forces.'

This ranting was an outrage both against the traditions of the South African courts and against the evidence. Not one single tittle of evidence laid any foundation for such a statement. On the contrary, there was Mandela's uncontradicted statement that he himself had undergone military training because if there was to be guerrilla warfare he wanted to be able to stand and fight with his people and share the hazards of war with them.

Once again Yutar's passionate hatred for Goldberg expressed itself: 'An aggravating thought is that a man like Goldberg, quite unnecessarily having created the Frankenstein monster and put it into action, would have gone abroad to join the band of brothers; this included that great and glorious guerrilla, Goldreich, the heroic Harmel and Hodgson, Slovo the soldier and the wise

Wolpe. From a safe distance of 6,000 miles or more they would behold the tragic works of their handiwork.'

Justice de Wet who had listened patiently to so much irrelevance and nonsense continued to listen without interruption to this, though why he should have done so, I do not know. Yutar was obviously trying to prejudice the judge's mind against the accused by oratory, not by evidence, by rhetoric, not by reference to the law. The judge, in permitting him to do so, showed himself to be less than totally objective and impartial.

'It is a great pity', said Yutar, 'that the rank and file of the Bantu in this country who are peaceful, law abiding, faithful and loyal should have been duped by false promises of free bread, free transport, free medical services and free holidays—they forgot to mention free holidays'.

This seemingly nonsensical claim based itself on a single leaflet issued by the Communist Party many years before the Rivonia trial ever started, which quoted the programme just adopted by the Soviet Communist Party in which they visualised such benefits as these for the Soviet people when communist society was completed.

In the midst of this rhetoric Dr Yutar reached a new height of hysteria, and proclaimed: 'The day of the mass uprising in connection with the launching of guerrilla warfare was to have been the 26th May 1963'. This mystified us. The accused had been arrested six weeks after this date. The evidence showed that the only armaments they possessed were an air rifle with which Mandela had once tried target practice. The suggestion that this date had been selected for an armed uprising had never previously been raised in this case. It was an innovation sprung at this very moment. Yutar built it up, repeating time after time that guerrilla warfare had not only been agreed on in principle but the date for it had actually been set.

For once Mr Justice de Wet intervened: 'Dr Yutar,' he said, 'you do concede that you failed to prove guerrilla warfare was ever decided upon, do you not?'.

Yutar looked stunned. It was precisely what he did not concede. He was proceeding on the wild assumption that he had proved absolutely that guerrilla warfare had been decided upon, and somewhere in his own imagination, had decided that it had not only been decided upon, but in fact had started on a particular date six weeks before the accused were arrested. We, on the other hand, realised that this remark of the judge fatally destroyed the main assumption of the State case. Guerrilla warfare had not been embarked upon; it had not been decided on.

Yutar stuttered, and stammered a submission that preparations were being made.

Mr Justice de Wet said testily: 'Yes, I know that. The defence concedes that. What they say is that preparations were made in case one day they found it necessary to resort to guerrilla warfare. But they say that prior to their arrest they never considered it necessary, and took no decision to engage in guerrilla warfare. I take it that you have no evidence contradicting that, and that you accept it?'.

Yutar for once was taken aback, and all he could do was stammer 'As your Lordship pleases,' which both de Wet and the defence construed as an admission that he conceded. But he did not, because he immediately went on arguing as though nothing at all had been said by the judge. He developed his argument by quoting from a document, found at Rivonia—'National acts of sabotage . . . appear to spring from mass action, although they are carefully planned'. With voice rising to crescendo he said 'This shows how the conspirators were deluding people. Kathrada has said that the State should be ashamed to mention Sharpeville and Langa. However, here in this document is evidence to show that what was supposed to be spontaneous uprisings were in fact engineered by the ANC and the Communist Party. For this reason I, on behalf of the State, am not ashamed to speak of these events.'

And so in his final hysteria he fastened responsibility for the shooting at Sharpeville, which a government appointed commission had found to result from policemen being unnecessarily fast on the trigger—on the African National Congress.

It is impossible to summarise this speech adequately. At one stage, turning to evidence against each individual accused, he began to read a summary of Mandela's statement. Mr Justice de

Wet stopped him. As he pointed out, Nelson had admitted his guilt on all charges, so Yutar's summary merely confused the issue. Yutar turned to Sisulu's evidence.

The same remarks applied to Sisulu, said the judge. Yutar was thwarted once more. But nothing could stop him when he came to Goldberg. The evidence against Goldberg was so overwhelming, he said, that he did not know where to start. There was a loud aside from Berrange: 'Well why try?'.

Yutar began to read the evidence of the forty-three witnesses who had mentioned Dennis. The judge sat through some hours of this, which appeared to encourage Yutar to new excess. 'My Lord, for the edification of your Lordship,' he said, 'I have decided to nominate a shadow cabinet for the provisional revolutionary government'.

We waited for de Wet to cut him off immediately, but he made no move. The function of the prosecution, we thought, is to try people, not to edify judges. But Yutar, encouraged by de Wet's silence, went on: 'Because Goldberg was alleged to have run a camp for spiritual and health purposes, I name him Minister of Health. But he will have to learn the truth first, which he will find difficult to do if one takes into consideration the lies he told in this court.'

The police surrounding Dr Yutar tittered appreciatively. Yutar smiled immodestly, and went on with renewed enthusiasm on his cabinet building. 'There is evidence before the court that despite appearances of solidarity all is not well in the relations between Africans and Indians. It is clear therefore that there will still have to be a Ministry of Indian Affairs in the proposed revolutionary State—who but Kathrada could be Minister of this department?' As 'Minister of European Affairs' he proceeded to nominate Govan Mbeki. I don't think he realised that in his self-satisfaction over this travesty, he showed a twisted understanding that the Ministry of Non-European Affairs which has always existed in South Africa is in fact a sinister office *against* the non-white people, much as he implied Mbeki's 'Ministry of European Affairs' would be against the whites. Bernstein, he said, despite all his restrictions, house arrest and so on, had found time to visit

Rivonia 'to give the men there his views on political matters'. Bernstein was the man consulted on political questions. He had said himself that he wrote extensively for political and other journals. He was regarded as a propaganda expert and there is no doubt that in the revolutionary government he would be named Minister of Information.

From this he went on to an indignant denial of Bernstein's allegation that the State coached witnesses. 'I deny, my Lord, that the State ever coached witnesses. I am a servant of the State, but I say now and I am prepared to say it under oath I have not been told what to say. In any case, I am an officer of this court. And I know your Lordship would not countenance from me or any of my colleagues any conduct which fell short of that expected from an officer of this court. I am disgusted and revolted by the allegations which the defence have made about the conduct of the State.'

And with this off his chest, Yutar proceeded to further improper conduct by naming Raymond Mhlaba as 'Minister of Foreign Affairs', by reason of his overseas trip which he refused to talk about. 'Elias Motsoaledi has told the court that he had to live on four acres of land while thousands of acres of white-owned land lay fallow. I accordingly name him Minister of Lands so that he can correct these disparities'.

Vernon was livid with Yutar, and there was an angry passage between them in which Vernon called Yutar a 'little man'. Yutar, with his incredible smugness of mind, seemed to think that Vernon was talking about his height off the ground. But Yutar was like a man drunk with his own cleverness. He went on cabinet building. Andrew Mlangeni—Minister of Transport. Jack Hodgson—Minister of Munitions. Duma Nokwe—Minister of Justice. 'From the information that Bob Hepple has given to the police I would like to make him Minister of Information. But because Bernstein already occupies that post I name Bob Hepple Minister of Informers instead.' When he came to Joe Slovo, one of the conspirators, Yutar really did himself proud: 'I wish I had the pen of a Pope and a Dryden to describe the infamy of this man who, with Goldreich, was one of the worst traitors to infest South African soil'. Slovo was named Minister of Munitions; Walter Sisulu,

Minister of Interior; Nelson Mandela, Defence and Deputy Prime Minister. Finally, having wound his way through this travesty of legal argument, he named Albert Luthuli as the President of the revolutionary government. Let it be remembered that although attempts had been made by the prosecution to implicate Luthuli in this case and to discredit him, he was not alleged in the indictment to be an accomplice, agent or a co-conspirator. Yet here he was being tried in absentia, with Justice de Wet sitting passive as sentence was passed on him by Dr Yutar.

This cabinet-making appealed to the sense of humour of the policemen who surrounded him, as did Yutar's final flourish on the subject. 'I have not been able to find portfolios for all the men involved. But if they run true to form, then if and when they come to power, there will be a lot of internal strife resulting in many casualties, and they will be able to fill the vacancies which will inevitably arise.

'At the outset of my argument I said that this case was one of High Treason par excellence. Because of the people who have lost their lives and suffered injury as a result of the activities of the accused it is apparent that this case is now one of murder and attempted murder as well.'

This was outrageous. There had been evidence led by one or two policemen that in certain petrol bomb attacks on occupied houses, some people had been injured and two had died. The evidence was inadmissible as it was hearsay. There was no allegation charging us with responsibility for any such deaths, and we had therefore not made any attempt to deal with this evidence. Yet Dr Yutar took full advantage of the free hand given by him by the judge to make allegations of murder now, at the close of the case.

Rising to the heights of oratory, with finger pointed dramatically in the air, he concluded: 'I make bold to say that every particular allegation in the indictment has been proved. There is not a single material allegation in the opening address that has not been proved'. Cynical laughter from the defence counsel's benches did nothing to daunt this little man who ended the travesty with a servile smile at the police sitting in packed ranks around him—'On the evidence it is clear that without the action of the police, South

Africa might have found itself in a bloody civil war. The public owes a great debt of gratitude to the police.' One felt that this was the signal for an outburst of public applause.

Customarily the defence reply answers the allegations of the State and deals in some detail with the prosecution's arguments. In this case there had not been an argument, only a summary and a lot of rhetoric. We decided we would not deal with Yutar's argument at all, nor would we follow a similar rhetorical approach. We would argue the case on the issues which had been formulated right at the beginning in Bram Fischer's opening address.

Arthur Chaskalson started off. Suddenly the court was no longer a forum for third rate amateur theatrics, but became a court of law. Arthur's task was to analyse the evidence, all given by police officers, about the 193 acts of sabotage alleged. 'May it please your Lordship,' said Arthur in his serious, clear, unemotional way, 'the State has told your Lordship that this trial is a trial for murder and attempted murder. The indictment alleges military training and sabotage. But despite this the accused have been subjected to cross-examination on murder, incitement to murder and attempted murder. The evidence presented to the court on these claims is all hearsay, and the existence of these claims has never been substantiated in this court. There has been a mass of inadmissible evidence which bears no relation to the indictment. The defence will not even deal with these allegations as they have nothing to do with the case. The defence concedes that Umkhonto we Sizwe recruited men for military training and that members of Umkhonto committed acts of sabotage. The defence denies, however, that they committed all the acts of sabotage with which they are charged. I will demonstrate to your Lordship, from the evidence, that there were other organisations in South Africa committing acts of sabotage at the time in question.'

Mr Justice de Wet seemed to warm to a proper legal argument. 'Mr Chaskalson,' he said, 'there is no need to pursue your argument on this aspect. I accept that there were other organisations committing sabotage at the same time, and choosing the same targets.'

In one stroke, a substantial part of the State case fell away. The State had produced evidence of every act of sabotage which had been committed in South Africa during the previous three years. Some, such as the removal of large sections of railway line on a busy passenger route, had resulted in serious danger to human life on a wide scale. Though both the accused and witnesses for the State such as Mtolo and Mthembu had testified that Umkhonto had at all times continued its sabotage to property and government installations in such a way that there was no danger to human life, these acts were charged. The reasoning of the State was that, since Umkhonto had been organising sabotage, any act of sabotage which had happened in this time must be the responsibility of Umkhonto and the accused. Sabotage merely had to be proved to have happened for the court to infer that Umkhonto was responsible.

Arthur Chaskalson said 'Even if the State had succeeded in proving that certain acts of sabotage were committed by Umkhonto, that is not the end of the matter. The accused who the State said were the leaders of Umkhonto are only responsible for the acts falling within the designated policy of Umkhonto. The evidence is that Umkhonto's policy was only to commit acts of sabotage against government and public property which it labelled symbols of apartheid. The evidence further shows and stands corroborated by the evidence of the State witnesses Mtolo and Mthembu that the clear policy of Umkhonto was sabotage without loss of life. The authorities show that if one member of the conspiracy goes out and commits an act falling outside the ambit of the conspiracy, his fellow conspirators are not legally liable for such acts. On this basis the accused, who adhered at all times to a policy designed to avoid danger to life, were not responsible for acts of sabotage committed even by proved members of Umkhonto against their instructions. The accused accordingly disclaim all responsibility of bomb attacks on private houses'.

Piece by piece Arthur launched a legal attack which destroyed most of the State evidence with regard to actual acts of sabotage. By the time it was finished it seemed that, of the 193 acts of sabotage which the State had proved to have happened, only about a dozen had been proved legally against Umkhonto we Sizwe and its High Command. Of these dozen acts, not one involved any danger whatsoever to human life. For the first time the argument began to resemble a legal struggle. When Arthur concluded his part of the argument, it was Bram Fischer's turn.

Bram, as senior counsel, had taken on the two most serious aspects of the case for argument. First, that though guerrilla warfare had at all times been in consideration as a possibility for the future, it had never in fact been decided upon by Umkhonto we Sizwe or the African National Congress. And second, that though the African National Congress had been aware of and some of its sections had even co-operated in the formation and the workings of Umkhonto we Sizwe, the two organisations were in fact separate, each independently controlled. Bram had prepared this ground with painstaking attention to detail and a thoroughness which had made him one of the country's foremost lawyers. The first point was obviously critical in determining sentence on the accused; the second was critical for the future of every member of the African National Congress who might ever be charged by the police.

On the determination of this point would hinge the question of whether an accused was charged merely with membership of an unlawful organisation, carrying a maximum penalty of ten years, or with treason or sabotage, carrying a maximum penalty of death.

As soon as Bram had stated the argument he would present on the first point, Mr Justice de Wet cut him short saying 'I thought I made my attitude clear. I accept no decision or date was fixed upon for guerrilla warfare.'

Bram accepted this statement gravely, and said he would then go on to argue his second point. Again Mr Justice de Wet intervened to say that it had been clearly established by the evidence that this was the position; that the two organisations were in fact separate though they overlapped. Bram's months of meticulous preparations had come to nothing, but he sat down very grateful indeed that he had not had to argue the case that he had prepared. We were over the two worst hurdles before the end.

Vernon Berrange was the next to argue. He was concerned particularly with the cases of Bernstein, Kathrada and Mhlaba, for whose discharge he applied on the grounds that the evidence did not sustain a conviction. Vernon, who had found such difficulty in containing his fury and outrage at the conduct of Yutar throughout the case, started off by delivering himself of a stinging rebuke. He said that during his address, Dr Yutar delivered himself of what he was pleased to term a number of 'observations' concerning the accused, the relevance of which 'we have found difficult to ascertain. On the assumption that these so-called observations, which consisted of a sarcastic and satirical attack on the accused, are relevant, we have consulted with our clients for the purpose of replying thereto. With the dignity that has characterised the accused throughout this trial,' he said, 'they have instructed us to ignore these remarks'.

Yutar was squirming and hopefully looking at the judge to intervene on his behalf. Mr Justice de Wet probably understood that this was as much an attack on his conduct of the case as on Yutar's. He remained silent.

'It is, however, unusual,' said Berrange, 'and not in the best traditions in which prosecutions are conducted in this country, for a prosecutor to deliver himself in this manner. It will be submitted that Dr Yutar in addressing the court has in instances not accurately set out the facts, and in no instance has he tried to evaluate or analyse the evidence of the witnesses upon whom he relies.'

Berrange proceeded to argue the case of Bernstein. He said that regardless of the fact that the indictment did not mention it, Dr Yutar had based his main attack on Bernstein on the fact that he had been shown to be 'a propaganda specialist'. He had thus been elevated by Dr Yutar to the position of 'propaganda expert' of both the African National Congress, Umkhonto we Sizwe and the Communist Party. There was no word of evidence to support this. 'Bernstein', he said, 'had denied the only piece of evidence against him. The cross-examination of Bernstein covers 153 pages of transcript. This is not remarkable in itself. But what is remarkable is that, in that 153 pages, there is not one word of cross-examination as to the facts deposed to by Bernstein. The only direct evidence against him related to the erection of the radio masts and this evidence had been given by a servant at Rivonia who was in police custody under 90-day detention when he gave it.'

Dr Yutar jumped to his feet. 'That is not so, my Lord. The witness was not in 90-day detention. He was in protective custody only.'

Dr Yutar should know that there is no provision in South African law for protective custody. But here finally Yutar was hoist with his own petard. Vernon produced the list of witnesses who were said by Yutar himself to be 90-day detainees—the list put by Yutar to Bernstein under cross-examination. Included on the list given by the prosecutor himself was the very Joseph Mashifane who had given evidence about the radio mast. Yutar coloured in confusion, and buried his face in his papers.

Vernon analysed Mashifane's evidence, and showed that it could not be believed. 'This' he said, 'was the only piece of evidence against Bernstein. And on this basis, he is entitled to his discharge.'

With Kathrada it was a somewhat different matter. Berrange demonstrated that the main case against Kathrada was that testified to by Essop Suliman, the clown who had been shown to have contradicted himself repeatedly in different trials. At one stage even Dr Yutar had jettisoned him as a witness. The State also sought to infer Kathrada's guilt from the fact that he had been at Rivonia on the day of the raid, that he was disguised, that he had lived at Rivonia for a while, that he had written one or two pamphlets and he had written a draft speech to be broadcast on the illegal radio. This showed that Kathrada was politically active, a fact that he did not deny. But it had not been proved that Kathrada had taken part in Umkhonto, or had had anything to do with the blowing up of buildings, preparing for guerrilla warfare or any of the other allegations made in the indictment.

Mhlaba's case Vernon argued with somewhat less assurance, not because the case was weaker, but because it was apparent that the judge was totally unsympathetic.

There were a few legal arguments by Arthur, Bram and George, and the defence case was closed.

The prosecution is permitted to reply, but only on questions of law raised by the defence. Dr Yutar chose to ignore this provision of the law and in his reply attempted desperately to seal the gaps which Berrange had torn in the case against Bernstein. He started once again reciting the evidence which he had said existed against Bernstein and which he had failed to put in cross-examination.

De Wet, perhaps mindful of Vemon's strictures at the beginning of his argument, stopped him. 'You know, Dr Yutar, you are only entitled to reply on questions of law', he said.

Yutar switched his tack, and even we, accustomed to the sudden veering and shifting of this somewhat unstable character, were quite taken aback. He announced that he now proposed to rely upon certain presumptions of legal liability which derived from recent proclamations by the government. These proclamations, gazetted during the course of the trial, declared the African National Congress to be the same thing as Umkhonto we Sizwe, and made this identity of the two organisations retrospective to the beginning of the period covered by the indictment in our case. Earlier Yutar had stated in court that he would not reply on these presumptions and so we had not bothered to argue them. Now he was calling them in, after our final say in the case, to repair the holes which Vernon had torn in the case against Kathrada. For all the evidence against Kathrada—including his own—showed only that he had taken part in the affairs of the African National Congress, including typing certain ANC circulars drafted by Mbeki at Rivonia. Yutar's argument now was suddenly that Kathrada had been proved to be doing Congress work, and that in terms of the proclamation that the African National Congress and Umkhonto were legally the same organisation, Kathrada was therefore proved to have worked for Umkhonto and was therefore guilty of plotting revolution and sabotage.

I can only assume that Yutar's casual undertaking given earlier in the case that he would not rely on this presumption arose from his confidence in the strength of the case against the accused—a confidence which he now found rather shaken. By this stage, it seemed that Mr Justice de Wet had finally had enough. He almost browbeat Yutar into a retreat, and Yutar announced that in view of de Wet's attitude, he was now 'abandoning presumption!'. Whether in law a presumption of this kind can be 'abandoned' is uncertain. But de Wet rather icily asked Yutar whether he expected the whole case to be re-opened to allow the defence to argue their case in the light of his latest switch. Yutar had no other way out. He replied meekly that he felt his case was still so strong that he did not need the presumption. His 'argument' was over.

The judge adjourned the case for three weeks to consider his verdict. For us the three weeks went quickly enough, though we were under tremendous tension and uncertainty. No doubt for the accused in the Pretoria Jail in the middle of winter, the time went more slowly. The tension in their minds, in a period in which they knew their very lives lay in the balance, must have been incredibly gruelling. On the day that judgement was to be given the police had again packed the court and all the squares and streets around it.

Downstairs, in their underground cell, the accused waiting for the court to assemble seemed fairly well balanced, serious but not grim. They were all aware of the position—that seven of them had admitted guilt and must be found guilty; that Bernstein and Kathrada, by rights, should be discharged; and that Mhlaba had a sporting outside chance but not much more. Their morale had been quite considerably raised by the judge's acknowledgement that, in his view, the launching of guerrilla warfare had not been decided upon. This I think they felt, as we did, was the hairline around which the prospect of a death sentence revolved. Mr Justice de Wet in all his contradictory nature seemed to have teetered over to their side of the line, though his conduct throughout had been so strange and variable that anything was possible.

We did not believe that de Wet was the type of man to find either Kathrada or Bernstein guilty for expedient reasons, if he believed them innocent. But we felt that his whole conduct was such as to make us doubtful whether he had understood all the intricacies of the evidence and the legal arguments. Both Bernstein and Kathrada were well aware that, even if they were acquitted that morning, their chances of walking out of the court were remote indeed. Both of them, even if acquitted, faced the virtual certainty of immediate re-arrest and new charges for other offences such as breaches of their banning orders, or technical offences of one kind or another to which they themselves had testified in evidence. On any one of these charges, they could be convicted and sentenced to from three to ten years.

Mr Justice de Wet delivered his judgement very quickly.

'I have very good reasons for the conclusions to which I have come. I don't propose to read these reasons. The verdict will be: Nelson Mandela is found guilty on all four counts; Walter Sisulu is found guilty on all four counts; Dennis Goldberg is found guilty on all four counts; Govan Mbeki is found guilty on all four counts. Ahmed Kathrada is found guilty on count two and not guilty on counts one, three and four. Lionel Bernstein is found not guilty. He will be discharged. Raymond Mhlaba is found guilty on all four counts; Andrew Mlangeni is found guilty on all four counts; Elias Motsoaledi is found guilty on all four counts. I do not propose to deal with the question of sentence today. My reasons will be made available in a statement. The defence will be given an opportunity to study these reasons and if so required, to address me on the question of sentence. I will deal with the question of sentence tomorrow morning at 10 o'clock.'

He stood up, the court was adjourned, and it was all over before most of the people in the court even knew what had happened. The judgment had been delivered in a quiet voice. The accused had heard it, but I don't think anyone in the public gallery had.

While the court was in session, there was no visible reaction from the men in the dock. Kathrada managed to hide his disappointment, Bernstein looked as solemn and as pale as he would have if the verdict had gone the other way. Immediately the judge was out of court the atmosphere changed. The accused turned and waved to their families, summarising the judgement for them. Bernstein's wife, Hilda, rushed across the well towards the dock, asking what had happened. Bernstein pushed his way out of the dock through the ranks of the rather bemused warders, trying to make his way towards her. Immediately police and senior prison officials rushed up to him, and demanded that he return to the cells below with the other accused. He refused, pushing his way through towards counsel's table. He was determined, so he told me beforehand, that if they wanted to re-arrest him after such an acquittal, they would have to do it in open court in the eyes of the whole world, not down below in the secret bowels of the court. He brushed off the warders and detectives who tried to restrain him and burst his way through to counsel's table. Finally, when restrained by police he challenged them loudly to say whether they were arresting him or not. They had obviously hoped to avoid such a scene. Even the Colonel of the Jail pleaded with him to come quietly down to the cells below, where everything would be fixed up. Finally Lieutenant Swanepoel, to bring the scene to an end, formally placed him under arrest in the court, and ushered him below to the cells. As he went he must have wondered what purpose there had been in defending himself through a judicial hearing of nine months, only to find himself re-arrested, back in jail, possibly to be charged again on precisely the same facts.

The Sabotage Act specifically provided that a person acquitted under the Act could be prosecuted again on the same facts for the same offence charged under a different statute.

As we left the court we found the police formed up in a solid phalanx between the African spectators and the court. Albertina Sisulu in tribal dress was leading the crowd in singing the African anthem, Nkosi Sikelel i'Africa. The crowd moved along to the back of the Palace of Justice, just in time to see the police convoy escorting the accused in their Black Marias from the court to the jail. As the trucks came into view the crowd raised their fists in the illegal African National Congress salute and the cry 'Amandla' (Power) echoed through the square. The prisoners with their hands thrust through the bars returned the salute with the traditional 'Ngawethu!' (It shall be ours).

We went back to Johannesburg with a typewritten copy of the judgement, to prepare for a plea in mitigation the following day. The accused made their views very clear. They were prepared to have a plea in mitigation only to persuade the court not to impose the death penalty. They were not prepared to have any apologies made on their behalf for what they had done, or any suggestion that they would behave themselves better in future. Even though Mr Justice de Wet had found in our favour on the question of whether guerrilla warfare had been decided upon or not, it would be difficult for us to argue that the death penalty would be excessive even for the offences admitted by the accused. The Sabotage Act, after all, permitted the imposition of the death penalty on a person who, for example, threw a stone with political motive through a window of a government building. We knew also that the South African courts take previous sentences as precedent. Less than six months before, an 18 year old youngster had been sent to jail for ten years for attempting to leave the country illegally in order to be trained by the ANC as a motor mechanic. In the same trial, another accused had received twenty years hard labour for recruiting a third man to leave the country to receive military training. Before that, several young men had been sentenced to ten years in jail for attending a single meeting at which sabotage had been discussed, although there was no evidence at all that the prisoners had done more than listen to the discussion.

On our way home we stopped at the jail to talk to the accused. They were calm, living now in the shadow of death. The strain and tension was becoming almost unbearable, yet the only matter that they wanted to discuss was how they should behave in court if the death sentence was passed. We told them that the judge would ask the first accused Nelson Mandela: 'Have you any reason to advance why the death sentence should not be passed?'. Nelson decided that he would have a lot to say. He would tell the court that if they thought by sentencing him to death they would oust the liberation movement, they were wrong; that he was prepared to die for his beliefs, and knew that his death would be an inspiration to his people in their struggle. As he had said before, in a document which was an exhibit in the case, 'there is no easy walk to freedom. We have to pass through the shadow of death again and again before we reach the mountain tops of our desires'.

We pointed out to him that such an address was hardly designed to facilitate an appeal. Nelson's answer was simple. If sentenced to death he would not appeal. It was hard to believe. He explained that he, Walter and Govan had discussed with their colleagues the question of an appeal against the death sentence. They thought that such an appeal might be interpreted by their supporters as an act of weakness. Their main concern was that their behaviour throughout should be such as would inspire their followers, and let them understand that no sacrifice was too great to be made in the cause of freedom. They had decided it was politically inadvisable to appeal against the death sentence.

On the other hand, they did not want this action to influence the case of the other accused, or to adversely affect any appeal they might make. None of the accused could see any reason for the others not to try to save their lives by an appeal. The fact that they elected to appeal would have little influence on popular feeling. They were not leaders of Umkhonto, and had no reason for making the stand of those who were. It was on this note that we left the accused—we to prepare our plea in mitigation, they to think over what George Bizos cynically called their 'pleas in aggravation of sentence!'.

We had only one witness to call in mitigation—Mr Alan Paton. He is best known to white South Africans, as to the outside world, as the author of the best selling novel on the problem of race relations in South Africa, *Cry the Beloved Country*. He was a lay-preacher, a Christian social worker, a leader of the South African Liberal Party, and well known for many years as a staunch opponent of communism. In happier times, when political discussions were more free he had clashed on occasion with some of the accused and found their views too radical, too revolutionary.

The accused had proposed several names of people who might give evidence in mitigation and we had approached most of them. A few had agreed; many had wriggled out, finding specious excuses. It took considerable courage at that time to stand up and speak for a group of men who had become the butt of the most tremendous barrage of hostile propaganda from the press and public platform of any accused in South African history, men who acknowledged themselves guilty of an offence which the white population of South Africa at least regarded with absolute horror. Alan Paton was one of the few who had agreed without hesitation to our request that he testify.

The court that morning was like a place under siege. All roads from Johannesburg had been blocked by police; road blocks were mounted throughout the Witwatersrand area; police check points were set up at railway stations and bus terminals. Africans were being stopped for passes and arrested. Yet through this screen, somehow or other, hundreds of Africans had made their way into Church Square outside the Palace of Justice. A large group of whites had gathered as well, mainly students from Pretoria University, rabid supporters of Afrikaner nationalism, coming, so they hoped, to hear death sentences pronounced on their enemies. These white youths were itching for an opportunity to beat up any of the blacks who were 'too cheeky'. Their vicious hostility to Africans in the Square was a product of their hostility to the accused within. Amongst the police in the building it was much the same. It was difficult to push one's way through the crowd into the court and some of the relations of the accused, like Mrs Motsoaledi, were unable to get in. I had to intercede for them, pushing them in through the police screen or they would not even have got inside the court building.

Boos and hisses and loud cries of 'kaffir-boetie' greeted me from the Pretoria students as I took Mrs Motsoaledi's arm to push her through. Three hefty young policemen at the door of the court told me curtly to clear off and stop looking for trouble. I insisted that Mrs Motsoaledi had a right to enter and eventually, by taking the matter over their heads to a brigadier in charge of security, I managed to find her a place inside the court.

The courtroom was jammed. The local press, BBC reporters and overseas correspondents were all packed in the well of the court and in the doorways. Police filled almost all the public benches. A policeman had occupied my chair behind the counsel's table and with typical arrogance refused to move. I had to get the officer in charge to order him out. Vernon Berrange was stopped outside by the police cordon. He had to show his driver's licence as proof of identity in order to gain entry to the building. We had a brief session with the accused down below, a quick handshake—it was too tense for anything else—and we were in court.

Advocate Harold Hanson rose to address the judge. He was one of the most eloquent of South Africa's counsel. He had a strong radical and democratic conviction, and fully understood what the accused expected of him—to explain why they had done what they had done and to impress the moral justifications they felt for what they had done. He was not, under any circumstances, to apologise on their behalf. Hanson called Alan Paton.

Paton put forward a very simple proposition—that the African people in South Africa had the same hopes and aspirations as people of any other race; that is, to live a decent life. 'And many of them feel that these aspirations can only be realised if they have some kind of political representation. 'He spoke of the men in the dock whom he had known before—Mandela, who he said was regarded by Africans as the heir apparent to Chief Luthuli, elder statesman of the African people; Sisulu and Mbeki, he said, were men well know for their courage, determination and ability. 'I have never had any doubt about their sincerity, their deep devotion to the cause of their people, and their desire to see that South Africa became a country in which all people participate.'

Hanson asked him why he had come to give evidence in such a case. 'Because I was asked to come. But primarily because, having been asked, I felt it was my duty to come here—a duty which I am glad to perform, because I love my country. And it seems to me, my Lord, with respect, that the exercise of clemency in this case is a thing which is very important for our future.'

Explaining his own beliefs, he said that he did not believe in violence either as a matter of principle or as a matter of expediency. He did not believe that in countries such as South Africa violence could achieve the end that some people hoped. But he understood how the failure of the peaceful methods pursued by the accused for many years had made them feel that there were only two alternatives left to them: to bow their heads and accept, or to resist by force. He himself, he said, did not believe that these were the only choices. But he understood very well that some people should believe it. The history of the Afrikaner people of South African showed that they, too, had refused to accept the position of subservience passively when the time for action had come.

Mr Justice de Wet interjected: 'There were many cases,' he said, 'where people resisted and were convicted of high treason and executed. I have in mind the famous gunpowder plot in England. In the light of subsequent history, these people had legitimate grievances. But they are not entitled to break the law by force. And what happens to people like that historically is that they get convicted of high treason and are condemned to death.'

It was a sinister note on which to end Paton's plea. The judge then asked Dr Yutar whether he had any questions to put to Mr Paton. It is rare indeed for a prosecutor to cross-examine a witness who appears in mitigation of sentence. The people he is prosecuting are, after all, already found guilty. Yutar had created many precedents in this case, and his behaviour now was not the least of them. He explained that he did not as a rule cross-examine people called in mitigation, 'But I propose to cross-examine this witness with your Lordship's leave. And I don't do so in order to aggravate the sentence, but in order to unmask this gentleman'—the sneer in Dr Yutar's voice was thick—'and make perfectly clear that his only reason for going into the witness box, in my submission, is to make political propaganda from the witness box'.

There followed the type of attack which a better man, a bigger man than Dr Yutar would not have attempted. It started like this:

Yutar: Mr Paton, are you a communist?

Paton: No.

Are you a fellow traveller?

I don't understand what a fellow traveller is, but I understand your implication. No, I am not a fellow traveller.

Your understanding of my implication is correct. Do you share the aims and objects of the Communist Party?

Some of the aims I would share.

Such as?

Such as a more equitable distribution of land and wealth, better economic opportunities.

What don't you approve of in the Communist Party?

I would disapprove entirely of the totalitarian methods which they adopt to bring about such changes.

You disapprove of that?

Entirely.

He was cross-examined then about Dr Yutar's belief that the African National Congress was dominated by the Communist Party. He denied it. He accepted that many communists had been active in the ANC and had held high positions. That was as far as he would go. Dr Yutar asked him whether he had 'moved a lot with communists in this country'. Paton pressed for a more specific phrasing of the question. Dr Yutar mentioned a certain Roley Arenstein, a lawyer, well known as a communist, who lived in Durban.

Yutar: Do you know him?

Paton: I know him.

Where did you meet him?

I met him largely through Defence and Aid.

That is another organisation with a high-sounding name which assists the saboteurs in this country, isn't that so?

No.

No? Well, what did it assist in?

It assisted in defending people who were brought before the courts so that they might get a fair and just trial.

Dr Yutar turned to Paton's views on the world boycott of South African trade. Paton had once advocated such a boycott, but he had changed his views, he said, a long time ago. 'I would say I feel less pessimistic than I felt in 1960 about the future of this country.'

Yutar: Why do you say that?

Paton: Well, I believe there are signs of a growing—a change in our rulers. I think that even a thing like the development in the Transkei although I think that it is fraudulent, is nevertheless a sign of change.

It is a strange thing, you know. What you have just said corresponds with what Govan Mbeki said in some of his documents. He is a Transkei expert and he said the scheme was fraudulent.

I don't find that strange.

You don't?

Not at all.

No? Perhaps you had a consultation with him?

I did not.

Yutar quoted from a newspaper cutting of a plea from Paton to people in Scandinavia, urging them to maintain the concern at the injustice of apartheid. Paton admitted he had made such pleas.

Yutar: Campaigning even from this country?

Paton: Yes.

Against your country?

Against my country? No, no! Against certain politics that are followed in this country, yes. But against my country, no.

You have spoken openly against the government?

I have.

That is not treason, is it?

I trust not.

Have you spoken against apartheid?

I have.

And that is not treason?

Not yet.

Do you think it will be?

I think it might become so.

You have spoken against the policies followed in this country with perfect freedom?

Not perfect freedom by any means.

Why, how are you . . .

It is extremely difficult for one thing to get a hall to hold meetings. It is extremely difficult because the security police often make it impossible to hold a meeting. We have actually had cases where people bringing people to the meeting in trucks and lorries have been stopped by the security police and advised not to go on. I call it intimidation.

I found the cross-examination a degrading exhibition. Dr Yutar had a paltry and crude collection of cliches and prejudices which he passed off for a political viewpoint. He was attempting to smear Paton using accusations and taunts. The police at least enjoyed it. They tittered gleefully as this honest man, of undeniable courage, was smeared and demeaned by Yutar. Mr Justice de Wet, probably by reason of his own political prejudice rather than of law, also appeared to be enjoying Paton's discomfiture.

For my part, I was pleased when it was over and Harold Hanson rose to make his own address. His plea was in part based on history. He urged the judge to understand that a nation's grievances cannot be suppressed, and that people find a way to voice these grievances as the African people and the accused had found.

In part it was a plea for the judge to remember that the Afrikaner people themselves, in their time of struggle against British imperialism, had also organised armed uprising, rebellion and treason, and had also appeared before the courts for that offence. The reason why the Afrikaner Nationalist government had the power of state with which to try these accused was that their own struggle had been carried on violently and illegally by people who were now recognised as the fathers of the Afrikaner nation.

In part it was a plea based on the precedents whereby South African courts had treated treason, armed rebellion and uprising with leniency for the very reason that it was not the crime alone which left its imprint on the history of the country, but the sentence which the court imposed on those found guilty. The sentence in this case, on the Rivonia men, would also echo down the hall of South African history for a long time to come.

Mr Justice de Wet scarcely appeared to be listening. It seemed likely that he had made up his mind on sentence, and that all Hanson's eloquence was merely delaying his opportunity to state his mind. As Hanson finished, Yutar rose to his feet to give his ego its last little puff before his hour of glory ended. He would not address the court on sentence, he said, but he had to affirm publicly his faith in the fairness of the court.

Mr Justice de Wet more or less brushed him aside. He nodded to the accused as a signal that they should rise, and barely waiting for them to get to their feet, began his judgment. The public galleries, handicapped by the awful acoustics in the court, could hardly hear his soft voice as he said: 'I have heard a great deal during the course of this case about the grievances of the non-European population. The accused have told and their counsel have told me that the accused who were all leaders of the non-European population were motivated entirely by a desire to ameliorate these grievances. I am by no means convinced that the motives of the accused were as altruistic as they wish the court to believe. People who organise a revolution usually take over the government, and personal ambition can't be excluded as a motive.

'The function of this court, as is the function of the court in any other country, is to enforce law and order, and to enforce the laws of the State within which it functions. The crime of which the accused have been convicted, that is the main crime, the crime of conspiracy, is in essence one of High Treason. The State has decided not to charge the crime in this form.

'Bearing this in mind and giving the matter very serious consideration, I have decided not to impose the supreme penalty, which in a case like this would usually be the proper penalty for the crime, but consistent with my duty that is the only leniency I can show. The sentence in the case of all the accused will be one of life imprisonment. In the case of the accused who have been convicted on more than one count, these counts will be taken together for the purpose of sentence.'

It was an abrupt end.

Yutar jumped to his feet again saying 'My Lord, the witnesses indemnity . . .', but it was too late. Mr Justice de Wet had swept out of the court, and it was over.

A strange feeling of anti-climax hung over us all after nine months of such tension. The men in the dock, who had shown no signs of emotion while de Wet was talking, turned to the public galleries and smiled.

And even then the people in the court had not heard it all. I heard Mlangeni's wife, Juni, call out 'How long, how long?' and Andrew saying 'Life'.

There was a silence in the court. Still smiling while the public stood hushed and shocked, the accused slowly disappeared out of sight for the last time, down the courtroom steps to the underground cells.

We looked at each other. There was nothing more to say. We had managed to save their lives, which I suppose is the most that we could have hoped to achieve. But there was nothing to cheer us in the fact that, though our friends were going to live, they would live out their lives in a South African jail.

We shook hands silently with Bram. It had been his responsibility in the first place to save their lives, and it was his victory in the first place that they would live. We sensed at the time, I think, that this was the last great trial of a great barrister and a great man. None of us thought at that time that his next appearance in court would be not at the counsel's table but in the dock, accused himself of participating in the very conspiracy for which these men had just been sentenced.

The crowd outside the court had grown close on 2,000. On one side of Church Square a long row of police, on the other the people waiting and hoping for their last chance to see the men who for so long had held their hopes and their inspirations. Posters unfolded amongst the crowd, held high overhead reading 'Our future is bright'. 'We are proud of our leaders'. 'Sentence or no sentence, we stand by our leaders'. 'They will not serve those years as long as we live.'

The women broke into song, as African women do so easily on every occasion when they are moved. Singing, they moved towards the back of the Palace of Justice, to see the men being driven away. So there, in the heart of Nationalist South Africa with an angry group of white students and white policemen looking on, they proclaimed the failure of the prosecution.

The political movement of the non-white people should have been broken, leaderless and without hope. Instead it was alive, singing, forming up in procession with flying banners and the African National Congress colours fluttering in the wind, moving round through Church Square, Pretoria, under the statue of Paul Kruger, in salute to the enemies of the South African State.

The whites looked on angrily. From the window of an upper floor of one building, some patriot poured water on to the heads of the people marching past. The students in Pretoria University blazers, hate in their faces, laughed without humour. The police with their dog handlers followed close on the women, egging their dogs on to snap at the women's heels. A couple of the women tripped, to the accompaniment of more laughter from the university students. The police moved in, obviously under strict orders to avoid violence at all costs. TV cameras from all over the world were recording every movement of the scene. Banners were roughly seized by the police, confiscated, torn up and thrown in the gutters. But still the crowd lined the route which the convoy from the court to the prison would take, waiting for the last glimpse of their leaders and their last salute.

For close on an hour nothing happened. The crowd stood singing. At last a convoy of traffic police on motorbikes formed up at the rear entrance. The walkie-talkie radios crackled, the massive iron gates swung open, and the convoy of police vehicles and prison vans turned sharp right instead of left, as it had done every day for the last nine months, the police trying to the bitter end to deny the people a chance of seeing their heroes. As the convoy shot off, a mighty roar of 'Amandla' (power) followed it. Through the bars of the Black Maria could be seen the waving arms of the accused, saluting as they disappeared in the distance.

It was Friday. We spoke to the police and prison authorities, and were given an undertaking that all the prisoners would be kept in Pretoria until we had an opportunity to discuss with them the question of an appeal. That undertaking was given on Friday. On Saturday morning we woke to read in the newspapers that all the non-white prisoners had been flown secretly the previous day to the prison camp on Robben Island, a thousand miles from Pretoria, off Cape Town. Dennis Goldberg, the only white convicted, was still in Pretoria.

That morning Bram Fischer left for Cape Town by car. He had planned to take a holiday. Now he would take time off to interview the accused on Robben Island. His wife Molly was with him. She was loved by us all. Throughout the trial she had catered for us, helped us with the backroom work, gathered the material we required and generally kept us going. That night on the road travelling through the dry and dusty Free State, Bram approached a bridge. A motor cyclist came the other way, swinging on to the wrong side of the road to pass another car. Bram swerved to avoid the motor cyclist. His car left the road, plunged into the bed of the river and dropped into a water-filled hole some thirty feet deep. The car filled with water and sank. Bram and a friend, Lis Lewin, who was with him scrambled out through the front windows. Molly was pinned in the back and drowned.

Bram's had been one of the happiest marriages I know. From that moment on, when tragedy ended thirty years of marriage, some vital spark seemed to have gone out of Bram. He came back to Johannesburg for a funeral attended by hundreds of people of all races and colours, from all walks of life, a tribute to the unique position which the Fischer family held in the hearts and minds of people of all political persuasions, from all occupations, from the highest in the land to the lowest. They were amongst those few South Africans who have people of all races who count themselves their friends.

Under this fearful blow, Bram bore up magnificently, devoting himself to the future of his friends on Robben Island. By sheer effort of will, he put his grief aside. Seven days later we flew together to Robben Island to see the prisoners.

In the world outside there was ferment. Fifty members of Parliament in London had marched to South Africa House to present a protest. In Canada, the Prime Minister, Lester Pearson, had stated that he and his government had followed the trial with grave concern. In the United Nations the sentences were attacked. Dr Joost de Blanc, the former Archbishop of Cape Town, flew to New York to present to Secretary-General U Thant a petition calling for the release of the Rivonia men signed by the representatives of organisations whose membership totalled 258 million, together with 92,000 individual names. The petition was said to have had wider support than any other petition in history. Dr Kaunda, Prime Minister of Zambia, wrote expressing his distress at the severity of the sentences. The International Federation of Trade Unions in Brussels sent a telegram to President Swart. There were protests in Scandinavia and many other countries.

In South Africa itself, so far as feeling was expressed in public, white opinion managed to remain unconcerned by these protests. This was the hour of Afrikaner Nationalism's jubilation. Now it could boast that it had broken the back of this radical enemy which had plagued it from its very beginnings. Now for the first time it could feel that it was really undisputed master of its own house. Yutar and the Chief of Police were being feted in interviews in the press in the manner of international celebrities. They had no inhibitions about boosting themselves. Carel Birkby reporting in the *Sunday Times* wrote: 'Percy Yutar made some fascinating comments on the trial itself. Dr Yutar said: 'I believe that the Rivonia people had an eminently fair trial. I did my best to ensure this, for I am a judicial officer, not a politician'. The Deputy Commissioner of Police also patted himself on the back, as though there was perhaps not enough back-patting being done by others to satisfy him. 'I deal with a large number of cases and this was just one of them. Just as I delegated this matter to Brigadier van den Berg, so the Attorney General delegated it to his deputy, Mr P Yutar. When it was decided that he would conduct the case we were happy that it was in able hands. He presented the case to the court in a masterly fashion. He is a very fair prosecutor but he can put his case firmly. We tried throughout the Rivonia affair to be as humane as possible.' The prosecutor and the police were allowed great latitude in the press to laud their ideas of their own behaviour.

Nobody bothered to interview me, or anybody else connected with the defence. What the defence thought of the trial did not matter in South Africa.

There was no flurry on Robben Island. When Bram and I arrived there by ferry boat, five or six miles from Cape Town, it was a bare, desolate and stark, forbidding place basking against the sunlit background of peace and serenity presented by Table Mountain and Table Bay.

The prison authorities were taking no chance that we should see anything of the conditions on the island. We were hustled into a room far from the prison itself and the seven prisoners were brought in. We had to get used to seeing them in prison clothes—short khaki trousers without underwear, rough shirts, a jersey and a sort of linen jacket which was all they were allowed to wear. Unlike less important prisoners, they had either shoes or sandals, and socks. Govan Mbeki, 53 years old, holder of two university degrees, looked strange and uncomfortable in short trousers, which he must last have worn as a lad at school. It was the middle of winter. He was shivering and cold. It was typical of him not to complain because with his thin jersey he was much better off than the other prisoners.

The prison department insisted on an officer being present at our interview, and listening in to our consultation. We objected. The colonel was summoned. There was a long harangue and dispute. Finally a complicated compromise was reached which required our returning to the mainland and coming back to the island a second time before consultation could be resumed, thus saving face for the colonel.

On the merits of the case, only Kathrada had any chance at all on appeal. Mr Justice de Wet had been unable to find any direct evidence against him, and had relied only on circumstantial evidence, more particularly on the fact that he had lived at Rivonia and at the Mountainview cottage, and that he had typed certain ANC documents. In his judgement he reasoned that these documents could well have had the result of encouraging the activities of Umkhonto even though Umkhonto was never mentioned in them. Kathrada must have known about Umkhonto and, therefore, in law, he reasoned, must be guilty of encouraging its policy. The argument was extremely shaky. It is permissible in law to convict on circumstantial evidence alone, but the rule is that the evidence must be consistent with the inference drawn and must exclude any other reasonable inference. In Kathrada's case it was manifestly obvious that the facts were consistent with the inference he had drawn. But they were equally consistent with the statement which Kathrada had made in the dock—that he had gone to Rivonia to pursue his political aims without violence; that his work before the birth of Umkhonto and after, had been the same— education of and agitation amongst the Indian population and their allies. We had little doubt that before a judge who judged the issue solely on legal grounds, Kathrada's appeal would succeed. Even more compelling was the second ground on which Mr Justice de Wet had decided against Kathrada. He had said 'In actively supporting the Free Mandela Campaign, Kathrada must have had in mind that the arrest of Mandela must have had a deleterious effect on the campaign for which he was working, and also on the activities of Umkhonto, and the object sought would be to enable Mandela to be free to continue the work which he was doing prior to his arrest. I am satisfied that the accused knew in essence what this work was. In spite of the fact that the accused was not asked what his motive was, I am satisfied that he would not be able to give an acceptable explanation consistent with an entirely innocent motive.'

This piece of legal reasoning was one which should be preserved for the text books. What it says in effect is: the prosecutor failed or forgot to ask Kathrada the critical question why he did what he did. But I am convinced that Kathrada could not in any event have answered it. I will, therefore, hold the failure of the prosecutor to ask the question not against the prosecutor but against the accused.

We felt fairly confident that this alone would be sufficient to sway a judge of appeal in Kathrada's favour. We asked Kathrada what his answer would have been if the question of motive had been put to him. He replied simply 'My motive in continuing to work for Mandela's release was simply that it was a political project. None of us for a moment expected the government to release him but we had to protest all the same.'

So much for Mr Justice de Wet's satisfaction that Kathrada could not have advanced an acceptable explanation not connected with violence or sabotage. On the merits then, Kathrada would probably succeed. Previous experience, however, taught all of us that this would not be the end of the matter. In his evidence Kathrada had admitted to a large number of offences. He had, he said, worked with the African National Congress when it was an illegal organisation. He had broken a house arrest order. He had been a member of the Communist Party when that was illegal. He had failed to notify the Minister of three changes of address during the time he had been underground (including his move from his flat to Rivonia!). We began to tot the offences up. Assisting the African National Congress, minimum sentence one year, maximum ten; for being a communist, the same. For failing to notify change of address, three sentences, a maximum of ten years each, a minimum of one year; under another section of the same Act, for thus breaking his house arrest order; for attending gatherings in contravention of a banning notice, three years. For failing to report to the police daily as required by his house arrest order, ten years; for leaving home after being house-arrested, three years; for speaking to each of the other banned or listed persons, including his co-accused, in breach of his house arrest order, three years for each offence; for printing documents of the ANC, three years. And so it went on. The exercise got tragically ludicrous. We stopped. If Kathrada appealed successfully, he would be charged with minor offences which could get him anything from 100 to 500 years imprisonment!—we had lost count. And even if the sentences ran concurrently, there was what was known as the 'Sobukwe Clause', which gave the Minister power to keep a political prisoner in jail indefinitely after the completion of his sentence. This was one of the provisions we knew this Minister, who had introduced it, would not hesitate to use against any or all of the Rivonia accused.

Kathrada was quite positive about his own position. He did not think there was any point whatsoever in an appeal. He preferred, he said, to take his chance on liberation five or ten years hence when the liberation movement changed the government, rather than go on to the Appeal Court.

Raymond Mhlaba had an outside chance of success. But the Appellate Division as we knew it—and he knew too—had also bowed to the winds of the time. It had recently upheld convictions in political cases where the flimsiest grounds for such a decision existed. Mhlaba might have an outside chance on appeal, but we felt that under the circumstances his chance was remote. We would appeal if he felt strongly that we ought to. He did not. Neither did the other accused, none of whom had any chance whatsoever on the merits. Their only prospects on appeal might be on the gravity of the sentence.

Here, we were in a quandary. It is a tradition in South African law, as in most other countries, that where conspiracy or common action by many people is proved, the leaders and organisers are deemed more culpable and are thus more harshly punished than their followers. On this basis, it could be argued that since Nelson, Walter and Govan were members of the High Command and members of the National Executive of the ANC and received life sentences, Elias, Andrew, Raymond and Kathrada should have received much lighter sentences. Kathrada, if one looked at it closely, had received a life sentence for typing one rather innocuous document for the African National Congress. But if we went to appeal on this basis, the results would only be of any significance if the sentences were so drastically shortened as to be of real significance.

All the men could, in fact, be recharged with other offences in much the same way as Kathrada. And all of them, if all else failed, could be held in jail indefinitely after the completion of any sentence. But, most importantly, if we did appeal on these grounds, the appeal court might not find that the sentence on the lesser lights in the conspiracy had been too heavy, but that the sentence on the leaders had been too light. All of this we put to them, so that they should understand fully what they were deciding. There was no division of opinion, and little time wasted. They saw no point in an appeal, and nobody wanted us to go ahead with it.

We flew back to Pretoria and saw Dennis Goldberg. He seemed more concerned about the health of one of his fellow prisoners than about an appeal. He also decided that an appeal would serve no purpose whatsoever.

And so the next day we released a statement to the press. 'The accused in the Rivonia trial have considered the verdict and sentence in their case and have discussed the question of their appeal with their legal advisers. Mr Mandela, Mr Sisulu and Mr Mbeki have throughout the trial accepted full responsibility for their actions, and accordingly no question of an appeal arises in their case. The rest of the accused have been advised that they have prospects for appealing successfully on their conviction or on their sentence or both. In view of the existing legislation in this country, a successful appeal against the conviction would in some cases mean the immediate re-arrest and re-charging of the accused. In other cases an appeal leading to a reduction in the length of the sentence could serve no purpose because of the power invested in the Minister of the Justice to retain for indefinite periods persons who have served their sentences. In all these circumstances the accused have instructed their legal advisers not to make any appeal either against their convictions or against their sentences. They would prefer that any funds that might become available for their appeal should be devoted to the defence of others charged with political offences, or should go towards the support of the families of those already sentenced.'

The trial was over and everything connected with it and all that we could do had been done. We could close our files and go on to other cases.

There was one minor side-light which I should record, which happened while all this was going on. On the Saturday that Bram set out on his ill-fated car trip to Cape Town, Bernstein had appeared in the Johannesburg Magistrate's Court—a formal appearance on three charges under the Suppression of Communism Act—belonging to an unlawful organisation and participating in gatherings. No further details were given at that time; he was formally remanded to a later date. Vernon Berrange appeared on his behalf and pulled off one of those spectacular pieces of legerdemain which Vernon managed so brilliantly from time to time. He persuaded the prosecutor and magistrate to do what everyone believed was quite impossible—to grant Bernstein bail. Bail was set at £1,000, and one at least of the Rivonia accused was free to walk again in the streets of Johannesburg while awaiting a new trial.

The press and commentators were still doing their post-mortems on the Rivonia case itself when our files were closed. Lawrence Gandar, the editor of the *Rand Daily Mail*, who had taken an uncompromising stand against the government's apartheid and injustice, referred to the case in an editorial to ask the vital question which had to be asked at the end of such a case: why had the non-white leaders resorted to violence in South Africa? Why had they not relied on the methods adopted by the Negro Freedom Movement in the United States of America—peaceful sit-ins and bus boycotts?

I don't think he expected any reply to this moralising, but from underground somewhere, a reply arrived in his office, signed in the name of the African National Congress. It answered the suggestions that the African leaders had followed the wrong road: 'What are the weapons of a political organisation? First of all an appeal must be made to the electorate and those who vote to choose the government that makes the laws of the land. In South Africa the African people, unlike their brothers in America, have no vote. They must, therefore, appeal to the whites who are in a privileged position and do not wish to give up their privileges. This has been demonstrated by the struggle of the African National Congress, which for fifty years, peacefully and politely pleaded for improvements in the conditions of the African people. It is a matter of history that the struggle was in vain and that the people's rights have become less, not more. We agree with you that violence is an unhappy method to seek for a solution to our problems, but can you blame our people? What else can they do? Our organisations are banned. If we start new ones, they can be banned with retrospective effect (this has since been done). Our leaders and members then become exposed to prosecution for acts which they may have performed openly at a time before the retrospective ban was announced. We dare not expose our people to this risk. We cannot therefore pursue any open agitation through mass organisation of the people.

'Nor can we act through individuals. Our leaders are in jail or have been banished. They are prohibited from addressing meetings or writing. Our Martin Luther Kings and James Baldwins have been silenced by law. If new leaders come out in the open the same fate awaits them. We have our leaders. We have those who have replaced Mandela, Sisulu, Luthuli, but their names are concealed today, their identity a secret. We will not have them banned, or put under house arrest or held for 90-days. They are too valuable to be sacrificed, therefore they cannot speak out nor can they make written public appeals. They must remain where they are, underground. Then there is the weapon of strikes. We have not abandoned this, but how do you call for a strike when all strikes by Africans are unlawful? And if the strike is organised in protest against any law of the country then all who take part are liable to long periods of imprisonment and to whipping.

'The same holds good for passive resistance. We tried that at the time of the Defiance Campaign. Over 8,500 people went to jail, but as the campaign gained momentum it was crushed by the vicious provisions of the Criminal Law Amendment Act and the Public Safety Act. We cannot allow our people to be exposed to legal whippings and jail for years in such a campaign. There can be civil rights demonstrations in America but not in South Africa. It is idle to compare political campaigning in America with political action in this country. If the laws of South Africa were similar to those in America there would be no need for sabotage and there would be none. If King or Baldwin lived in South Africa, or Christ

Himself, today they would be banned, banished, house arrested or in jail. You must be realistic. Our organisations have been banned, our leaders silenced. Strikes and passive resistance campaigns crushed by legislation. Do you think we like sabotage? Have those who condemn us ever thought of the terrors through which each one must walk, the fearful difficulty each one must face? People don't risk their lives because they like the sound of the explosions. Committing sabotage is a last desperate act when no other means are left. Do you sincerely believe there is any other way that is effective? We are held in a fist of iron and only force can prise it open'.

This summed up the attitude of the African National Congress and of the Rivonia men. I believe it is their conviction still to this day, despite all the sentences, all the terror and horror which has been heaped upon them. It is the attitude of the members of the African National Congress in South Africa, unknown and secret, as of the thousands of men and women who have been sentenced for taking greater or lesser part in the struggle to prise that fist open.

Sentenced, crushed, imprisoned, perhaps, but still convinced that in the end of ends, force will be needed to prise that fist open.

And so, they are in the jails throughout the country. Nobody knows any longer how many there are. I suspect the numbers are now seven or eight thousand men and women, all of them convinced in their own minds that they will live to see the day when that fist will be prised open and with it the doors of the jails behind which they wait for their countrymen and for the world to act effectively for their freedom.

December 1965

Dennis Goldberg was released in 1985 after spending 22 years in gaol.
Govan Mbeki was released in 1988 after spending 25 years in gaol.
Walter Sisulu, Ahmed Kathrada, Raymond Mhlaba, Elias Motsoaledi and Andrew Mlangeni were released in 1989 after spending 26 years in gaol.
Nelson Mandela was released in February 1990 after spending 27 years in gaol.

Epilogue

Epilogue written by Edelgard Nkobi-Goldberg in *Joel Joffe, Der Staat gegen Mandela*, 2006, Karl Dietz Verlag Berlin, translated into German by Edelgard Nkobi-Goldberg from *Joel Joffe, The Story of the Rivonia Trial*. The Epilogue has been translated into English by Denis Goldberg.

Today the Rivonia Trial is history. More than 40 years have passed. The ANC has been the government for over ten years and now has a two-thirds majority in Parliament. Nelson Mandela left his jail in the triumph of the victory over apartheid and was elected to be the first black President of South Africa. For all eight of those convicted, the prison doors were eventually opened.

Denis Goldberg, the engineer, is still working. He has remained true to technical matters, and with his now more than 73 years (born 11 April 1933), is still a Special Adviser to the Minister of Water Affairs and Forestry, Ms Buyelwa Sonjica. Andrew Mlangeni was elected to parliament in 1994 and now, nearly 80 years old, he wants to see through his third term in the legislature. Ahmed Kathrada went into retirement after two terms as a Member of Parliament but is still active as the Chairperson of the Board of the Robben Island Museum. Arthur Goldreich, who after his escape went first to Britain and later settled in Israel, still teaches architecture in Tel Aviv.

In 2001, we laid to rest Govan Mbeki, who became the Deputy President of the Senate in South Africa's first post-Apartheid parliament following release. With his son, Thabo Mbeki, now in his second term of office as President, the sons have taken over from their fathers. Elias Motsoaledi came out of prison with a severe illness of the lungs and died on 11 May 1994. He did, however, experience the first democratic election. Walter Sisulu died in 2003 and Raymond Mhlaba in February 2005. Lionel Bernstein, James Kantor and Harold Wolpe have also passed on.

For the Rivonia group, imprisonment on Robben Island came to an end after 18 years. With the start of Nelson Mandela's secret negotiations with the regime, they were taken in 1982 to a separate section of Pollsmoor Prison in Cape Town, and there Nelson Mandela was separated from the others. In 1988, the 78 year old Govan Mbeki was released. In 1989, the releases of Walter Sisulu, Raymond Mhlaba, Andrew Mlangeni, Elias Matsoaledi and Ahmed Kathrada followed. The only white Rivonia prisoner, Denis Goldberg, who had been held in the high security prison in Pretoria, had been released earlier in 1985. Nelson Mandela lived for the last two years of his imprisonment in a bungalow in the grounds of the Victor Verster Prison near to Paarl, a town not far from Cape Town. This was more for his security from attack by ultra right-wing elements opposed to the negotiations.

On 16 December of 2001, there was a great reunion of the men of the Rivonia trial at the Liliesleaf Farm in Rivonia. Relatives and friends as well as those who fled or had gone underground and who now live in many parts of the world were also there to celebrate. The members of the High Command of Umkhonto we Sizwe who were arrested there in 1963 returned there in honour. Arthur Chaskalson, George Bizos and Joel Joffe, the lawyers of that time, were also present.

Walter Sisulu could no longer participate. Now 89 years old and seriously ill, he was visited by his struggle companions Nelson Mandela, Ahmed Kathrada, Andrew Mlangeni, Denis Goldberg, Arthur Goldreich, Raymond Mhlaba and James Kantor's daughter who was born during the trial (Nelson Mandela is her godfather).

During the days around 16 December 2001, there were media briefings, press conferences and meetings with journalists during which they and the old guerillas could look into the Rivonia trial documents and the police files from 1963/64. These materials had been kept securely among the treasures of the Oppenheimer Foundation in Johannesburg. In a small exhibition, copies of old police photographs and items of so-called military material that were introduced in evidence at the trial were displayed.

The Capetonian Denis Goldberg, who now lives in South Africa, flew in from London where he spent 18 years in exile after his release from prison. Now he no longer needed to try to get his descriptions and drawings of weapons out of his jacket pocket to destroy them as he had done when the police raided the farm. During their search of Liliesleaf, and later of Travallyn, they found further documentation for the development of weapons manufacturing facilities. Because of this, the apartheid regime had thought of him as the most dangerous white man in the country. Goldberg also attempted to escape during the 90-days detention for police investigation. He was recaptured and put into leg irons for a time.

Rivonia is today an exclusive area of fine houses, part of Sandton, the poshest area of Johannesburg. The previous owner of the nearly original main house on Liliesleaf farm was a German. Helmut Schneider was born in Bavaria and went to South Africa on an employment contract.

Out of the blue Nelson Mandela and the journalist Alistair Sparks arrived at their door. They had been looking for the farm and later there were negotiations to buy the farm back again. For that part of the farm that the Schneiders owned – the main house and the one time farm outbuildings, now living quarters – required a sum of 12 million Rands. Since then, more of the properties that formed the original Liliesleaf Farm have also been bought back. The 28 acre farm is being reconstructed to become a national memorial but with access for social scientists to a research complex. The tourist museum will be complemented by a library and archive relevant to the Rivonia events.

Nicholas Wolpe, son of Harold Wolpe, is responsible for the reconstruction, which has made good progress since the founding of a Trust launched in 2001 on the fortieth anniversary of Umkhonto we Sizwe. There have been numerous generous private donations. When the Liliesleaf Farm is properly integrated into the consciousness of international tourists it will be talked about in the same way as Robben Island is at present.

How the police discovered the Rivonia hideout is today still not known. The actors in the events still discuss the matter. Was it the systematic stone for stone work of the police and state security? Was it the adventurous story told by Bruno Mtolo as state witness in the trial? Was it due to one of the many visitors or perhaps the radio? It was clearly a mistake to have so many visitors and also that relatives of those who had gone underground came to the farm without great security precautions being taken over the comings and goings. Or was there a tip off from the CIA?

Since then other sources have become known and they reveal that the American CIA and the British MI5 kept Liliesleaf under observation. Both secret services had long been actively engaged in these activities at latest from the time of Nelson Mandela's international travels in 1962. They had informed the South African security service about everything that happened during his journey and followed his movements after his return to South Africa. And that might have led to his arrest.

The Americans and British, according to newly discovered documents – materials from all over the world relating to the Rivonia events are being collected and will form part of the Liliesleaf research archives – must have been keeping the activities leading up to the founding of Umkhonto we Sizwe and the activities at Liliesleaf under observation. The South African Communist Party was already a CIA target, and so the tip-off that led to the Rivonia arrests could have come from the Americans or the British.

It is known that after the escape of Goldreich and Wolpe, the CIA knew of the complicated escape route they had followed through several African countries to Britain, and that they had whistled the South Africans back when they wanted to recapture them in neighbouring countries. The grounds for this were that the British would not permit the South Africans to operate in places that were clearly spheres of British influence or even Protectorates, and the Americans supported them in this.

After the arrest of Umkonto we Sizwe's first National High Command, a second one appeared on the scene. Its members were soon captured by the Security Police. Among them were Wilton Mkwayi (who had been trained in China with Mhlaba and Mlangeni), Dave Kitson, Mac Maharaj and others. Kitson, who after being sentenced to 20 years imprisonment, was taken to the same prison as Denis Goldberg in Pretoria because he too was white. Mkwayi followed the Rivonia prisoners to Robben Island having also been sentenced to life imprisonment. Important leaders of the ANC left South Africa for asylum in other African countries, where they not only sought to build up Umkhonto we Sizwe as the military wing of the liberation movement, but also to rebuild the political structures of the ANC that had been destroyed, and also to win further international support. On his release from Robben Island after his 12 year sentence, Maharaj played a key role in Umkhonto and the ANC eventually returning to work underground in South Africa.

The leader of the legal defence team in the Rivonia Trial, Abram Fischer QC, was arrested shortly after the end of the Rivonia Trial and was himself put on trial. Fischer was not only a well-known lawyer, but also secretly the Chairperson of the illegal Communist Party and was therefore on the apartheid regime's Wanted List. He could have gone abroad but saw it as his duty to fight for the lives of his comrades in the Rivonia Trial. Only a few months later he was also sentenced to life imprisonment and joined Denis Goldberg and others in prison in Pretoria. He died as a prisoner in 1975.

The lawyers Vernon Berrange and Harold Hanson, already elderly men at the time of the trial, have both died. Arthur Chaskalson became Chief Justice of the new South African Constitutional Court and later the Chief Justice. Last year he went into retirement. His colleague, George Bizos, honoured with the highest awards that can be given to lawyers and defenders of human rights, still undertakes cases that bring him further respect. He defended the Zimbabwean opposition politician, Morgan Tsvangirai, whom Mugabe had charged with High Treason in order to silence him. Joel Joffe, the author of this book, lives in England and is now a member of the House of Lords.

Mr. Justice de Wet and the prosecutor, Dr Yutar, have both died. The Rivonia Trial was for Percy Yutar the most significant case in his career. His ambition was to be appointed to be the State Advocate, the highest ranking lawyer in the public service. Yutar had no shame. He sold his beautifully bound official copies of the record of the Rivonia Trial to Harry Oppenheimer, the head of Anglo American Corporation, for his private Brenthurst Library. Oppenheimer with his Brenthurst Trust is world famous as a collector of art and historical materials relating to South Africa (and Africa).

Friends and co-survivors still cannot understand why Nelson Mandela 'white washed' Yutar in 1994. He invited Yutar not only to his inauguration as president but also on one occasion to a meal at the President's Residence. The press was present on that occasion and he shook Yutar's hand. Perhaps it was a public relations gesture to show the world that South Africa under its first black government did not have the intention to charge the apartheid murderers and to convict them. They would all be left to the Truth and Reconciliation Commission which could grant them amnesty. Yutar drew out of all this the conclusion that after all he had not done anything really bad in his life and until his death in 2002 at the age of 90 years, he appealed to Mandela's handshake as proof that he bore no responsibility for apartheid oppression. When Joffe asked Nelson Mandela how he could treat Yutar so generously after his appalling conduct in the Trial, Mandela's response was that in reconciling the different races in South Africa, he could not afford the luxury of revenge.

My involvement in the struggle started years ago in 1964. The first group of ANC students came to be educated in the German Democratic Republic from Dar es Salaam, and among them was my future husband, Zenzo Nkobi, who died in Bulawayo, Zimbabwe, in 1993. The members of this group never tired of discussing the political situation in South Africa. The South Africans shook us up and called upon us East Germans to show our humanity and to participate in determining their fate.

Edelgard Nkobi
Cape Town, 2006

The Indictment

IN THE SUPREME COURT OF SOUTH AFRICA

(TRANSVAAL PROVINCIAL DIVISION)

THE STATE

against

NELSON MANDELA and OTHERS

IN THE SUPREME COURT OF SOUTH AFRICA

(TRANSVAAL PROVINCIAL DIVISION)

RUDOLF WERNER REIN, Attorney–General for the Province of the Transvaal, who prosecutes for and on behalf of the STATE, presents and gives the Court to be informed that:

1. NELSON MANDELA,
2. WALTER SISULU,
3. DENNIS GOLDBERG,
4. GOVAN MBEKI,
5. AHMED MOHAMED KATHRADA,
6. LIONEL BERNSTEIN,
7. RAYMOND MAHLABA,
8. JAMES KANTOR,
9. ELIAS MOTSOALEDI and
10. ANDREW MLANGENI,

hereinafter called the accused, are guilty of the offences of:

SABOTAGE, in contravention of section 21 (1) of Act No. 76 of 1962, (two counts),

Contravening section 11 (a), read with sections 1 and 12, of Act No. 44 of 1950, as amended, and

Contravening Section 3(l) (b), read with Section 2, of Act No. 8 of 1953, as amended.

COUNT1 1.   SABOTAGE in contravention of Section 21(1) of Act No. 76 of 1962.

In that, during the period 27th June, 1962, to 11th July, 1963, and at Rivonia, Travallyn and Mountain View in the Province of the Transvaal, as well as at other places within the Republic of South Africa, the accused Nos. 1 to 7 personally and by virtue of their being members of an associations of persons, within the purview of section 381 (7) of Act No. 56 of 1955, as amended, known as the NATIONAL HIGH COMMAND, the accused No. 8 personally and by virtue of his being a member of an association of persons within the purview of section 381 (7) of Act No. 56 of 1955, as amended, styled JAMES KANTOR AND PARTNERS under which name he conducted his profession in partnership with HAROLD WOLPE, and the accused Nos 9 and 10, together with

ARTHUR JOSEPH GOLDREICH and HAROLD WOLPE, who were also members of the NATIONAL HIGH COMMAND, VIVIAN EZRA, JULIUS FIRST, MICHAEL HARMEL, BOB ALEXANDER HEPPLE, PERCY JOHN (JACK) HODGSON, RONALD (RONNIE) KASRILS, MOSES KOTANE, ARTHUR LETELE, TENNYSON MAKIWANE, JOHN JOSEPH MARKS, JOHANNES MODISE, GEORGE NAICKER, BILLY NAIR, LOOK SMART SAULWANDLE NGUDLE, PHILLE-MON DUMA NOKWE, JAMES JOBE RADEBE, ROBERT RESHA, JOSEPH (JOE) SLOVO, HAROLD STRACHAN, OLIVER TAMBO, BENJAMIN TUROK, CECIL GEORGE WILLIAMS, as well as the persons name in paragraphs B.8 and B.9 of the particular furnished in Annexure 'A', attached hereto, and THE SOUTH AFRICAN COMMU-NIST PARTY, THE AFRICAN NATIONAL CONGRESS, and the UMKONTO WE SIZWE (The Spear of the Nation), as well as other persons unknown to the Prosecutor,

did, acting in concert and in the execution of a common purpose, wrongfully and unlawfully, through their agents and servants, commit the following wrongful and wilful acts, namely:

(i) the recruitment of persons for instruction and training, both within and outside the Republic of South Africa, in

(a) the preparation, manufacture and use of explosives—for the purpose of commiting acts of violence and destruction in the aforesaid Republic, and

(b) the art of warfare, including guerilla warfare, and military training generally—for the purpose of causing a violent revolution in the aforesaid Republic, and

(ii) the acts particularised and numbered 40 to 193 in Annexure 'B', attached hereto,

whereby the accused, injured, damaged, destroyed, rendered useless or unserviceable, put out of action, obstructed, tampered with or endangered—

(a) the health or safety of the public;
(b) the maintenance of law and order;
(c) the supply and distribution of light, power or fuel;
(d) postal, telephone or telegraph services or installations;
(e) the free movement of traffic on land, and
(f) the property, movable or immovable, of other persons or of the State.

COUNT 2. SABOTAGE in contravention of section 21(1), of Act No. 76 of 1962.

In that, during the period 27th June, 1962, to 11th July, 1963, and at Rivonia, Travallyn and Mountain View in the Province of the Transvaal, as well as at other places within the Republic of South Africa, the accused Nos. 1 to 7 personally and by virtue of their being members of an association of persons, within the purview of section 381 (7) of Act No.56 of 1955, as amended, known as the NATIONAL HIGH COMMAND, the accused No. 8 personally and by virtue of his being a member of an association of persons within the purview of section 381 (7) of Act No. 56 of 1955, as amended, styled JAMES KANTOR AND PARTNERS under which name he conducted his profession in partnership with HAROLD WOLPE, and the accused Nos. 9 and 10, did wrongfully and unlawfully conspire each with one another and with

ARTHUR JOSEPH GOLDREICH and HAROLD WOLPE, who were also members of the NATIONAL HIGH COMMAND, VIVIAN EZRA, JULIUS FIRST, MICHAEL HARMEL, BOB ALEXANDER HEPPLE, PERCY JOHN (JACK) HODGSON, RONALD (RONNIE) KASRILS, MOSES KOTANE, ARTHUR LETELE, TENNYSON MAKIWANE, JOHN JOSEPH MARKS, JOHANNES MODISE, GEORGE NAICKER, BILLY NAIR, LOOK SMART SAULWANDLE NGUDLE, PHILLEMON DUMA NOKWE, JAMES JOBE RADEBE, ROBERT RESHA, JOSEPH (JOE) SLOVO, HAROLD STRACHAN, OLIVER TAMBO, BENJAMIN TUROK, CECIL GEORGE WILLIAMS, as well as the persons name in paragraphs B.8 and B.9 of the particular furnished in Annexure 'B', attached hereto, and THE SOUTH AFRICAN COMMUNIST PARTY, THE AFRICAN NATIONAL CONGRESS, and the UMKONTO WE SIZWE (The Spear of the Nation), as well as other persons unknown to the Prosecutor,

to aid or procure the commission of or to commit the following wrongful and wilful acts, namely:

(i) the further recruitment of persons for instruction and training, both within and outside the Republic of South Africa, in

  (a) the preparation, manufacture and use of explosives—for the purpose of commiting acts of violence and destruction inthe aforesaid Republic, and

  (b) the art of warfare, including guerilla warfare, and military training generally for the purpose of causing a violent revolution in the aforesaid Republic,

(ii) further acts of violence and destruction of the nature described in Annexure 'B', attached hereto,

(iii) acts of guerilla warfare in the aforesaid Republic,

(iv) acts of assistance to military units of foreign countries when invading the aforesaid Republic, and

(v) acts of participation in a violent revolution in the aforesaid Republic,

whereby they would have injured, damaged, destroyed, rendered useless or unserviceable, put out of action, obstructed, tampered with or endangered—

(a) the health or safety of the public;

(b) the maintenance of law and order;

(c) the supply and distribution of light, power or fuel;

(d) postal, telephone or telegraph services or installations;

(e) the free movement of traffic on land, and

(f) the property, movable or immovable, of other persons or of the State.

COUNT 3.   Contravening section 11 (a), read with sections 1 and 12, of Act No. 44 of 1950, as amended.

In that, during the period 1st July, 1961, to 11th July, 1963, and at Rivonia, Travallyn and Mountain View in the Province of the Transvaal, as well as at other places within the Republic of South Africa, the accused Nos. 1 to 7 personally and by virtue of their being members of an association of persons, within the purview of section 381 (7) of Act No. 56 of 1955, as amended, known as the NATIONAL HIGH COMMAND, the accused No. 8 personally and by virtue of his being a member of an association of persons within the purview of section 381 (7) of Act No. 56 of 1955, as amended, styled JAMES KANTOR AND PARTNERS under which name he conducted his profession in partnership with HAROLD WOLPE, and the accused Nos. 9 and 10, together with

ARTHUR JOSEPH GOLDREICH and HAROLD WOLPE, who were also members of the NATIONAL HIGH COMMAND, VIVIAN EZRA, JULIUS FIRST, MICHAEL HARMEL, BOB ALEXANDER HEPPLE, PERCY JOHN (JACK) HODGSON, RONALD (RONNIE) KASRILS, MOSES KOTANE, ARTHUR LETELE, TENNYSON MAKIWANE, JOHN JOSEPH MARKS, JOHANNES MODISE, GEORGE NAICKER, BILLY NAIR, LOOK SMART SAULWANDLE NGUDLE, PHILLEMON

DUMA NOKWE, JAMES JOBE RADEBE, ROBERT RESHA, JOSEPH (JOE) SLOVO, HAROLD STRACHAN, OLIVER TAMBO, BENJAMIN TUROK, CECIL GEORGE WILLIAMS, as well as the persons named in paragraphs B.8 and B.9 of the particular furnished in Annexure 'A', attached hereto, and THE SOUTH AFRICAN COMMUNIST PARTY, THE AFRICAN NATIONAL CONGRESS, and the UMKONTO WE SIZWE (The Spear of the Nation), as well as other persons unknown to the Prosecutor,

did, acting in concert and in the execution of a common purpose, wrongfully and unlawfully, through their agents and servants, commit the following acts, namely:

(i) the recruitment of persons for instruction and training, both within and outside the Republic of South Africa, in

   (a) the preparation, manufacture and use of explosives—for the purpose of commiting acts of violence and destruction in the aforesaid Republic, and
   (b) the art of warfare, including guerilla warfare, and military training generally for the purpose of causing a violent revolution in the aforesaid Republic, and

(ii) the acts particularised in Annexure 'B', attached hereto, which acts were calculated to further the achievement of one or more of the objects of Communism, as defined in section 1 (l) (ii) (b) of act No. 44 of 1950, as amended.

COUNT 4.   Contravening section 3(1) (b), read with section 2, of Act No. 8 of 1953, as amended.

In that, during the period 1st July, 1961, to 11th July, 1963, and at Rivonia, Travallyn and Mountain View in the Province of the Transvaal, as well as at other places within the Republic of South Africa, the accused Nos. 1 to 7 personally and by virtue of their being members of an association of persons, within the purview of section 381 (7) of Act No. 56 of 1955, as amended, known as the NATIONAL HIGH COMMAND, the accused No. 8 personally and by virtue of his being a member of an association of persons within the purview of section 381 (7) of Act No. 56 of 1955, as amended, styled JAMES KANTOR AND PARTNERS under which name he conducted his profession in partnership with HAROLD WOLPE, and the accused Nos. 9 and 10, together with

ARTHUR JOSEPH GOLDREICH and HAROLD WOLPE, who were also members of the NATIONAL HIGH COMMAND, VIVIAN EZRA, JULIUS FIRST, MICHAEL HARMEL, BOB ALEXANDER HEPPLE, PERCY JOHN (JACK) HODGSON, RONALD (RONNIE) KASRILS, MOSES KOTANE, ARTHUR LETELE, TENNYSON MAKIWANE, JOHN JOSEPH MARKS, JOHANNES MODISE, GEORGE NAICKER, BILLY NAIR, LOOK SMART SAULWANDLE NGUDLE, PHILLEMON DUMA NOKWE, JAMES JOBE RADEBE, ROBERT RESHA, JOSEPH (JOE) SLOVO, HAROLD STRACHAN, OLIVER TAMBO, BENJAMIN TUROK, CECIL GEORGE WILLIAMS, as well as the persons name in paragraphs B.8 and B.9 of the particular furnished in Annexure 'A', attached hereto, and THE SOUTH AFRICAN COMMUNIST PARTY, THE AFRICAN NATIONAL CONGRESS, and the UMKONTO WE SIZWE (The Spear of the Nation), as well as other persons unknown to the Prosecutor,

did, acting in concert and in the execution of a common purpose, wrongfully and unlawfully, personally and through their agents and servants, solicit, accept and receive money from various persons or bodies of persons, both within and outside the Republic of South Africa, and give money to various persons or bodies of persons, for the purpose of enabling or assisting the commission of offences, namely, SABOTAGE in contravention of section 21 (1) of Act No. 76 of 1962, and contravening section 11 (a), read with sections 1 and 12, of Act No. 44 of 1950, as amended, in support of a campaign against some of the laws of the Republic of South Africa or in support of a campaign for the repeal or modification of such laws or variation or limitation of the application or administration of such laws.

WHEREFORE, upon due proof and conviction thereof, the said ATTORNEY–GENERAL prays the judgment of the Court according to law.

(sgd) R. W. REIN
ATTORNEY–GENERAL
(TRANSVAAL PROVINCE.)

PARTICULARS.

Particulars to the aforementioned counts are contained in the schedules, Annexures 'A' and 'B', attached hereto, which form part of this indictment.

Index